One of Our Pilots is Safe

One of Our Pilots is Safe

A Battle of France Airman's Story of
Survival and Road to Recovery

Squadron Leader William Simpson DFC, OBE

AIR WORLD

ONE OF OUR PILOTS IS SAFE
A Battle of France Airman's Story of Survival and Road to Recovery

Part 1, *One of our Pilots is Safe*, was first published by Hamish Hamilton, London, in November 1942. Part 2, *The Way of Recovery*, was first published by Hamish Hamilton, London, in July 1944.

This edition published in 2024 by Air World Books, an imprint of Pen & Sword Books Ltd, 47 Church Street, Barnsley, S. Yorkshire, S70 2AS.

ISBN: 978-1-03611-558-6

Typeset in INDIA by IMPEC eSolutions
Printed and bound in the UK by CPI Group (UK) Ltd, Croydon, CR0 4YY.

Printed on paper from a sustainable source by
CPI Group (UK) Ltd, Croydon, CR0 4YY

Pen & Sword Books Ltd incorporates the imprints of Air World Books, Pen & Sword Archaeology, Atlas, Aviation, Battleground, Discovery, Family History, History, Maritime, Military, Naval, Politics, Social History, Transport, True Crime, Claymore Press, Frontline Books, Praetorian Press, Seaforth Publishing and White Owl.

For a complete list of Pen & Sword titles please contact:

PEN & SWORD BOOKS LTD
47 Church Street, Barnsley, South Yorkshire, S70 2AS, UK.
E-mail: enquiries@pen-and-sword.co.uk
Website: www.pen-and-sword.co.uk

or

PEN AND SWORD BOOKS,
1950 Lawrence Road, Havertown, PA 19083, USA
E-mail: Uspen-and-sword@casematepublishers.com
Website: www.penandswordbooks.com

Contents

APPENDICES

Abbreviations

A.A.	Anti-Aircraft
A.A.S.F.	Advanced Air Striking Force
B.B.C.	British Broadcasting Corporation
B.E.F.	British Expeditionary Force
D.B.S.	Distressed British Subject
D.F.C.	Distinguished Flying Cross
D.F.M.	Distinguished Flying Medal
E.N.S.A.	Entertainments National Service Association
H.E.	High Explosive
K.L.M.	Koninklijke Luchtvaart Maatschappij (Royal Dutch Airlines)
N.A.A.F.I.	Navy, Army and Air Force Institutes
N.C.O.	Non-Commissioned Officer
P.O.W.	Prisoners of War
R.A.F.	Royal Air Force
R.A.O.C.	Royal Army Ordnance Corps
R.A.S.C.	Royal Army Service Corps
R.C.A.F.	Royal Canadian Air Force
R.T.O.	Rail Transport Officer
V.A.D.	Voluntary Aid Detachment
V.C.	Victoria Cross
W.A.A.F.	Women's Auxiliary Air Force
Y.M.C.A.	Young Men's Christian Association

Preface

I feel very privileged to be invited to play a part in bringing my father's amazing story back to life again after more than eighty years!

I am so proud of my father and the extraordinary bravery, forbearance and resilience he displayed as such a young pilot. His story is that of a young man who not only endured such horrific life-changing injuries, but grew as a person through his terrible ordeal and gave much back to his country and to others suffering disability throughout the rest of his life.

I would like to dedicate this book to my late father to whom we all owe so much. I would also like to dedicate it to his seven grandchildren and their offspring who only knew the author affectionately as 'Grandpa Billy'.

As a family we will always remember him as a modest, wise, brave, warm, amusing and loving man.

Long may his memory and legacy live on.

Anne Burness,
daughter of William Simpson

Foreword

They called it 'The Lost Weekend'. Once a year veterans of the Guinea Pig Club would get together in East Grinstead to swap stories and to support each other. It was at one of those weekends that I first met Bill Simpson.

I had already trained at the RAF Medical Training Centre at Lytham St Anne's and was subsequently posted to RAF Moreton-in-Marsh with the rank of Senior Air Craftsman. During this time, I carried out advance training for air casualty evacuation, which enabled me to travel to Germany, Egypt and Malta, being part of a team helping to bring injured personnel back to the UK for further treatment.

After the RAF, I started at East Grinstead's Queen Victoria Hospital in 1956 as a theatre attendant. During my RAF training I had read about the ground-breaking achievements of Archibald McIndoe and his work on the casualties suffering from burns and other crash related injuries which had been treated at East Grinstead, but I never thought I would end up working with the great man. I soon realised that this was the career I wanted to follow.

It was not until 1960, that I was introduced to the Guinea Pig Club, and I soon found myself helping with fundraising at their annual weekends – I used to run the tombola – held at the Felbridge Hotel in East Grinstead. It was at these gatherings that I got to know Bill Simpson well. By that time, he was one of the senior Guinea Pigs. He was always very sociable and very well respected within the club. Because of my fundraising and involvement with club, in 1976 I was made an Honorary Member and subsequently I was invited to become the Club's Honorary Secretary.

For a number of years, items relating to the Guinea Pig Club and its members were accumulated with the ultimate intention of displaying them in a museum. This became reality in 1994, with the opening of the museum in the ante-room of the lecture theatre above the A-Wing theatres.

I had also the idea of collating all the information concerning each of the 649 Guinea Pigs and bringing it all together in a database. I suggested this to the base commander when I was at RAF Benson one weekend with the Guinea Pigs. He was immediately supportive of the proposal, and seconded an RAF sergeant to the project for three days a week to help compile the database.

Bill Simpson did much to promote the Guinea Pig Club, and his two books have helped to bring the work of McIndoe and his teams to the attention of the wider public. Individually, they describe the harrowing experiences of Bill Simpson through his awful accident, and the dreadful injuries from which few people expected him to survive, the repeated, seemingly endless operations, and his often faltering, but eventually uplifting, story of his road to recovery. Together, they make an immensely powerful statement of determination to carry on despite the odds, not just on Bill's part but also on that of all those who never gave up on him, especially the staff at Queen Victoria Hospital.

I am immensely pleased that these books will now be made available again for the current and future generations.

Bob Marchant
July 2024

PART 1

One of Our Pilots is Safe

Dedicated to
Flight Sergeant Odell D.F.M. and
Corporal Tomlinson D.F.M.,
who together saved my life.

Chapter 1

Battle Bombers Fly to France

A t Shoreham-on-Sea, and for several miles east and west along the south coast, on the afternoon of Saturday, 2nd September 1939, the peace of the holidaymakers of an England as yet undisturbed by war was broken by the sound of aircraft engines.

All that afternoon formations of Battle bombers, dark silhouettes patterned against the pale blue of the late summer sky, were flying high overhead in waves. They rose up from their bases in the heart of England, flew south to the coast, turned out to sea at Shoreham, and disappeared from sight in the general direction of the north of France.

How many of the people who watched from the ground those bombers passing overhead realised that they were witnesses of the making of history? How many saw, in that sight high up in the sky, a portent of war? Probably very few. After all, it was no unusual sight. During the past months of summer there had been many large-scale manoeuvres in the air over the south and east coastlines; manoeuvres calculated to test the air defences of the country and at the same time to provide practice for our fighters and bombers under conditions approaching as near as possible to real air warfare.

Formations of bombers flew far out to sea, turned and raced back low over the water; rose up over the cliffs and houses and made straight for points on the coast and far inland, where they simulated bombing attacks on their imaginary targets. On the way they were attacked by Spitfires and Hurricanes, which swooped down like hawks on the Battles, Blenheims and Wellingtons and chased them over the hills and down along the valleys.

The people of England, who had never as yet had occasion to use the word "blitz," were nevertheless becoming quite blasé to the sight and sound of military aircraft. Some of them, particularly the farmers and landowners, looked upon the youthful Air Force with an unfavourable and even baleful eye. They asked themselves, naturally enough, whether or not the young airmen were being allowed too much scope to let off the steam of their high spirits at the cost of frightening livestock and of disturbing the public peace. Some went so far as to vent their feelings on the public through the correspondence columns of the daily Press. Fortunately for themselves, in the end they received little change out of the Air Ministry, which, while taking every reasonable care to prevent unnecessary low flying, still allowed and encouraged pilots to carry out their war training in a realistic manner. So, the Air Ministry in its wisdom gave to the air crews in the squadrons the necessary scope and encouragement they needed, and the foundations of the great Royal Air Force of this war were laid.

While to the onlookers below there was nothing unusual in the sight of large formations of bombers flying out to sea overhead that Saturday afternoon, the crews of the bombers were experiencing new and serious sensations. For once they were not taking part in mimic war. This time at last it was the real thing.

The British public as a whole had yet to hear from Mr. Chamberlain, in his memorable Sunday morning broadcast the next day, that war had been declared on Germany. The Royal Air Force, however, had already made its first war disposition. One of these was the dispatch to France of the Advanced Air Striking Force.

It was the Battle bombers of the A.A.S.F. – some one hundred and sixty of them, ten squadrons organised in five wings – that turned out to sea high overhead that Saturday afternoon and disappeared out of sight. They were bound for secret bases in France – a number of landing grounds and aerodromes prepared in advance by the French *Armée de l'Air* – spread out around the countryside surrounding the old cathedral town of Rheims.

Several books about the A.A.S.F. in France have already appeared. On the whole they give an accurate account, as far as I know, of the incidents which they describe in the life and work of the A.A.S.F. from September 1939 until the withdrawal from France in June 1940. There is, however, a possibility that the public, after reading these accounts, may be left with the impression that the A.A.S.F. consisted of two first-rate fighter squadrons (1 and 73) and a few obscure bomber squadrons. In actual fact the ten bomber squadrons were specially selected and trained by Bomber Command long before the war began and were as much the elite of the bombers as 1 and 73 were of the fighters.

The two fighter squadrons have already received full recognition for their legendary achievements. The achievements of the bomber squadrons were also legendary. They were faced with odds as great as – perhaps greater than – the fighters. The losses amongst fighter pilots – all honour to their skill – were small. Those of the bomber crews were very large.

The name Advanced Air Striking Force would have had no meaning without the bomber squadrons, for they were the real striking force. It was with bombs that the German Army columns were attacked, while the fighters were occupied mainly with the Luftwaffe's bombers attacking France. It was with bombs that the bridges at Maastricht, Mouzon and Sedan were destroyed.

Little as yet has been written about these bomber squadrons. However, the best account of the work of the Battles and Blenheims in France is contained in the publication *Bomber Command*. It is restrained and to the point. That is good and may the heroism of the many bomber crews never be denied by exaggeration and cheap repetition. In this account it is recorded how in aircraft that were ill-armed and lightly armoured – no self-sealing petrol tanks, for instance – the crews of the bombers were ordered out on raids over small targets that were difficult to find and difficult to hit, and always highly defended by light and heavy flak. Often, they had no friendly fighters to protect them; at best the few fighters were hopelessly outnumbered by the squadrons of Messerschmitts lurking always high overhead.

It seems a long time ago now since that Saturday afternoon – the afternoon before the war was declared – when, with the other pilots of 12 Squadron, I took off from Bicester Aerodrome in my Battle aircraft to fly to France.

Many details and impressions of that day have since faded from my memory, but a few still remain. We took off in sections – four aircraft to each – and formed up into flight, squadron, and finally wing formation. The two squadrons of our wing were 12 and 142 – both until that day based at Bicester, now to be based in France and called 76 Wing, A.A.S.F.

For the first time every one of us had his eyes skinned, looking around keenly for any signs of German fighters – not that there was much chance of being intercepted by Messerschmitts so far from the bases in Germany. In past practice operations we had become well accustomed to watching out for our own fighters, waiting above us to carry out their dummy attacks. The sensation of watching for the black crosses on the wings of Messerschmitts was new and very real. I had a feeling of intense excitement. At last, after many months of waiting since Munich, the year before, the war was upon us.

What a relief to pent-up feelings and worn nerves that now, at long last, something definite was happening. About the war I had a great curiosity, and surprisingly few misgivings. I was filled with a strong *sehnsucht*, a longing to go forth in search of all that lay hidden beyond the far horizon; a strong and savage lust for great moments, no matter what they might cost. These irresponsible emotions were mixed up with and offset by others which struggled for supremacy, among them a sober realisation of the great responsibility that was ours and of the tremendous odds we were bound to face – we, the few squadrons that were about to challenge the mighty Luftwaffe built up by Goering with feverish haste during the last few years.

Then there were memories of the day before, of our Wing Commander saying: "Well, the balloon's going up at last. We are to take off for France tomorrow after lunch. All aircraft are to be bombed up and loaded, as already arranged. Here are the full details …" The party that night in the ladies' room of the mess – smoke, beer, excitable chatter of the officers and the girls – genuine hilarity of a few, forced cheerfulness of the majority. The ever-present question in each of our minds – would we ever have any more parties like this again? Last minute packing, writing letters on through the night and into the first hours of the morning – letters to my mother, to friends and to my wife, who lay sick in hospital, slowly recovering from a serious operation. Worst memory of all this – leaving Hope when she needed me most.

Looking down on the shimmering water of the Channel and ahead to the faintly discernible coast of France, I could not accustom myself to the idea that I was in control of a machine of terrible destruction. I dreaded the time to come when I should have to let loose its powers. How senseless it all seemed – everything so beautiful, yet the necessity to destroy some of it. I felt like a small boy who sees a butterfly and has to tear off its wings to satisfy some obscure instinct inside him.

Now the wing was flying over Le Tréport, and then the rich green countryside of France – what a difference in the shape of the fields, the towns and lonely farmsteads, from the English countryside behind us, and yet sane, and with so much of the same peacefulness. How insignificant man seemed – out of sight from this height. On over a French aerodrome – the name POIX marked in white in its centre, and the dark shapes of ancient bombers marked with the French roundels dispersed around the perimeter. Soon we were circling around our new landing ground, a flat square of green, bordered on one side by one of Napoleon's straight military roads and on the others by woods, beet fields and golden corn. Here and there, dotted over the countryside, were the red and white villages we were soon to know so well.

We landed by sections in formation and taxied to the filling points. There were three of them, one in each of three corners of the landing ground: petrol tanks sunk out of sight below the ground, each with its hand-operated pump and length of hose.

There followed incidents typical of the seemingly haphazard arrangements made by the ground personnel of the *Armée de l'Air* for our arrival. First, two of the pump handles broke. On examination we found they were very badly made, having flaws in the light metal from which they had been moulded. This delayed refuelling, and it was almost dark before we had dispersed our refuelled aircraft, covered up the cockpits, and picketed them down. Then we were driven with our baggage to the nearest village, Berry-au-Bac, to find further snags about billets. There were about a hundred of us, all air crews. The ground personnel of the two squadrons and Wing Headquarters were following us by boat, rail and motor transport, the whole wing consisting of some three hundred officers and airmen. It appeared that all were to be accommodated in this one village of Berry-au-Bac.

However, when we arrived in the village, after bumping over the road in two decrepit old buses, we found that practically nothing had been arranged about our billets. It was two o'clock the next morning – we had landed at four in the afternoon – before the Wing adjutant had completed the allotment of billets to all our aircrews. The N.C.O.s were installed in the school, where they rolled themselves up in their blankets and slept on the floor. The airmen laid their blankets on the straw of a number of evil-smelling barns and stables. The officers were more fortunate. Some had real beds and the others camp-beds in such houses as had room to spare.

Peter, who later commanded "A" Flight, and I visited most of the billets that night before turning in ourselves. Peter's knowledge of French had already proved very useful to us in the *Mairie* when billets were being arranged, and from then on until the official interpreters arrived he was hard at work arguing in two languages.

My billet was in one of the jerry-built labourer's houses. There I shared a three-quarter bed with Spencer, my deputy Flight Commander. Such remaining floor space as was not covered by the bed was filled by the camp-bed of another officer. There were many smells in our billet, but those of boiled cabbage water and dirty rabbit-hutch predominated. The house belonged to a young French labourer and his wife. He had been called up and she was left alone to look after their three small children. She was very upset, and always looked as if she had been crying. Every now and then she hurled filthy epithets (that I did not then understand) at the *sâles Boches* who had broken up her home with their war.

Berry-au-Bac, like all the other villages in the vicinity, had been completely razed to the ground by the shelling of the last war. After the Armistice it was reconstructed by building new houses on the foundations of the ruins. From the air it had looked most attractive, but in reality, it was ugly and untidy. Most of the rubble had been left after the rebuilding, and lay, overgrown by weeds, in the open spaces between the houses. The houses were badly built. Sanitation was of the crudest kind. The roads, with the exception of the cobbled main street, were made of rough flints and were pitted with potholes. The gardens behind the houses at least might have been beautiful, but instead they were ill-kept and filled with vegetable plots and rickety hutches full of grey domestic rabbits bred for food.

The *Mairie* was an ugly building, its porch plastered with mobilisation notices. The church, with its tall spire, was little better. Bordering the main street were a few estaminets, one with a petrol pump outside, a ramshackle garage, and several small stores. The River Aisne and a broad canal ran together past one end of the village. Leading away to Laon to the north and Rheims to the south stretched the great tree-lined military road.

We made our officers' mess in a tin shack behind one of the estaminets. There on our first night we drank champagne to the downfall of our mutual enemy, with the *capitaine*, the *médécin-lieutenant*, and the other officers of the *Armée de l'Air* company in charge of the landing ground. Champagne was cheap and plentiful, but food supplies were short for the officers, who, unlike the airmen, had no service ration. No special provisions had been laid in for our arrival, even although we appeared a day later than the French expected. Money was another difficulty. We had only English currency, and at first there was no means of exchanging it for francs.

The lives of the people of Berry-au-Bac were simple and rather crude. Most of the men were farm labourers who worked in the beet fields which surrounded the village. Mobilisation had been thorough, and men of military age had already disappeared before we arrived. The women carried on the work of their menfolk, just as they had done in the last war. Apart from the estaminets and the church, there were no facilities for social life. Our presence was accepted with nonchalance. There was no enthusiasm. On the whole, the people were friendly and did what little was in their power to help us. The relative wealth of our airmen was a sore point with the women, whose husbands were getting only 50 centimes a day and themselves a very meagre marriage allowance.

Chapter 2

Wings Over France

The first few days in France passed quickly for the pilots, air observers and gunners of 12 and 142 Squadrons. It was several days before our ground crews arrived in force, although a few appeared every day, flown over from England with urgently required spares and stores in the motley collection of ancient and modern civilian aircraft commissioned for that purpose by the R.A.F. So it was that the burden of camouflaging our landing-ground fell on the air crews.

From early in the morning until dusk we were hard at work each day. It was really the work of a pioneer corps – digging, felling trees, building ramps. We worked stripped to the waist, our braces tied round our uniform trousers. Luckily the weather was perfect. There was hardly a cloud in the sky for days. Soon we were bronzed and extremely fit, as a result of the unusually hard exercise in the open air and the simplicity of our life, bounded as it was by the landing ground and the village of Berry-au-Bac.

The first essential was to hide our aircraft, petrol and bomb dumps and the temporary headquarter tents. The same good weather that helped us in our pioneer work below was even more useful to the enemy reconnaissance aircraft and their prying cameras. Already the wavering note of German engines had been detected overhead – although looking up into the sky there was nothing to see, for they were flying very high.

The landing ground was a large square field, flat and covered with grass. On one side it was bordered by the Rheims-Laon military road. On another it merged into fields of beet and corn. The two remaining sides were skirted by scrubby woods, through which flowed a stream, just inside the borders nearest the landing ground. We chose parts of the wood where the ground was firmest, and at regular intervals cut away the trees and scrub to make lanes just wide enough to allow the tails and fuselages of our Battles to be pushed in among the trees.

The aircraft, after being pushed into their hiding places, were picketed down and covered with cut branches. Fortunately for us the trees were still in full leaf, and by the time all the positions had been completed and the Battles picketed in place it was practically impossible to tell that our landing ground was inhabited. Our few camouflaged tents were pitched in the woods near the aircraft and the bomb and petrol dumps were covered with scrub.

The work was difficult. At first, we had to commandeer and buy all the picks, shovels, axes, saws and lengths of rope that we needed. Some of the positions were on soft ground and had to be strengthened with logs. Others were so near the stream that stout log ramps and bridges had to be built. Here Aussie Mac, one of the officers of "B" Flight, was in his element. He was a natural wood-craftsman and directed all the building operations for the squadron. Airmen stood looking on with awe while he wielded his axe, felling trees and shaping logs for his ramps and bridges.

We ate our midday meal in the open. It consisted of tinned bully beef and ration biscuits, and hot stew served by a ragged and bearded French *Armée de l'Air* cook from the rickety old portable field kitchen which was dragged onto the landing ground behind one of the buses each day. It was washed down by *pinard* (French Army wine). I liked the *pinard* from the start, but it was most unpopular with the airmen.

At first the landing ground was defended against possible air attack by three French machine-guns – one in each of three pits. Our only radio station and battery charging point was situated in a French wireless lorry. There was one small French ambulance and no fire tender. As the days and the weeks passed all this was changed by the arrival of the hundred odd vehicles of our M.T. columns – petrol bowsers, tractors, office trailers, store trailers, radio trucks, water and cooking trailers, etc. Later still huts were built, and camouflage netting was issued to replace the branches, which soon lost their leaves as autumn turned to winter.

With the arrival of our ground crews and equipment, we, the pilots, observers and air gunners, were freed to concentrate on our real work. Our first operations were high level reconnaissance over the frontier. Formations flew over the chosen areas at about 20,000 feet. They met heavy and fairly accurate anti-aircraft fire, but, at first, no fighters. They brought back valuable photographs.

As the operations were carried out regularly over approximately the same areas, it was not surprising that after the first few days the Luftwaffe sent up their Messerschmitts to intercept us. One formation of five Battles from another squadron was badly caught out. It was intercepted at high altitude and only the squadron leader escaped to crash on landing at his base. The formation was spread out wide when attacked. It did not, or could not, close up in time. Two Messerschmitts were definitely shot down. After this we carried out no more high level reconnaissances. We were fitted with armour plating and given an extra gun – firing downwards and backwards out of the bomb-aiming hatch.

Leading a section of three Battles sometime after this, I was sent on a low-level reconnaissance, flying at tree-top level over the Siegfried Line and along a stretch of the Rhine. We managed to take a large number of photographs of guns, encampments and forts, half-concealed in the woods and along the banks of the river. As we flew over the German villages, soldiers waved to us, apparently mistaking us for their own Luftwaffe. We were only fired on once and returned with two bullet-holes in the wing of one Battle. We saw no fighters.

That was the last "recco." flight we made, and for months we had to content ourselves with mock air battles with the French Morane and Curtiss fighters and our own Hurricanes, practice bombing on a range, dummy attacks on columns of the B.E.F. near Arras, and night "cross-countries." Most of our time was spent moping about the aerodrome, getting thoroughly "browned-off" and hoping against hope for some real action.

Sometimes Spencer and I would get permission to take the Magister – a light training aircraft used for wing communication – and fly around the countryside. We were particularly interested in looking for French bombers. In the air we had seen only a few Morane and Curtiss fighters and an occasional Potez reconnaissance machine. Once a very antiquated and slow bomber landed at Berry-au-Bac. It made our obsolescent Battles look like something out of Wells' *Things to Come*. However, after several flights in the Magister we had still seen nothing of the *Armée de l'Air* bombing force. This is not now surprising, as it has since appeared that the French had only forty bombers fit for operation – by night only – over the Western Front.

As we waited by our aircraft, we would often see long streams of old Paris buses, camouflaged with green and brown paint and loaded with troops, passing, sometimes north, sometimes south, along the military road. The troops looked uninterested and disillusioned. They were untidy, ill-clad, armed only with old rifles – and bored. We were repeatedly told that they were only reserves, but I have often doubted it since. Even as reserves they left an impression on us that the great French Army was largely a myth.

Before the end of the month the officers were comfortably installed in a château at Guignicourt, the largest of the villages near the landing ground.

This château was a typical product of post-war reparations. It was not definitely ugly and seen from one direction standing out above the trees, it looked beautiful, but the architecture lacked character. The earlier château, upon the foundations of which the present house had been erected, was probably a gem, for the site had been well chosen. This oblong red-brick building, with its white stone facings and grey-tiled deep-gabled roof, stood on a wooded slope above the north banks of the River Aisne. The interior of the house – it was far more like a house than a château – was plain, but very comfortable. Even after the furniture had been removed – with the exception of a few beds and four armchairs – we still had central heating, plenty of hot water and five bathrooms.

Spencer, the Doc., Michael and I shared a room. We had managed to scrounge two of the four armchairs, and our room had a fireplace. Later on, when the snow came, we used to spend our evenings lying on our camp beds or sitting in the old armchairs in front of the fire, writing letters home or reading.

The owner of the château was the Marquise de Nazelle. She was altogether charming. Her hair was white and her features delicate; her smile was sweet, and her expression was that of a young girl grown wise. I thought her very beautiful and used to like to be invited to dine with her in the *dépendence* – the house inside the château grounds into which she had moved with her six sons, her daughter and the English governess, before we took over the château for our mess. Her eldest son was seventeen. She was a widow, but never allowed the great sadness she undoubtedly felt to be shown in her face or reflected in her ways and conversation.

Sometimes I saw it for a moment in her eyes – but it would suddenly disappear again, and she would smile. Dinner was served at a round table. The Marquise was always vivacious, and stimulated the rush of lively discussion that crisscrossed over the table from all directions. I preferred this way of dining to the traditional English "dinner-club-and-mess" style, the latter so dull and stodgy, rather like the food, talking usually with the one diner present who bored one most, but happened to be sitting beside one.

I understood very little of the conversation, my French being terrible at that time. I remember, as the months passed, an impression of considerable apprehension in the Marquise's salon – when the conversation became more serious as we sipped our coffee and liqueurs. I sensed a suggestion of mistrust of the French Army. We heard stories of gross inefficiency from the young French officers who visited the Marquise. The de Nazelles, like most honest French people, tried hard to refute these rumours and to disbelieve the evidence of their own eyes. After all, the French Army had no parade ground aspirations – the slovenliness of dress and marching was supposed to reflect the rugged individualism of the French soldier, who would be sure, by reason of his very individualistic ideas, to defend to the death his own sacred spot of the soil of France.

I often wonder now what has happened to the Marquise de Nazelle and her splendid young sons. I can well imagine them leaving Guignicourt to join the pitiful stream of refugees. I can see, too, the village and the château ruined and in flames, the simple and good people of north France homeless for the third time in the living memory of the *grande mère*.

The hot sun of September faded out, and by the middle of October heavy rains had transformed the dispersal points into quagmires. Mud became our greatest enemy. It lay like a sea of thick brown liquid all around our Battles. Petrol bowsers and tractors stuck in it, mechanics and pilots dragged through it in their gumboots. Our Wing Commander, a huge man with a red face, whom we nicknamed "Two-Ton," was often to be seen pushing his staff car through the slime. Iron grille was delivered in lengths and laid over the mud. There was very little flying. When we did succeed in taxiing our Battles through the mud on to the aerodrome the tail units of many were damaged. We were now thoroughly fed-up with the war. The excitement we had felt on coming to France had worn off. It was replaced by a feeling of anti-climax and of frustration.

We dug ourselves into the ground for the winter. All along the edge of the woods dug-outs were constructed, cut deep down into the ground. Ostensibly they provided some protection against enemy bombs, in reality their construction gave us something to do, they kept us out of the rain, and provided good hide-outs. Our earlier experience constructing the aircraft position was useful now, and many of the dugouts were solid and quite comfortable. They had roofs of logs and tin sheeting; some had windows, and most had fireplaces. The rooms were almost flush with the ground and covered with mud. We became a colony of cave-dwellers. How incongruous it was to see the noses of our Battles sticking out of the woods, surrounded by these odd little mud dugouts, each with its chimney belching forth smoke.

My air gunner, Roberts, was an excellent cook, and an even better scrounger. Sometimes in the middle of the morning he would disappear. Eventually he would be seen crossing the horizon from the direction of a farm and would arrive laden with spoils – eggs, vegetables, coffee, and sometimes a chicken. The chimneys gave forth so much black smoke that Flight Commanders were ordered to restrict the use of fire. On one of my periodic smoke inspections I saw Roberts standing in front of our dug-out. Behind him thick black clouds of smoke poured out of the chimney and spiralled up over the tree tops. Before I had time to speak Roberts called out: "How about a hot pancake, sir, with fig jam?"

Inside the dug-out, in front of the fire, the question of smoke was debated amicably from every angle as I ate my pancakes. Later on, Roberts became the flight cook, and transformed the daily stew, which arrived at midday in hay-boxes, into concoctions that were more palatable and varied. One day he was filmed by a news-reel man, standing ankle deep in mud, covered in soot and grime, stirring one of his most successful culinary efforts in a pot hung from a branch over his fire.

The winter wore on, the coldest for many years. Rain turned to snow. Still there was no real activity for the squadrons. Every day we huddled in our tents and dugouts, shivering over oil-stoves and wood fires. It was particularly severe for the mechanics, working on the Battles with bare hands out in the biting cold. When their work was finished the billets to which they returned were miserable places to go to for a little comfort. We began to think of two things: amusement and leave.

The amusement was provided for us in several ways. Sometimes we had a visit from the N.A.A.F.I. film projectors and sometimes E.N.S.A. gave concerts. The films were shown in a big shed which we had commandeered in Berry-au-Bac as a N.A.A.F.I. They were modern and good, but we saw very few of them. The E.N.S.A. concerts were probably appreciated more, although I always felt that the principle of sending concerts to us was wrong, and that we should have organised our own with our own talent. Of course, there would have been no women in our shows. E.N.S.A. in France had many good artistes. They put on good shows, and they must have found us most appreciative audiences. On concert evenings Air Force lorries and buses used to roll into the village from the four or five other villages then occupied by the wing.

Another source of amusement was the periodic visits by our transport buses to Rheims. Here, in spite of the war, we found plenty to amuse us. There was no dancing and no music – but plenty of good food and wine. Other places of diversion usually to be found flourishing in continental towns were working overtime. Then there were the cinemas – two of which showed English films on certain days of the week – the town itself, the champagne cave and the cathedral.

The cathedral, scarred in the last war, still retained its dignity and austerity, as befitted the crowning place of the medieval French kings, the scene of the triumph of Joan of Arc. The great porch was heavily protected by embankments of sandbags, twenty to thirty feet high. Stained glass had been removed from the windows. It was still magnificent.

Some of the squadron paid a visit to the champagne caves – many miles of tunnel running underground below the outskirts of the city, where the champagne of France is collected and matured.

The shops were as yet little affected by the war. Shopping was profitable for us, with the good exchange from pounds to francs and the difference in price standards between France and England.

Rheims was always crowded with military vehicles of every kind. It was full of gold braid, French Army and British Air Force. It was the home of the headquarters of the A.A.S.F. It was strange to see the grey-blue R.A.F. uniform mingled with the civilians and the French Army khaki – and occasionally the royal blue and gold of the *Armée de l'Air*. On the street were camouflaged lorries, light vans and staff cars mixed with the civilian traffic and the French officers' Peugeots and Citroens.

The movement, the animation of the city, the bright lights inside the cafés, even the complication of finding the bus home in the black-out, all these little things in themselves gave us some link with modern life, which we could not get in our dug-outs or on the icy aerodrome.

Back in the château during those freezing winter nights we used often to wonder just where the nerve war was leading to. Most of us were sceptical of the British and French propaganda, which left an impression that we would succeed in defeating the Germans without a fight, by a combination of Maginot Line, naval blockade, and Air Force leaflets. It was maddening for us to have to wait there all those months, not even being re-equipped with more formidable bombers, while the Germans were making feverish preparations for the Spring offensive that was rumoured to be planned.

We had come to France to fight. I doubt if any of us realised just how great were the issues for which we were fighting. None of us was particularly anxious to fight – but we were determined that when we got the chance we would fight well. It was infuriating to have to sit around our fast Battles while other squadrons at home were submarine chasing and bombing the German fleet. Even to have dropped a few leaflets would have been something.

The Headquarters staff of the A.A.S.F. was quick to realize that a short spell of leave at home would have a very beneficial effect. By the middle of December arrangements had been completed for leave trains and boats; and parties of officers and men were sent back to England for ten days leave at home.

Jimmy, who commanded "A" Flight, myself, two observer sergeants and two air gunners, made up the first party from 12 Squadron.

The snow was crisp underfoot and the air biting cold as we climbed into the bus that was to take us from Guignicourt to Rheims railway station. We arrived at the station just as dawn was breaking. From Rheims we travelled by train to Paris, and left Paris by the night train for Cherbourg. This was the second time I had been in Paris since the beginning of the war. The first had been with the Doc. about a month before, at a time when we were all being allowed a 72-hour local leave. So far, Paris had changed very little. It was very much the same gay, irresponsible place that I had visited before the war. True, there was the black-out, which spoilt the effect of the thousands of lamps that used to blink all along the Champs-Élysées, round the Place de la Concorde and along the broad way in the direction of Les Invalides. The lamps were still there, and many of them still alight, but dowsed down to a glimmer. The theory seemed to be to keep Paris lit up to a certain extent and to extinguish all lights from the source of power when there was an *alerte*.

In the streets there were many more khaki uniforms than in peacetime, but the contrast was slight, for Paris had always been full of khaki, especially in the summer of 1938, when I had passed through on my way to Switzerland. The Paris amusements were as gay and irresistible as ever; cafés, restaurants and bars were packed and noisy. The Parisiens and Parisiennes seemed to have adopted the war like a new craze. Women dressed themselves in artistic caricatures of military uniforms, soldiers were admitted half-price to the cinemas, those wearing the distinctive badge of the Maginot Line were heroes. Everyone seemed keen to get all the glitter and glamour possible out of the excitement – the war-fever – that was entirely vicarious for most of them. They seemed to have forgotten that war meant toil, blood, sweat, pain and utter misery. They had lost their scale of values. They were nearly all Maginot-conscious.

Jimmy and I took things very quietly. We had a good lunch in the Champs-Élysées and afterwards walked around the Arc de Triomphe, visited one or two of the various bars frequented by the Air Force, and ended up at the station in the evening in time to collect our party and take the express for Cherbourg. This train was fast, stuffy and crowded. We stood in the bar, jostled-by a number of French pupil pilots, who were in high spirits and itching to get into fighter squadrons at the front.

We arrived at Cherbourg at midnight and were met at the station by an open British army truck, which carried us and our baggage through the dingy streets of the town and pulled up in the backyard of an ancient barracks. There was just enough light showing for us to see that the buildings were dirty and ugly – they looked as if they must have been built by Napoleon and ought long ago to have been condemned. However, it was occupied by a French colonial infantry regiment – as far as I remember, they were Moroccans – the British R.T.O. and a few Tommies.

The Assistant R.T.O. who received us was a lanky, lugubrious second lieutenant, who had been left behind, for some reason or other, when his regiment had passed through on the way to the front. I think all the moribund misery, the smell and air of decay of the place had eaten right into his soul. There was a meal for the N.C.O.s, but Jimmy and I had to satisfy ourselves with a mug of tepid, stewed army tea. Then we were shown into our "bedroom." It was a small stone-floored, cell-like apartment on the second floor. It was lit by a single weak and naked electric globe; the window was barred; there were two iron army bedsteads. We threw off the filthy mattresses which covered them and curled up on the bed in our greatcoats and tried to forget how cold we were.

There was no breakfast to be had in the barracks next morning. We washed ourselves with the trickle of icy water that flowed from a tap into a sink downstairs. Then we left with the rest of our party for the R.T.O.'s office, where we received our instructions. Soon we were on board the boat for Southampton and were zigzagging across the Channel for England and home.

The next morning, I was in Edinburgh, and in the afternoon was met by Hope, my wife, in a little village in the hills of Scotland. I shall never forget that leave; the simplicity of life in our cottage; long walks over the hills with Hope's cairn terrier, and a thousand other things, both large and small, which brought me back into the reality and companionship of the sane life I had left behind me when I first flew out to France. The weather was bright and cold; the hills were peaceful and quiet; there were just a few sheep, an occasional deer, the rabbits and ourselves.

We had, it seemed, a whole lifetime to discuss; we lived again our sweetest moments of the past; we planned with hope greater happiness and a richer life for the future. It seemed impossible to us then that anything could happen that would mar our happiness. Life was perhaps too simple, too beautiful, and too happy. Perhaps if it had always remained like that, our senses would have been dulled and we would have lost the art of appreciation. We were in the clouds then. Pain brought us back to earth again.

Hope came to Southampton with me on my way back to France. We stayed one day in Edinburgh, where we walked around the shops and along Princes Street. We were there in daylight only, so there was no black-out to bring the memory of the war back to us – only the khaki and blue uniform, so seldom seen in English and Scottish towns in times of peace. Edinburgh has always stirred something deep inside me – something pagan – a feeling of defiance and of national pride that is the birthright of all Scots and is the more strongly felt by the exile when he returns to his native Scotland.

Looking across at the castle from Princes Street, I saw the grim granite towers outlined against the faint smoke haze that usually hangs over "Auld Reekie." I was transported hundreds of years back into history; I could not realise that greater and more painful history was, being made at that moment.

We arrived in London in the black-out. What a comparison – the black-out of London and the fade-out of Paris. The next day we visited my mother, then left for Southampton, and so back to France and the war of nerves again.

We arrived back at Guignicourt on Christmas Eve. Snow lay thick on the ground, and it was freezing hard.

Christmas Day for 12 Squadron was to be celebrated in traditional manner. Work was to stop at midday and the afternoon spent in festivities.

After a hurried breakfast we, the officers, set out in our transport coach for the landing ground. About a month before we had moved to a new landing ground near the village of Amifontaine and across the road from the French aerodrome of La Malmaison. This left the whole of the Berry-au-Bac landing ground to 142 Squadron, whose aircraft positions had been better situated than, ours.

We were driven over the quiet countryside, over which sound had been muffled by the crisp carpet of snow which lay deep on the fields and hard on the roads. Above us was the promise of a further storm in the grey overcast sky. We went through villages that were almost empty of life, and out again across the snow-covered beet fields which stretched away on both sides, their monotony broken only by an occasional house or a clump of trees; on under the railway arch, to emerge in the little village of Amifontaine. Here our squadron N.C.O.s and airmen were billeted. Passing through the village, we overtook the lorries, petrol tankers, tractors and trailers; the ambulance and fire tender; all going to the landing ground, like ourselves.

The landing ground was bounded on one side by the road connecting La Malmaison to Amifontaine. It was practically flat near the road, but half-way across it rose up in a deep, steady slope, to flatten out once more and stop a hundred yards in front of a thick line of stately pine trees, which ran parallel to the line of the road. In this row of pines was concealed our operations hut, various headquarter offices, and "A" flight commander's tent. Our Battles were dispersed in flights, "A" near the pine wood and "B" on the edge of another wood of scrub in one of the corners. Each Battle crew – air and ground – had its own tent pitched somewhere near its aircraft. In the cold weather our Battles had their noses tucked into shelter tents, each one heated by an incandescent stove. They looked more like great living monsters than machines; grotesque with their noses covered up.

We got out of the bus and crunched over the snow, some of us making for "B," the others for "A" flight. In "B" flight commander's tent all the officers of the flight sat down and started to censor the airmen's mail, which lay in a bundle on my home-made table. The flight sergeant, who had been waiting for us, to wish us "Merry Christmas," disappeared outside to supervise the daily inspections of the Battles. The mechanics had to look over the air frames and engines also; wireless operators check their radio sets; armourers inspect the bombs on their racks and examine the guns. That morning the inspections were soon over, for there had been no flying the day before, and there would be none on Christmas Day.

Soon we had permission from the C.O. to pack up for the day. A few minutes afterwards the white surface of the landing ground was spotted with blue, as officers and airmen made their own individual way back to the road and the buses and lorries which were to carry them to Amifontaine village, where the airmen's Christmas dinner was to be served.

How peaceful it all looked! There was nothing warlike or vicious in the sight of our big Air Force lorries and buses, nor in the officers and airmen approaching them. After four months we were still playing at war. Most of the officers behaved like the overgrown schoolboys they were. Jake, tall, thin, with a big nose set in his long pallid face and an unruly ginger-brown moustache, was probably the biggest kid of all. He liked to ride on the bonnet of the bus, or, failing that, stand on a seat inside and put his head through the sunshine roof. Barevski, dark, good-looking in a swarthy way, sat in the bus, giving realistic renderings of classical music on his mouth-organ or whistling a waltz of Tchaikovsky's in such a way that I could hear all the orchestrations in my head. Don, tall, fair, and proud of his Irish blood, lashing with his witty tongue all the bureaucratic institutions he hated so much. Blackie, short, red-headed Canadian, with a cheery, india-rubber face, cracking jokes at me or at his fellow-Canadians. And all the others, each one so different in temperament – English, Scots, Canadian, Australian, and Irish – yet with so much in common. None of us were over twenty-seven. We knew nothing of war.

There were some three hundred airmen in the squadron, all billeted in the houses of Amifontaine. The airmen's dining-room was a badly-lit, mean little meeting hall. It was filled completely by trestle tables and forms. In a yard just outside stood the mobile cooking trailers, equipped with petrol cooking stoves, where the squadron cooks were putting the finishing touches to the Christmas dinner, consisting of turkey, ham, vegetables and Christmas pudding. There were also large quantities of beer – for the local wines and champagnes meant nothing to the airmen, and anyway this was to be a British Christmas.

The officers and N.C.O.s acted as waiters, this being an old-established tradition in the Air Force. The Group Captain who commanded our wing came in to give us his greetings. There followed toasts and a few impromptu speeches, and then we crept out to leave the airmen with their beer. We were driven back to the château for our own dinner. This was not so uproariously convivial as the airmen's, nevertheless, it was very cheerful – one of the best Christmas dinners I could remember.

When it was all over, I slipped away and out into the grounds down by the side of the river. Wandering slowly along the snow-covered path on the wooded banks of the river, its grey swirling waters swollen by snow and rain, I felt completely detached from all the festivities going on in the mess behind me. A thick mist had settled down over everything. The only sound was the soft mumbling of the water. Peace and goodwill unto all men. At home in England the children would be singing carols. There would be Christmas trees and crackers, games, too much to eat, and shrill laughter. No doubt in Germany, too, the "Weihnachstbaum" would be lit and placed in the windows – at least until black-out time – and German children would be happy too. They would sing the most beautiful of all carols – *Stille Nacht* – and would hear stories of past Christmases when there had been more butter and less guns. Yes, there was still plenty of peace and good-will, but it was not extended unto all men.

Elsewhere in Europe a bloody war was raging. Men's hearts were turned unwillingly to savage controversy. Young men were bleeding out in the cold or lying stiff and still on the frozen fields of Poland. The little villages all around me had been robbed of their menfolk, who were waiting, bored, in the Maginot Line or on the Belgian frontier. How senseless it all seemed; how out of place the big words of international politicians; what a poor, miserable, crazy kind of civilisation. What a waste of Christ's blood on the cross. It was a Christmas Day stained with blood; of murder, born of greed and stupidity. This quiet, snow-covered countryside, in all its natural peace, was a delusion. Man, who had been given a noble gift in the earth, was hard at work destroying it. Back in the mess there was champagne and hilarity. We listened to the radio with its usual Christmas Day messages. The party spirit was alive well into the morning.

The snow lay long after the New Year; in fact, there were intermittent snowstorms right on until April. Our two main preoccupations were keeping warm and keeping in flying practice.

There were many restrictions to flying in France. Some of them were relaxed sufficiently to allow us to carry out practice bombing with live H.E. bombs on an inland range; low flying "cross-countries," in certain specially selected areas; dummy attacks on B.E.F. motorised columns; and defence against fighters with the Hurricanes of 1 Squadron.

Before the end of January 1940, I was sent down to Perpignan, the last town of any size before the Spanish border, near the Mediterranean coast. I was to open up for 12 Squadron an aerodrome at Saint-Laurent-de-la-Salanque. With this aerodrome as base, the squadron was to practise air gunnery over the sea.

Perpignan fascinated me. It had a Moorish atmosphere. The streets were narrow and smelt, amongst other things, of musk. The people spoke Catalan. The sand-brown plains were covered with vineyards, the roads lined with plane-trees. The Pyrenees, at their southern end, were majestic; the highest peak, Canigou, was covered in snow. The wind was freakish and very violent; it blew down from Canigou, whistled through Perpignan and across the plains most days of the week.

While at Perpignan, the officers of the squadron were invited to a *vin d'honneur* at the military encampment of La Barcarès, where a regiment of foreign volunteer infantry was under training. The encampment was constructed on the shore of the Mediterranean – pasteboard huts set up on the loose grey dirt. Next to it there was a concentration camp for Spanish refugees, an evil relic of the Spanish civil war. There was little difference between the two camps – perhaps there was thicker barbed wire around the Spaniards than the foreign volunteers. Downwind, just past the last row of hutments, stood open stone troughs, into which the contents of latrine buckets were emptied and covered with lime. The wind whirled the grey dust from one end of the two camps to the other. The wretched Spanish refugees worked in guarded gangs on the road; the foreign volunteers sweated in their heavy ill-fitting uniforms on route marches and at the ranges. It was at La Barcarès that I first prayed that I should never be behind the barbed wire of a French concentration camp.

The French officers received us in a canteen hut. We drank champagne to the King and M. le President. Outside the band played a squeaky but stirring

Marseillaise and followed it with its best effort at a dignified rendering of "God Save the King," which they had probably only learnt the day before. The officers were mostly middle-aged men, covered in Great War decorations, who had seen many years' service in the Foreign Legion and other colonial regiments.

The soldiers were a mixture of all the foreign nationalities who lived in France. Many of them had a tough and resolute air. The others looked plainly bored. They were pitifully badly armed. I saw nothing except old-fashioned rifles. Most wore khaki, but some had the old blue uniform worn by the poilus in the last war.

So, this was a French infantry regiment, and one which was later to fight the Germans at the front!

Flying back from Perpignan, we were routed by way of Nantes, where we stayed weather-bound for a week. This great rambling Breton town, one of the largest in France, depressed me. It had that air of decay that is typical of so many French towns and villages. Most of the houses were old and in a bad state of repair; a coat of paint might have helped. Dirty trams rattled through the crowded streets, untidy French soldiers, neat officers, and hundreds of British Tommies crowded the cafés and cinemas or strolled past the shop windows. Nantes was dirty and ugly – worse than most English industrial towns. The greatest attraction was its food and wine.

For months my wife had been trying hard to get to France. At last, at the end of February, she succeeded in getting permission to visit the French Riviera for health reasons. I was given eight days leave, and on the 5th March I set out for Nice to join Hope.

It was colder than ever at Amifontaine when I left. There had been new and heavier falls of snow, followed by harder frosts. In Paris it was much warmer when I arrived there from Rheims on my way south. I had an hour or two to wait before my train – the Blue Train express – was due to leave the Gare de Lyon for Nice. For a while I loitered in the Gare de l'Est.

This was the terminus station for trains coming in from Rheims and the Maginot Line, and already I had come to know it well. It was always crowded with troops, some arriving dishevelled and tired, dirty and unshaven, from the Maginot Line, to be met by their wives and children; others, spruced up, coming into the station, their sweethearts clinging to their arms, happy after their leave, but dreading the parting and the relentless train journey which would take them farther and farther away from their homes and back to the strained, unnatural atmosphere that pervaded the underground fortifications.

Inside the crowded space of the Gare de l'Est the atmosphere was electric. Thousands of human dramas took place every minute. There were tearful partings, excited and equally tearful reunions. Gallic sentiment and emotion, stirred up by war fever, made a great commotion. Figures crisscrossed hurriedly in all directions, each one like a thread in a great pattern, so complicated that its form was impossible to distinguish. Each individual wove his own predestined line, always in fleeting contact, yet never confused with his fellows. Terminus railway stations have always fascinated me, and the Gare de l'Est in war time perhaps most of all.

At the Gare de Lyon I had dinner in the station restaurant and left on the Blue Train for Nice. Hope had travelled down from Paris by motor coach – a two-day trip, stopping one night at Lyon. When I arrived in Nice we stayed in a little pension. The patron was French-Swiss and his wife English. The cuisine was a mixture of Italian and Midi-French, which was strange, for it was the English wife who did all the cooking. Altogether she was a very busy woman. In addition to the cooking, she did nearly all the housework, and still managed to find enough time to look after the baby. Her husband was lazy and selfish. He was mean and looked it. Fair and quite good-looking, in spite of something rather rat-like in his expression, he spent most of his time serving at table, keeping the accounts and shopping. In the evening he left his wife at home and went out to a café to play *belote* and drink with his friends.

The food was quite good, but there was not nearly enough of it to satisfy our fresh-air appetites. Pension terms were very cheap, and everything was spotlessly clean.

The eight days passed far too quickly. Sometimes in the morning we hired horses and rode along the promenade. Afterwards we drank our aperitifs, sitting in the sun outside a café on the Promenade des Anglais. In the afternoons we would take a bus up into the hills or along the coast to Monte Carlo or walk through the flower market and up the hill into the old Italian quarter of Nice. On some evenings we danced in one of the few places remaining open for dancing. All the casinos were closed in Nice.

Nice was a long way away from the war. It was completely detached from the discomforts of the north, but, like all Riviera resorts, had undergone a great change since September 1939. The most expensive hotels were almost empty. Most of the rich American and English residents had gone away. Yachts had been laid up and dismantled in the harbour. The Promenade des Anglais was crowded with foreign officers serving in the French Army – particularly Poles and Czechs. There seemed to be more Jews than Frenchmen in the fashionable quarters. There were large numbers of French Army doctors, easily distinguished by their plum-coloured velvet képis and the tabs on their khaki tunics – and here and there the distinctive blue uniforms and *berets basques* of the Chasseurs Alpins regiment, stationed on the Franco-Italian frontier.

One day we took a bus up into the hills behind Nice to a little town built on a peak and completely surrounded by a citadel wall. Here we stayed all day. It was a perfect day, too, the sun shining down on us out of a very deep blue sky. The view across the hills and valleys was magnificent. The valleys and hillsides were terraced with vineyards, broken up by groves of oranges and olives and dotted with grey stone villages, built on spots as hard of access as St. Pol (I think that was the name of our little town). We wandered about on top of the town wall, watched men playing *boule* – a game of bowls over rough ground, very popular in Provence, and gazed away into the distance over the hill-tops and the mountains beyond. Here there was very little connection with the rush and nervous excitement of the mechanical age.

The peasants seemed quite content to live out their lives simply, free from the ties of ambition. The rich earth provided them with most of their wants – certainly all the bare necessities of life in abundance. The sun was hot and shone regularly. The children grew up fat and healthy. There was music and laughter, and they were happy. For some time, we strolled through the narrow cobbled streets – all either up or down hill – until on a corner we found a little café-restaurant in the basement of a small house. After reading the menu outside we decided to have lunch. We had to go down five or six stone steps, for the restaurant was half underground, only the tops of the windows being above street level.

We found ourselves in a small square room, one side of which was taken up by an enormous open fireplace hung around with antique cooking utensils. It had been a kitchen several generations ago. Small tables were set for lunch with clean check linen cloths. One corner of the room was cut off by a curved bar. On the bar lay a guitar, and behind it stood the *patron*, an insignificant-looking man with thick glasses and dirt-ingrained hands. Lunch was simple but good. We sat over a bottle of good vintage wine. The room was almost full. The art of conversation, the absence of which is so marked in England, was well cultivated here. After a while the *patron* picked up his guitar, strummed a few chords as warning, and then began to play and sing. He sang with great feeling and rich expression the Provençal songs of his repertoire. His dark wife, gigantic and swollen, but smiling and good-natured, came in and stood behind him proudly, wiping her hands the while on her apron, for she was the cook.

Too soon the last day of my leave arrived. I left Hope in Nice, where she stayed for another week or two before returning to England.

Soon after I arrived back in my squadron tension increased, and from then on until the 10th May, when the blitz started in Holland and Belgium, we were subjected to a series of "flaps." They usually occurred in the middle of the night. The French General Staff would suspect that the Germans, massed on the Dutch and Belgian frontiers, were going to start an offensive at dawn. A.A.S.F. Headquarters would then be informed and would send orders by telephone to the squadron to stand by ready to take off and bomb the German mechanised columns and communications, according to plans long since prepared.

In the early hours of the morning, while it was still dark, "Two-Ton" would come round to my room. I became quite used to waking up to see his massive figure towering over me and to hear the words: "Get your flight up right away, there's a flap on." Soon we were all dressed and ready to leave for the landing ground. There was always a great deal of individuality about our clothing, no two officers in the squadron being dressed alike; the severe winter had made us reinforce our Air Force uniform below and above with all kinds of comforts, such as polo-neck sweaters, seamen's stockings under our flying boots, mufflers, balaclavas and silk scarves of many colours. Some of us had white overalls turned grey with oil and dirt, others blue.

In the bus there was an air of carefully suppressed excitement – and some foreboding. As the dawn came and nothing happened, we would become completely browned-off, and cursed everyone who might have been responsible for the flap, from Hitler downwards.

April brought the first signs of spring. The snow melted and the weather improved. As the German Army had not made a move and there was no sign of a Franco-British offensive taking place, we were told to concentrate on night-flying practice. For night-flying we operated from our old landing ground at Berry-au-Bac.

At first, we were only allowed to make practice cross-country flights over certain districts in northern France; but these flights were good practice for the work we had to do later on. During the day each aircraft received a special check-up and was test-flown by its pilot and crew to make sure that all the night-flying equipment – particularly lights and radio – was in good working order. At the end of the test flight pilots landed at Berry-au-Bac landing ground. The Battles were picketed down and the cockpits covered up. At dusk the control officer for the night arrived and arranged a path of small electric glim lamps in the form of a capital L, the long stroke of which was made longer than the distance required for a Battle to take off and made in line with the wind direct.

At the bottom, or downwind end, of the L a searchlight mounted on a mobile chassis was parked so that its beam was cast along the line of glim lamps, lighting up the path for take-off and landing. As darkness fell there would be a splutter and roar from one Merlin engine after the other, as the Battles were started up. Then they would appear; dark shadowy shapes bounded by the bright little navigation lights, one red, the other green, like coloured stars on the wingtips. At the base of the L they would stop and wink out the Morse letter of the aircraft with the top signalling lamp (behind the pilot's head on top of the fuselage). The signal would be answered by the control officer's signaller – green for "take-off" and red for "wait." After each pilot had received his "green" he would taxi out, turn the nose of his Battle into wind along the L-space line of light, open up the throttle, and, with a roar that quickly diminished for those who were listening on the ground, take off and climb away out of sight, into the pitch black of the night.

Inside the two cockpits of each Battle flying through the night lighting was dowsed down to a pale orange glow. The pilot, all dressed up in flying suit and helmet and strapped with his parachute into the seat, would be concentrating on his instruments to keep the aircraft straight and level on its course at the correct air speed, r.p.m. and boost. Every now and then he would glance at his map and at the chart showing his courses marked as lines and dotted with the relative positions of the light beacons, he should see on his way. Beside each dot representing a beacon was marked the letter which the beacon would be flashing in Morse during that night's "cross-country." One or other hand would leave the throttle every few minutes to carry out some necessary adjustment – to twist the trimming tab controls for rudder and elevator, to reset the compass or the directional gyro, or alter the strength and setting of the little orange lamps set at intervals around the cockpits to light up instruments and controls.

Behind the pilot's cockpit the observer and wireless-operator-cum-air-gunner would be fully occupied. The observer had his maps and navigation instruments, his log sheet and the position message forms to work out. The position messages would be passed by him to the wireless operator, who would send them back to base, tapping them out with his Morse key. Sometimes he would switch the radio set over so that the pilot could talk to the observer. All three members of the crew would be keeping a sharp look out for enemy aircraft, although there was small chance of meeting any at night over France at that time. They would make mental and written notes on the weather and watch out for the French A.A., which, although inaccurate, was nevertheless keen, and not very particular about the nationality of the target it chose.

The captain on board a Battle was always the pilot. It was he who made all the decisions affecting the movement of the aircraft. As well as being captain, however, he was an active member of the crew. He was the key man, but the other two members of the crew had responsibilities as great as his. Navigation and most types of bombing were the responsibility of the observer; protection from attack by fighters and the emergency homing by radio was that of the wireless operator-cum-gunner. All three members formed a team, each depending on the other two for his safety. Successful missions were the result of good teamwork.

On returning from these night cross-country flights the Battles would be landed – after obtaining permission from the control officer – and taxied back to their dispersal positions. The engine stopped and the lights turned out, the crew would climb down and walk over to the operations hut, where the flight would be discussed with the flight commander and the intelligence officer. Sometimes the C.O. would also be there.

These flights were small things in themselves, and only served as the best effort we could make at training inside the limitations to flying, which were considerable, laid down by the French General Staff.

One day we were told that at last we were to take a real part in the war – we were to be given a real job of work operating against the enemy. We knew it was to be at night, and had visions of attacking the Ruhr, perhaps-bombing Cologne, or laying parachute mines on the Rhine. However, we were due for a sad disappointment, for our job turned out to be leaflet raids on moonlight nights, combined with reconnaissance duties on the same flights. On the first moonlight night, if the weather was favourable, two Battles from 12 Squadron were to take off independently and fly over Germany, dropping leaflets over selected towns in the Rhineland at about 10,000 feet.

I was one of those first two pilots. My usual crew – Sergeant Odell and Corporal Tomlinson – were to fly with me, and, in fact, share between them the donkey work of the flight. During the afternoon we tested our Battle – "V" for Victor, trying out carefully all the night-flying equipment. Then we visited the operations hut, where we studied the large-scale map of Germany pinned to the wall and marked with flags and coloured pins to represent flak concentration, enemy fighter aerodromes, balloon barrages, etc. We made a note of the requisition letter of the night – the letter to be flashed back at the ground if we were challenged to prove our identity by the French A.A. We took down a list of the letters that would be flashed in Morse by the various light beacons we would pass in France on our way. We were given our emergency ration and other material and moral aid and advice, useful in the event of a forced landing in enemy territory.

As we took off that night, loaded with leaflets, and our heads full of information and good advice, we felt a glow of satisfaction. For once, at least, in this war of nerves we were to be allowed to cross German territory. We would be a nuisance and keep many Germans out of bed. Also, we would offer the direct lie to Goering's boast that no British aircraft could pierce Germany's anti-aircraft defences. So far the Whitley squadron had dropped leaflets well in the heart of Germany. If we could get away with it, too, in our obsolete Battles, Goering's boast was going to look sillier than it did already.

The full moon shone down on the landing ground out of a sky almost clear of cloud. The countryside was bathed in its soft light, as we took off and climbed up in a curve. Woods, rivers, roads, stood out clearly in detail. For the first 2,000 feet we climbed around the landing ground, watching the L-shaped flare-path getting smaller and smaller below. Then we straightened out and climbed up to 10,000 feet on our course for Germany.

About halfway up on our climb we passed through a gap between scattered clumps of cumulus cloud, outlined in silver by the moonlight. We flew on over the top of the banks of cumulus – great white puffs like steam from a railway engine on a cold, clear day. Through the gap between the clouds the countryside was half lit by the ghostly light of the moon and half covered by the shadows cast by clouds.

As we plied steadily on, with the moon above us and clouds and the earth far below, I was filled with that curious, almost mystical feeling of elation which I believe must be the prerogative of airmen and mountaineers, elation having as part of it a strong sense of mastery over the elements, a great loneliness of spirit, and an extraordinary state of mental peace. Even at 10,000 fcct, only a quarter of the operational height of the most modern aircraft, the earth stands in miniature. Houses are minute and human beings invisible. Nobody possessing an imagination could fail to be impressed repeatedly on such occasions by the smallness of man, his insignificance, and the relative unimportance to the universe of his acts.

Our course took us very close to the southern borderline of the Duchy of Luxembourg; in fact, to the point where the frontiers of France, Luxembourg and Germany meet. Here the Luxembourgeois had placed electric-lighted Ls all along the frontier of their territory. The idea of this was to discourage the pilots of belligerent military aircraft from flying over Luxembourg, a neutral State. For us it served as a very valuable aid to air navigation at night.

As we crossed over the frontier into Germany the clouds had cleared. Spread out below us lay enemy territory, but I could not bring myself to think of it as such at first. There was a great dark forest spreading itself away out to our left, covering hills separated by river-filled valleys. There were broad stretches of undulating downland, with every here and there small towns and villages, the houses standing out clearly in the moonlight, even from 10,000 feet. Not a sign of life anywhere – no lights, nothing. It was difficult to believe that there below us lay anything but a peaceful, sleeping nation. That impression was rudely obliterated as we approached the Rhine.

We were looking down upon the Rhine, which was a silver grey, standing out clearly against the darker grey of its background, when suddenly searchlights began to light up and the sky was criss-crossed by the ranging beams of light blue and orange. Then groups of little red balls began to pop up from below us like bubbles in a glass of champagne, to vanish as unexpectedly as they had appeared on reaching a certain height. Then came the "flaming onions," which looked like orange tadpoles wriggling up into the air, and snuffing out as suddenly as the red balls, some uncomfortably near to us.

We were already jinking, turning, climbing and dropping down again in an attempt to keep out of the searchlight beams and escape from the heavy flak which was bursting continuously just behind our tail and too close to be lightly dismissed. At the same time, we had to concentrate on flying to a certain spot before Odell could push out his bundles of leaflets, which we had orders to spread over Coblenz.

Dropping leaflets from a height is neither a haphazard nor an easy business, for if they are to fall in the right place a careful study must be made of the meteorological position at the height at which the aircraft is going to fly; this in order that it may be directed by the pilot on a course in such a way as to insure tracking over a given line on the ground. An equally careful study of the wind force in between the height at which the aircraft is going to fly and ground level must be made to determine how far from the town the track lines must be to ensure that the leaflets, once they have started fluttering down, are blown in the right direction to cover the town.

As for most flying operations, detailed preparation for the flight must be made on the ground before taking off, for once in the air and the job begun, there is neither time nor the facilities necessary for accurate readjustment. Leaflet dropping can only be successful if the navigation is careful; this necessitates good teamwork between pilot and observer. In France, navigation at night was based on dead reckoning, for we had neither the sextants nor the detailed knowledge necessary for astro-navigation and could only use our radio for homing.

When Odell estimated that we were over the point for releasing our leaflets I straightened out and flew straight and level for a short time, while he pushed out the leaflets in bundles, which separated clear of the tail and floated down behind us out of sight.

Then we started to jink violently again, for the heavy flak had become more accurate. It seemed as if a giant firework display was going on all around us. The colours were beautiful; blue and orange searchlights, red balls of fire, yellow gun flashes, orange "flaming onions," and green tracer shells. Now we were over Coblenz. We had lost height, taking avoiding action, and had to come down lower still to complete the second part of our task – a reconnaissance of shipping on the Rhine.

At about 2,500 feet the light flak opened up, red and green tracer shells flashing past us from all directions. We circled round Coblenz at about 2,000 feet, looking for white smoke coming up from electric transformer plants and searching for signs of blast furnaces at work. We saw nothing, so we flew on down the Rhine to Bingen. The river was shining brightly in the moonlight, and still the tracer shells leaped up at us from gun emplacements on both banks. Not a sign of any other movement anywhere. The roads and railways seemed empty; on the river there were groups of barges tied together and other small craft motionless at their moorings. Had it not been for the searchlights and flak, it would have been difficult to believe that any life existed on and around the great river below.

Eventually, after we had reconnoitred the sector of the Rhine which had been allotted to us – weaving from side to side to escape from the light flak which had been uncomfortably close while we were low down over the river – we turned away and climbed as quickly as possible in the direction of France. Behind us, as we flew away, the firework display rapidly diminished. It had blazed up with tremendous suddenness, and almost as suddenly it now died away. Once more we were passing over the quiet sleeping villages, the valleys, the forests and the wooded hills.

Once more we were approaching the Luxembourg frontier, with its illuminated Ls. And now, back in France, we could relax a little, while setting out to find our landing ground, mainly by means of the light beacons set unevenly on either side of our route. As we were passing close to Metz

I suddenly became aware of a dark shape casting its shadow across our Battle – a mysterious something between us and the moon. On closer examination I recognised it as a barrage balloon and very close, too. There is something very unfriendly about these dark monsters floating in the air when you come across them unexpectedly at night.

There were plenty of light beacons to guide us – almost too many, for it was difficult to keep a check on all the different Morse letters which they were flashing. We made a slip. One of the lights was sending out the wrong letter according to our chart – or more likely we misread it. We turned too late on our final course for home, and when our estimated time of arrival was up the light beacon on the landing ground at Berry-au-Bac was nowhere to be seen. It was now up to the wireless operator to get us safely back.

Corporal Tomlinson soon got a bearing by radio, and we calculated from it that we were far south of Berry-au-Bac. We turned on to the homing course we had been given, and soon the light beacon and the flare path appeared in front of us. This was a good example of the importance of radio for night flying and the necessity for teamwork in a bomber. Odell had navigated us to the target and dropped the leaflets. Tomlinson brought us faithfully back, and my responsibilities had been confined to piloting.

Back in the operations hut, we reported the details of the flight, drank a cup of tea, ate a few sandwiches, and went off to bed.

A few weeks later the war started in earnest. Germany invaded Belgium, Holland and Luxembourg. For me, the first day of that invasion was to change the whole future course of my life. To many of my friends it brought death, to others, the dreary existence of a German prison camp. For few of the original 12 Squadron air crews went home from France.

Chapter 3

Broken Wings

As dawn was breaking on May 10th, 1940, the anti-aircraft guns in the vicinity of the château at Guignicourt opened fire. The firing was only spasmodic, but it woke me up, and I rushed over to the window just in time to see a formation of five Dornier bombers coming out of the mist to bank round our mess and fly on in the direction of the landing ground at Berry-au-Bac. Soon the whole mess was aroused, and we were all out in the grounds together, hiding under cover of the trees, watching other formations like the first wheeling overhead. They were flying at only about 2,000 feet, for they had little to worry about.

In the first place, the A.A. fire from the French and British batteries was very wide of the mark; in the second, there were no Hurricanes nearby to intercept them – only a few Moranes from which the Dorniers could easily escape after their bomb-loads had been dropped. It was infuriating to have to stand there hiding under the trees, knowing that we were powerless to defend our aircraft or to attack the German bombers. One anti-aircraft shell burst near a bomber, but it did not break formation, and soon all the Dorniers flew back to Germany unperturbed – still in good formation.

I got into the Hillman van with the squadron leader and one or two other officers, and we set off as quickly as possible for our landing ground, to see if it had been attacked. The orderly officer had rung through from Amifontaine to say that he did not think the landing ground had been bombed. Now we wanted to make sure. We found that no bombs had in fact dropped on the hillside at Amifontaine that even the British and French would be fools enough to risk using the side of a hill for taking off and landing modern aircraft; perhaps they thought our Battles were wooden dummies. Whatever they thought, they had completely ignored Amifontaine, and instead had laid a stick of H.E. bombs across the French aerodrome of La Malmaison, on the other side of the road, leaving one hangar and other buildings damaged and a line of craters over the aerodrome surface.

For months we had been waiting for dummy wooden aircraft to disperse in fields near our landing ground. How ironical it was that our Battles should be treated as dummies – that the Germans should treat our landing ground as unfit for use, when it was the best bit of ground that the French and British air staff had found for us. Our Battles, sixteen of them, all with their bombs fitted ready to take off on a raid, were left untouched – while at La Malmaison the Luftwaffe had only damaged a few antique communication aircraft.

In the Operations hut, hidden in the line of pines, we telephoned through to Headquarters. There were no orders, so we left a skeleton staff on the landing-ground and went back to the château for breakfast, there to await further developments. Our organisation for flaps had become almost routine – there had been so many cries of "wolf" from the French staff throughout the last month.

On our way back to the château we made a circuit to pass Berry-au-Bac landing ground, in order to see what damage had been suffered by 142 Squadron. A large number of bombs had been dropped, mainly amongst the aircraft, which for once were dispersed over the landing ground instead of being hidden in their prepared positions on the edge of the wood. Most of the bombs were delayed action. This accounted for the small number of explosions we had heard while the Dorniers were circling overhead.

While we were having breakfast, reports began to come through that Belgium, Holland and Luxembourg had all been invaded. There was a parachute scare; we were to trust no-one; everyone was to be armed at all times; we were to be extra careful about sabotage attempts, etc. – all the usual ingredients that made up a flap. As usual, the first move had come from the Germans, and the French High Command seemed to be largely unprepared. In spite of all the flaps spread out over the last month, the real attack had come as a surprise. The day before no one had suggested the likelihood of its arrival.

Back at Amifontaine we found further reports waiting for us. All the other aerodromes and landing grounds used by the A.A.S.F. had been bombed at dawn. Ours was the only exception – our impossible-looking hillside which had been treated as a dummy. Lille, Armentières, Arras, Douai, Verdun, Metz, Charleville, Mézières, etc. – towns in the north known to be concentration points for the B.E.F. and the French Army, had all been bombed simultaneously with the landing grounds.

And so, at last this was the day. The "sitzkrieg" was over and the "blitzkrieg" begun.

That morning, as far as I can remember, all the eight Battles in my flight, and six in "A" flight, were completely serviceable – fit in every respect to take off immediately and carry out a bombing raid. Later on, all sixteen were serviceable. All day our air and ground crews sat around impatiently, waiting for the order we all expected, to get the whole squadron into the air on its first bombing raids against enemy columns.

In the event of an invasion of the Low Countries the bomber squadrons of the A.A.S.F. were to attack the enemy columns advancing along the roads, bridges and railway junctions, and so delay the advance of the German Army by road and rail. It was naturally expected that Dutch and Belgian sappers would systematically destroy bridges, roads and railway tracks behind the rearguard of their retreating armies. Large areas of Holland were to be flooded. Each bomber squadron of the A.A.S.F. had a large-scale map of the Low Countries, including parts of Germany and France. These maps were marked with circles around every possible target, the destruction of which was calculated to delay the German advance at strategic points. There were thousands of these circles, and they covered the roads – subsidiary as well as main – canals, rivers, and railways in Belgium, Holland and Luxembourg. With this system it was a simple matter for the French General Staff to select targets as the German advance progressed and transmit orders to the squadrons.

However, we sat about apprehensively for hours, expecting at any moment to be called upon to send all our serviceable aircraft up in sections to bomb the enemy columns. Meanwhile, the Heinkels and Dorniers continued to fly over French territory – near us and over us. I remember talking to Peter, the other Flight Commander, about the losses we were likely to have on each raid. We decided it would be about eighty per cent aircraft and sixty per cent pilots. It was not until well on in the afternoon that the orders for 12 Squadron came through. We were to send two Battles to attack a large German column reported to be in Luxembourg, on a road leading from Germany to the capital of the Grand Duchy.

As Senior Flight Commander, it was my privilege to lead the first raid in my old Battle, "V" for Victor, with my regular crew, Sergeant Odell and Corporal Tomlinson. The Battle which was to follow me would be piloted by Al, a Canadian, with another of the best crews in the flight.

We marked our maps, prepared our navigation logs, and decided on our plan of attack. We would take off in formation and set course direct for the target. This would take us over the southern end of the Belgian Ardennes, and from there onwards the ground would be mainly undulating and heavily wooded. If we went down low at the frontier of France and Belgium and stayed down for the rest of the distance to the target in Luxembourg, our chances of escaping detection would be good, either by enemy fighters high above or sound detectors on the ground. Ground observation posts would be less likely to see us either, low down, and we would be free from long-range flak.

Our two aircraft were started up, and we took off with our full load of four 250 lb. bombs. We climbed up and set course for the target. The day was still fine and hot. Hitler had certainly made no mistake about the weather. The sky was clear, and there was still a slight haze – at half past four in the afternoon. Away we flew in close formation at 2,000 feet above the ground. The most striking thing about our approach to the frontier was that there was nothing unusual to see.

There were no visible signs of the French Army. Even right on the Belgian frontier there was still nothing – no lorries, guns, troops. Was there any army at all there? If so, it was perfectly concealed. Now we were right down low – hedge-hopping, banking round the houses, sweeping down the valleys and up again over the tree-tops, dodging high-tension cables. Low down like this, navigation was difficult; however, we were well on our course, and soon my heart started pounding when I knew that we were within five minutes flying time of the target. Still no sign of troops or guns. High up there were wisps of white – trails from the exhausts of fighters. We passed unnoticed.

After another two minutes we came upon one or two small parties of motor cyclists, probably the advance reconnaissance scouting units belonging to the columns we were to attack. As we flew over them they opened fire on us but missed both Battles. We dived on one group, and I gave them two short bursts from my single forward-firing Browning gun, partly to keep up my spirits and partly to disorganise their fire. Before the target was in sight Al dropped back a little, so that when we attacked he would be able to follow me yet take his own aim.

We flew down a wooded valley, and on coming over the rise at the far end we caught our first glimpse of the target. There was a moon-shaped clearing in a great wood; in the clearing, leading diagonally in our direction, lay the road coming out of Germany and on towards the town of Luxembourg – we could see the town over to our right. The enemy column had halted. It stood on the road. At its head were mule-drawn vehicles. Spread away behind were all kinds of other vehicles. Many more must have been hidden where the road ran back into the wood. It was impossible to estimate the size and length of this mixed caravan.

Things were happening quickly. Even our obsolete Battles could make 210 m.p.h. at full throttle low down. We had to sweep round a little to the left and then turn right to make sure of running up along the road and dropping our bombs on the leading vehicles. We opened up our bomb doors and got ready to release the bombs. Before we had time to turn in on our attack, I saw Al's Battle diving down behind the trees with a white trail streaming back from the engine – but there was no time to follow him and see where he had landed.

I turned to the right, and dived slightly with such little height as remained, firing with my Browning gun. Then I pulled out straight again, and skimmed at thirty feet over the tops of the vehicles and dropped the bombs on the leaders. They went off in a stick, one after the other. All of this time Tomlinson was standing up in the back, taking photographs. We were so low down, so dead over the top of the column that some of our bombs were bound to hit.

Turning violently from one side to the other, in an attempt to escape from the heavy fire that was spraying us, I saw four puffs of grey-white smoke drifting downwind lazily from the bombed vehicles. It was then that I noticed for the first time that we had been hit. The cockpit was full of petrol fumes and I was sticky with escaping glycol. I opened the hood of the cockpit to allow the fumes to escape.

Suddenly there was a heavy thud. Flames started pouring from a great jagged hole on the left side of the engine – two cylinders had been hit. Lumps of molten metal shot past my head. Miraculously my Rolls-Royce Merlin continued to turn.

I opened the throttle wide, and just managed to keep flying at about 100 feet above the ground. We had seen little sign of anti-aircraft defences. We must have been hit mainly by light flak, well concealed in the woods. The column had obviously been expecting attack from the air – certainly it was well prepared when we arrived. If only we could have attacked with a stronger force!

With the engine on fire, it was obvious that we would not be able to keep flying for long, nor could we climb up and escape by parachute. We would have to make a forced landing somewhere. But where? Certainly, as far from the Germans as possible. So, we flew on in the direction of home, the engines spluttering and backfiring, flames pouring out of the damaged cylinders. I looked anxiously around for somewhere to land. At first there was nowhere – just woods and hills, with here and there tiny clearings too small even for a landing with wheels retracted, but at least we were now in Belgium.

Just when I felt that we were bound to crash I saw a grass-covered clearing rather larger than the others we had passed. It was on a hill – rounded off like the top of a mushroom. Across it ran a sandy track. The engine was giving its last few despairing coughs as I turned in and made a "belly-landing" along the track. Two blades of the metal air-screw ploughed into the ground. There were a series of sickening crunches, and we stopped.

While we were still in the air the flames from the engine had been blown clear of my cockpit. Now they settled down, and the fire in the engines burned furiously. Before I had time to undo the straps which secured me in the cockpit the flames had rushed back from the engine. Suddenly the petrol vapour which had escaped from the burst tanks and permeated the cockpit was touched off. There was a tremendous "woof."

My hands were searching frantically for the release clip holding my straps together. Great sheets of searing flames rushed between my legs and up to thirty feet above me. In that first rush of heat my hands were burned and they seized up solid. They were completely useless. I was trapped by my straps and could not move. The awful realisation that I was about to be burned to death took possession of my mind. A tremendous white heat enveloped me. I could feel my flesh burning, but the pain I felt was mostly mental.

I shall never be able to describe the agony of spirit that I knew when it seemed certain that I should burn to death. Having found that it was impossible for me to escape from my trap by my own efforts, I let my hands drop on to my knees and curled myself up, waiting for the release of death. My whole mind was full of a bloodcurdling scream; but no sound came. If it had it might have relieved the shock.

For some reason I never lost consciousness. I sat there for what seemed to be hours, but could only have been seconds, filled with the awful horror and fear of a drawn-out death. I was convinced that it was certain and inevitable. Behind my head the electric klaxon screamed out its strident note, reminding me to lower my wheels before making a landing. That sound pierced my senses for days afterwards.

As I sat there waiting to die my mind raced back over the years. I saw a kaleidoscope of scattered, ever-changing scenes. Some were happy, many sad – the most vivid moments of my life. Afterwards I was surprised to find that it was really true that on the point of death life is lived in vivid retrospect, the mind grasping for a last time at the memories which had stimulated it in life. A feeling of great solitude filled me. I realised more strongly than ever before my own identity as a solitary soul; the loneliness of my spirit, which could never be shared by anyone else; how inarticulate was the soul of man; and that it had no language. It was only through certain obvious similarities that two souls could be brought together at all – unity of two souls was impossible. I – we were all – as alone in this world as ghosts, ghosts having no complete communion one with another. These were not new sensations to me, but they were a thousand times, stronger than ever before. It needed the shadow of death to teach me how separate is the soul of man from its fellows and from the clumsy body which carries it.

But I did not die. Odell and Tomlinson appeared on the side of the wing – I heard Odell's gasp of horror – and they dragged me from the flames. Tomlinson burnt his hands on the metal release which secured my parachute and was pressing into my stomach. It was red-hot. The other straps had all burnt through.

They dragged me down over the wing and rolled me in the long damp grass, trying to extinguish the flames that still clung to me. The few rags of clothing that still hung on my shoulders were blackened and smouldering. Molten metal had fallen on to the top of my left flying boot. It had already burnt through the thick leather, the sheepskin lining and three pairs of socks. It was now biting into the top of my foot. The pain was great. Odell cut off the boot with his knife. At last, my foot was free, but the pain hardly diminished.

With one of them on each side of me, propping me up, we staggered away from the burning Battle and flopped down 200 yards away. V for Victor was burning like a torch. Every now and then the flames would discover something explosive: the Verey signal cartridges in the cockpit, or the machine-gun ammunition, which would pop and crackle like burning twigs. Then the petrol tanks caught fire. There was a tremendous explosion, and still the Battle burned. V for Victor. Victor over what? Certainly not fire. A stupid thought, this, but it kept coming back into my mind like a hated jazz tune that runs for hours through the brain and cannot be got rid of.

The first-aid kit burnt with Victor. Tomlinson had saved the camera. He said that he was sure he had taken plenty of good photographs of the enemy column. Could all this be real? Had I been burnt – yes, I could see and feel the physical evidence. Yet we were chatting about photographs; Tomlinson was trying to cheer me up – yes, that must be it. Part of my mind still seemed to be detached – to be a long way off, somewhere in space, looking back at the rest of the mind, which was still imprisoned in my burnt body, watching every reaction, feeling each sensation, living vicariously the tortures and bewilderments of the rest of my mind and my body.

They left me sitting in the grass, my back to the burning aircraft, and ran towards a little group of peasants who were standing on the edge of the clearing, as far away as possible from the scene of the accident. They seemed to have difficulty in interesting the Belgians.

"They took us for Germans," said Odell, when he got back to me, "but they say they'll help. One of them has gone off for a car. They're still a bit suspicious."

They went back to the group to try and hurry things up. While they were away I had time to think and feel.

The pain had not become as intense as might have been expected. There was a peculiar drawn feeling about my face; the left side of my nose and my left eye felt completely distorted – as indeed they were. Ragged lumps of blackened clothing hung on me. The smell of burning was everywhere – above all, the smell of my own burnt flesh – very frightening, this. My left side, arm and leg, and the top of my foot were badly burnt. My right leg, from below the knee to the top of the thigh, was as bad; but my face and hands were worst of all. My whole body was stiff. I shivered in the cool evening air. There was physical pain, but it was still endurable.

What horrified me most of all was the sight of my hands. I stared at them with an unbelieving terror. They were the hands of a ghost, bone-white. The skin hung from them like long icicles. The fingers were curled and pointed, like the claws of a great wild bird – distorted, pointed at the ends like talons, ghastly thin. What would I do now? What use would these paralysed talons be to me for the rest of my life if I did live?

There was great relief in being out of that flaming trap, being once more a part of the living world; but the mental horror that now besieged me was more than long drawn out. On top of the shock, both physical and mental, that I had already experienced this final thought was almost more than I could bear. I was unlucky in that I never lost consciousness.

I felt weaker now, and the pain was increasing. I played every trick I knew on my mind to try and stop thinking.

Odell, having at last convinced the Belgians of our friendly intentions towards their country, arrived back at last in a battered old Citroen driven by a fat Flemish farmer. It was like a little grey box on wheels. Thank God, it was closed and not an open tourer! The back seat had been removed. I was pushed in beside one of the Belgians, who put his arm around me to support my drooping form. He kept repeating: "Quel malheur. Les sáles Boches!" We bumped away on the worst and most uncomfortable journey of my life.

We were driven for ten or fifteen minutes over roads already packed with refugees. We passed through villages in which peasants were rushing about wildly, trying to make up their minds whether or not to join the crowds who were fleeing south to the French frontier. Everywhere carts and cars were loaded with mattresses and personal belongings of every kind. Eventually we arrived in front of the entrance to a large red building – clean, new and pleasant. It was a convent.

I was carried inside and laid on an emergency operating table. Nuns bustled around me, chattering in Flemish. They gave me an injection of morphia. This dulled my senses but did not completely block out the ever-increasing pain. They cut off the rags of clothing that still stuck to me and wrapped up my burnt body in bits of torn sheets. They had no medicaments apart from the morphia. I was laid down gently on a sofa, covered up with a blanket, and left to wait for the ambulance. The nuns were packing up as quickly as possible, preparing to leave. They said the Germans were only ten kilometres away. I did not believe them and said so. Whether or not it was true I never found out, for soon I was lying on a stretcher inside a French ambulance bound for the frontier.

Odell and Tomlinson were still with me. I don't think I was ever so grateful for human companionship. We had been good comrades in the air, priding ourselves on our teamwork. In my moment of greatest need they had not hesitated. They had pulled me out of the flames and saved my life. One moment of hesitation on their part, and I would have been burned to death. But there was no hesitation. They did not stop to count the cost. Nobody could have blamed them had they left me there. We had been together on many pleasant flights in peacetime. Then when I needed them most they did not fail me.

So began the first of a series of nightmare journeys that I was to make in ambulances and trains during the next five weeks. It was not later than seven o'clock when we left the Belgian convent on our way to the French frontier. We crossed into France less than an hour later and stopped outside a French Army casualty clearing station. They took my stretcher out of the ambulance and placed it on the ground. Then followed a long delay. No one seemed to be able to decide what hospital to send me to for the night. I was too exhausted to take part in the heated discussions that were going on. I wanted only three things – a soft bed, cold drinks and the dark – and I could get none of them.

After a while I asked to be taken out of the light and the cold, which I felt keenly, although it was a warm evening. Two big, raw-looking French soldiers picked up my stretcher and carried me underground, below the stone building of the clearing station. Frenchmen, Senegalese and Arabs lay around on the stretchers which covered most of the floor space. They were all wounded – mostly as the result of air-raids – few seriously. There were no signs of food. I asked for a drink. They poured a lukewarm infusion into a soldier's aluminium mug and gave it to me.

While still in the clearing station my left eye closed up, in spite of the fact that the eyelids had been burned off. I could now see only through a space between the burnt eyelids covering my right eye. I did not care very much. I had no desire to see. The pain was still increasing, and I had a great thirst which nothing could satisfy. The morphia had made me drowsy, without relieving the pain sufficiently to let me sleep or get any rest. Altogether I felt very miserable but thanked God for Odell and Tomlinson.

At last, it was decided to take me to Verdun, which was not very far away. By now it was dark – too dark for me to see Tomlinson, who sat by my stretcher in the back of the ambulance. Was it really as dark as I thought? Was I going blind? How much had my eyes been affected? Would I see again? These thoughts tortured me as we were jolted along the road. On and on we went. Every now and then the driver, who was soon hopelessly lost, would stop, get out and search for someone who could tell him the way. Then back he would come, and off we would go again, only to stop after a few minutes, lost once more. It was between one and two in the morning when we finally arrived at the hospital.

It was a château somewhere on the outskirts of Verdun, which had been converted into a military hospital. They laid me on the operating table and began to tear off all the bits of unsterilized linen sheet which had been wrapped around me by the Belgian nuns. I suppose they could not have given me another injection of morphia. They used no anaesthetic – perhaps because I was suffering badly from shock. The pulling-off process was therefore very unpleasant. When the linen rags were removed they picked off the loose skin which remained from around the burnt areas with forceps, covered me with tannic acid, and wrapped me up again in gauze, cotton wool and bandages. They left my face uncovered, painted with scarlet mercurochrome. A nurse from Brittany with pretty eyes and a comforting smile held my head and gave me cold *limonade* and Vichy water mixed to drink. "Courage, mon petit, ça sera vite fini."

When they had finished they laid me in a soft bed. I was completely exhausted. No further pain could have kept me awake.

The rest of my first week in hospital is a confused memory of delirium and nightmare. Sometimes I could see quite well, but most of the time I was totally blind. Often guns could be heard quite close. Bombs fell not very far away. The château was never touched while I was there. I was told afterwards that a handful of doctors were treating a thousand serious cases a day in the château. They were mainly casualties from the French and Belgian armies; there were also a few British, but I did not see any of them. Then there were bombed and machine-gunned refugees – the Luftwaffe's military objectives – that crammed all the roads.

I was in a small room packed tightly with beds – so tightly in fact that the beds were all practically touching. I could move nothing but my head – and that only very slightly up and down. My whole body, including my hands, was locked together tightly. I felt all trussed up like an Egyptian mummy. They only changed my dressings once while I was there. I stank of decay.

They gave me nothing to eat, keeping me alive on rectal salines and drinks of Vichy water mixed with *limonade*. Once Tomlinson smuggled in some goat's milk for me, but I vomited it. Once they gave me a few small pieces of orange. They were broken up and left by my bedside on a plate. I could not wait until they came to feed me. I managed to raise my right arm to try and push the plate on to my bed near my mouth. The plate fell to the floor. They had no more oranges.

Most of the time I lay in wild delirium. My nightmares were horrible. Often I would wake up in the pitch darkness, not knowing whether it was night or day in my blindness. I forgot where I was. I was filled with terror; the darkness was full of mocking voices and weird sounds. Sometimes I thought I was back in the squadron mess at Guignicourt. We were giving a party for some senior naval officers. I had hidden all their clothes. They lay all around me where I sat on the floor near the main staircase. Now they were covering me; I was slowly suffocating. I tried to call for help, but no one could hear me. Then I would dream that tunnels were being dug under the château (there was always the sound of men working below). Everyone was down there tunnelling furiously. They would have nothing to do with me. Instead, they shut me up in a dark room. I had no clothes, and it was bitterly cold. I had many other dreams too horrible to record. Once I fell out of bed unconscious – how I do not know, for I was all trussed up like a chicken and terribly weak with fever and lack of food.

When I came to I could see a little. I was lying on the floor, and a strange face was close to mine. Someone was bending over me to see if my eyes were open. It was a man, and he was bathing my head. In answer to my whisper: "J'ai soif," he gave me a drink of water. Then I sank back into oblivion, unconscious, asleep or blind, I never could tell which. What did it matter, anyway? In those days I had no wish for life. Luckily my brain was too worn out with nightmares to let me reason out the fact that I was a cripple for life. I knew it – yet somehow at Verdun it never seemed quite real.

Odell had gone back to the squadron, but Tomlinson was still beside me, in the same room, sleeping in a bed near mine. Our room-mates were French officers. Sometimes when I could see a little I would watch them eating their lunch. I asked the nurse from Brittany for food, but she just shook her head sadly, smiled and went out. My lust for food approached madness. Thank God for Tomlinson – without him I should have been lost in the middle of voices babbling continuously in a language I could not understand properly. I could have no part in the conversation that went on all around me. I knew none of the words and expressions necessary to a patient in bed.

One day, after the shelling had sounded nearer than usual, a young woman walked into the room. She wore the uniform of an ambulance driver in the French-American Ambulance Corps. She was American, and it was a most refreshing sound to hear her speaking English with her slight and attractive American accent. She told me that the hospital was to be evacuated, and she was going to drive Tomlinson and myself to Bar-le-Duc.

The French nurses – I seemed to have seen practically nothing of them in that week at Verdun – lifted me on the stretcher and carried me outside. They then pushed me into the back of a large Packard ambulance. Tomlinson, his hands swathed in bandages, and the Breton nurse with the pretty eyes climbed in beside me. In spite of everything I felt ridiculously happy. My Breton nurse, who seemed to have adopted me, told me that Bar-le-Duc was famous for its *confitures*. My mouth filled with saliva at the very thought of fruit, let alone French fruit jam. I made up my mind to gorge myself at the first opportunity. The next hospital, she said, would be comfortable, and I would soon be up and well again.

I believed her, not realising even then how extensive my burns were. She herself was on her way home to Brittany for two days' leave with her parents. We did not talk about the war. She put her arm under my head to support me and waved the flies away from my face. The inside of the ambulance was painted light green – it was restful to my burning eyes. I could see quite well that afternoon. When I was thirsty they gave me drinks of lemonade. I was conscious of how much I owed to these two – Tomlinson and the girl from Brittany. They seemed to be my whole existence; but I was soon to lose them both.

At Bar-le-Duc the ambulance stopped outside the railway station. They carried my stretcher into a waiting-room. My Breton nurse with the soft eyes said good-bye; "Bon voyage, mon petit, vous serez vite guéri." Good luck, you will soon be well again now. And I believed her. I hated saying good-bye.

For a while Tomlinson stayed with me, then he was taken away to the military hospital. I pleaded with a French army doctor to send us both to the same hospital, but he said it was quite impossible. I was to be sent to L'Hôpital Mixte, which was reserved for civilians and officers. I never saw Tomlinson again. Later, when I got back to England, I heard that he had been killed during a bombing raid over Germany.[1]

For a while I lay alone. Then a stretcher-bearer in a steel helmet came in and brought me a bowl of soup. I knew I was not allowed to eat, but the savoury smell which rose from the bowl completely undermined my morale. He fed me with the soup. It tasted wonderful. It was the first food I had had since I had been burnt. After a while another stretcher-bearer arrived. I was put back in the Packard ambulance and taken to the hospital.

They carried me through an open ward at the far end of which were cubicles and put me into bed in one of the cubicles. The American ambulance driver wrote a postcard to my wife.

"Thank you for bringing me safely here – and comfortably too."

"We were lucky. Usually, I get machine-gunned by German fighters. Good luck, and I hope you'll soon get home to your wife."

They left me alone in the tiny cubicle for years it seemed. There was absolutely nothing for me to do but think. I was cut off from the world by the cubicle walls. I was too weak to call out – it hurt me even to speak. My eyes had gummed up and I was nearly blind again. I could not ring the bell or hold a urine bottle. Only a week ago I had been a fit young man. Now I was as weak and helpless as a new-born child. I smelt food and could hear the clatter of plates outside in the ward. This was too much. I managed to utter a few feeble cries, and then a nun appeared. Most of the nurses here were nuns.

"Qu'est-ce que vous voulez, mon petit?"

---

[1] Having returned to 12 Squadron, Tomlinson was killed, aged 22 and with the rank of Sergeant, on 8 February 1941. He lost his life when the Vickers Wellington he was crewing, Mk.II W5365, stalled and crashed while trying to land at RAF Tollerton. The oldest son of Captain Thomas Singleton and Ida Gertrude Tomlinson, of Dublin, where he was educated at the High School, his body was taken back to Dublin for burial in Mount Jerome Cemetery.

I opened my mouth as wide as my burnt lips would allow. She understood. At first she said I must not eat, but my look of dejection won, for she went out and came back with what seemed to me to be the most wonderful of meals – soup, meat and vegetables, *confiture*, white bread and red wine. She was small and timid. Only her face and hands were uncovered. Her starched clothes were not quite clean. She did not speak with her lips – but her eyes were full of compassion. When she had finished feeding me I was left alone once more.

Nearly all the time I was at Bar-le-Duc I was left alone. The loneliness was unbearable. I lay there longing for human company and wondering how long it would be before the Air Force doctors arrived to take me away and send me back to England. But they never came; and I lay there for a week.

All day and night I lay and sweated. I hardly ever slept at all. The slightest movement was agony, and my whole body throbbed continuously. I could not lie flat on my back, for my left buttock had been burned. They gave me no more meals – just rectal salines and occasional infiltrations of plasma. I was always thirsty but had to cry out every time I wanted a drink, and then wait a long time before anyone answered me. It was almost impossible to make myself heard, and there seemed to be very few orderlies. My bladder, weakened by fever, had lost its elasticity. I thought I would burst it a hundred times while I waited for relief. At last, two days before I left, they gave in to my pleadings to be put outside in the open ward. It was while I was in the ward that I overheard two doctors talking about me. My French was then very bad – but I understood this conversation.

"Does he understand French?"

"No."

"There's nothing we can do for him."

"No."

So, they thought I was going to die. Surely that could not be true. Life was grim enough at present, but I was not afraid of it. But death – that was another matter. I did not want to die.

They dressed my wounds once at this hospital. It took two hours. I had never known such pain before. They tore off the gauze, which had become as hard as brick with pus and blood. They used no anaesthetic – no warm salt water – they just tugged, and I bled like a stuck pig. When all my burns were exposed they wiped them with ether, and wrapped them up in gauze soaked with mercurochrome, which in turn was covered with cotton wool and then bandages. During the dressing one of the few Red Cross nurses there sat on my bed and held my head in her lap.

She knew a few words of English and made me sing "Tipperary" with her while the doctors pulled at the sticking gauze. I think she thought "Tipperary" was the British national anthem. It was she who gave me the foundations of a "hospital vocabulary." For days I had been shocking the nuns with the crude expressions I had picked up somewhere which described all the body's natural functions.

One day while I was still in the cubicle the wing commander of 150 Squadron came in. He was paying a visit to one of his air gunners, Leading Aircraftman Summerson, who had had his face, both hands and arms badly burned and a gun-shot wound in one leg. Summerson had been in the next-door cubicle for a day, and no one had told me! I asked for news of the war and my own squadron, but the wing commander was in a great hurry and said very little. He had to move his squadron to a new landing ground further south. So, the rumours I had picked up about the French Army being in full retreat must be true!

This seemed even more certain a day or two after, when I was told by a doctor that Summerson and I were going to be evacuated. The word "evacuated" sounded ominous. What could have happened to my own squadron? It must have left Amifontaine, if Summerson's squadron had been moved. For 12 and 142 Squadrons lay further north than nearly all the others. Now there was talk of evacuation from Bar-le-Duc. I asked where we were to be sent, and they told me Chalon-sur-Saône.

For some reason that I cannot explain I connected Chalon-sur-Saône with the Atlantic coast near Bordeaux and built up in my mind a vision of a wonderful modern sanatorium set high on a hill overlooking the sea, equipped with *chaises-longues* and some lounge verandahs. From there I would be put on a hospital ship at Bordeaux. I would soon be back in England. By August I would be fit to swim during my convalescence, which I had decided already to spend in Cornwall. I suppose it was on fantasies such as this that I kept myself alive. I longed for sunshine and sea – for a sight of the blue sky; the refreshing sound of children's laughter; bright colours and movement; fields and hills and "hearts at peace under an English heaven."

I saw Alan Summerson for the first time as we lay on stretchers in the ward, waiting to be taken by ambulance to the station. His dark hair was unkempt, his face black and red in patches – scab and mercurochrome. His lower eyelids and his bottom lip were drawn down, giving him a tired expression. His eyes were brown. God, I thought, surely I can't look as bad as that. So far I had not been allowed to look in a mirror.

We left Bar-le-Duc with some regrets. The doctors had been kind, and we had not been allowed to feel that we were foreigners. The nurses seemed proud to look after "la Royale Air Force." However, we were both convinced that our next move would bring us nearer to home. They took us together in an ambulance to the station and carried us aboard the hospital train. There, for some reason, we were separated and did not see each other again until we arrived at Chalon-sur-Saône.

This was a real hospital train. The long compartments were fitted to carry rows of stretchers two deep along the sides against the windows, leaving a clear passage down the centre from one end of the compartment to the other. My compartment had a kitchen attached. During the journey I managed to scrounge a mug of army wine, a plateful of savoury rice and a bowl of coffee. After a fortnight of rectal salines, I knew how to appreciate this food.

Alan was less fortunate. He had nothing to eat during the twelve hours it took us to cover the short distance between Bar-le-Duc and Chalons-sur-Sâone. Just before we left the station an R.A.F. doctor came into the compartment and left me two packets of cigarettes, which I could not smoke. I asked him when we were going back to England. He said he did not know, but I was not to worry everything would be all right. Then he went away again.

We arrived at our destination after midnight – we had left the hospital at half-past ten in the morning. The journey had been very uncomfortable. Every time the train braked – as it seemed to do once every two or three minutes – the carriages clattered together, and we were jarred on our stretchers. So, we were glad to find ourselves in an ambulance again, climbing the hill from the station to our new hospital.

The Hôpital Carnot stood on a hill overlooking the town of Chalon-sur-Saône. It had no sun-lounge. We saw no *chaises-longues*. There was no sea. It was a huge military hospital, and although I saw only one small room and a passageway all the time I was there, I learnt that it was built rather like an old-fashioned barracks.

Alan Summerson and I were carried on our stretchers along a stone passageway and into a small room with a tiled floor. A single weak and naked electric globe cast a little light over its gloomy interior. Two iron beds were pushed with their backs to the window and touching the walls – one on each side. Between the beds stood two enamelled bedside tables. Near the door, which was opposite the window, there was a plain wooden wardrobe, a table and a chair. The beds and the room were clean. We were put into the beds, which were hard, by a group of Red Cross nurses who smiled at us and seemed very friendly. We were so weak that they gave us an injection to stimulate the action of our hearts, and an infiltration of plasma. They asked us if we would like an *infusion*. I told them we would prefer *café-au-lait*. They gave it to us, but expressed surprise at the Englishmen who did not like tea. It was impossible to explain to them the difference between English tea and a French "infusion." In spite of the coffee, we slept soundly.

The next morning, we wakened early. The little night-nurse, who had several hundred patients to attend to every night, was standing between our beds. In one hand she held a large enamel jug full of steaming *café-au-lait* and in the other a bowl. We had three bowls each of the steaming coffee. While we drank, the night-nurse chirupped like a young thrush. She spoke a special pidgin French of her own, and we understood her quite well. She was a nice little thing – always very lively and cheerful. We kept her pretty busy at night emptying our urine bottles. At first, when we wanted her we had to shout: "*Infirmière!*" at the top of our voices. This would have kept us amused, had it not been for the urgency of our call. Later Alan taught himself to ring the bell with his toes.

Later on in the morning the ward maid came in and washed the floor. She was soon one of our best friends. A middle-aged woman of the peasant class, she had many of the best qualities which have won the French peasant the reputation for hard work and kindliness. We never really talked with her. It was too much effort to think out the French words we could pool together between us and make them into sentences. Alan spoke much better French than I, but we still had a great deal to learn. She would do some little thing or other for us, for which we would thank her, and then she would say: "It is nothing at all." That was all. Yet when we left the hospital she wept bitterly, and we cried a little too – rather to my surprise.

Madame Gentille, the nurse who looked after us almost exclusively, was the equivalent of one of our British V.A.D.s. She was a good-looking woman of about thirty-five. She had a striking personality, generous in all things and full of fun. Her husband was a *garde mobile*, and they had a son. She did everything for us until she fell sick a few days before we left. She was tickled pink at the idea of having two inarticulate foreigners on her hands and teased us a great deal about our ignorance of French. She did her best to spoil us in every way. Once she brought her husband and son to see us. The father was a typical French policeman. The only thing outstanding about him was his sweeping walrus moustache. The son was small and rather skinny. I don't think he enjoyed either seeing or smelling us.

When lunch time arrived that first day Madame Gentille brought us eggs, ham, bread and butter, vegetables and milk pudding. From then on every day, we were asked in the morning what we would like for lunch; and usually we got what we asked for. There was chicken, ham, milk and many different fruits in abundance. I doubt if any of the French patients were better provided for.

Most of the time we just lay still – too worn out even to talk to each other. It was only at night, when sleep would not come, that we talked at length. Alan would tell me of his home in Lincolnshire, of swimming expeditions in the summer, and skating on the fens in winter; of rough shooting and hay-making, and his pet hobby – ornithology. His mind was retentive. He was as informative as an encyclopaedia. We talked little of France and the war – it was all too close.

Our dressings were changed every three days. Whereas the nursing and our general care were perfect, and we were as happy as possible under the circumstances, the doctors' methods seemed crude and unnecessarily painful. We always lost a lot of blood which should not have been necessary with burns. The dressings were never removed by soaking in warm water. Doctors, with forceps in each hand, tugged violently at the hardened gauze which was sticking fast to our burns. Oils and softening ointments were scarce, and usually the gauze dressing was put on dry.

The doctors were overworked and had to hurry. Worse than the pain of the treatment were the awful moments of waiting for Alan's dressings to be finished before they started with mine. His hands had reached a more painful stage than mine, and the pain brought out the sweat all over him. His fingers were a jumbled mass of scarlet, and blood gushed freely from them all over the rubber sheet laid over his bed.

On our first Sunday we received quite a stream of visitors, each bringing a gift of flowers, fruit or chocolate. Some of them stayed and wrote letters for us. They all reiterated their belief in England and the alliance of our two countries. Later in the afternoon Madame Gentille brought in six very small girls, each carrying a bouquet of flowers from her own garden. They must have seen a terrifying sight, for we were both horribly disfigured and smelt of decaying flesh. With perfect composure they came in, smiled at us, laid their flowers on the foot of our beds, and then filed out again quietly. We were deeply touched. Of all our visitors we appreciated them most.

With typical kindliness the nurses lent us the only public radio in the hospital. We listened in occasionally to the British news, but usually it was blocked out by atmospherics – probably of German manufacture. The French news was gloomy. Each day brought accounts of a new disaster, a further retreat. Weygand would soon make the counter-attack he was preparing, said the Government spokesmen, but it was difficult to believe. I shall never forget the day that it was announced that the Germans were in the outskirts of Paris. There was a group of nurses, doctors, and a few wounded soldiers in our little room. Many of the nurses cried openly. On every face was a look of intense sorrow – of shame and despair, which increased at the end of the news, when the Marseillaise was played with its usual vigour. It still sounded the same as ever, but we all felt it was the swan song of France.

France would undoubtedly lose Paris – it had already been declared an open city, and the Government had fled to Bordeaux. Would the loss of the capital mean the end of this great nation? I could not believe it would be so. Surely the spirit of the French people, their love of the homes they seldom left, would be strong enough to prevent the collapse of France. The French Army would stand and fight somewhere, even with Paris gone. I did not realise then that France had been betrayed and lost long before the first tank appeared on her soil.

Once on the B.B.C. news I heard how Don Garland, who had taken over the command of my flight after I was wounded, had won the V.C. for his suicidal attack on the bridges at Maastricht. I wondered whether I should ever see any of "B" flight air crews again. They had destroyed their target, but the French Army had failed to check the German advance.

Our only visitor from the Air Force was the padre from my wing. He brought me all my kit, letters from Hope and news that I had been awarded the D.F.C. I was most embarrassed, for Alan had received no letters from his squadron and had not been decorated. He was compensated a little later on, for the French awarded him the *Médaille Militaire* and the *Croix de Guerre avec Palme.* I had wormed out of him the details of his adventure.

He was a wireless operator and air gunner in 150 Squadron, equipped with Battles. He was the gunner in one of three Battles carrying out a raid against a concentration of German troops halted in a valley. While they were in the middle of their bombing run they were attacked by a large number of Messerschmitt 109s. They carried on with their bombing while Alan and the other two air gunners in the formation dealt with the attackers. The Messerschmitts came in very close, for they knew that the Battles were easy meat – slow and ill-defended in the rear.

Alan was hit in the leg, and the observer behind him killed. Two Messerschmitts crashed to the ground in flames. Alan's Battle suddenly struck the ground, and he was thrown out some distance clear of the aircraft. He got up and found that apart from the gun-shot wound in his leg he was not hurt. He stumbled back to the Battle, which was now in flames, his one idea to save the pilot trapped in the cockpit. He climbed on to the wing, and standing in the middle of the flames, pulled out the pilot and dragged him clear. The pilot was already dead. He himself was severely burned. Now he was determined not to fall into the hands of the Germans. He set out for some woods not far away. His leg was bleeding profusely, and the skin hung down in loose shreds from his face and hands. He reached the wood and lay there in hiding until dark.

For two days and nights he was at large in territory already largely occupied by the enemy. He hid in houses and cafes which had been deserted by their owners. Once he was upstairs in a bedroom when he heard German soldiers talking in a café below. He stumbled out of bed and hid beneath it for hours, while in the room below the Germans soldier made merry with the café's stock of wine. A long counterpane covered the bed and drooped to the floor on either side. Had the Germans come upstairs and stood opposite the foot of the bed, they could not have failed to see him. Luckily they never did. When their party was over they rolled out into the night and left him undisturbed.

All the time he suffered great pain from his burns and wounded leg. For food he had only dried cereals and stale bread which he soaked in wine. He was nearly blind. In spite of everything he managed to walk many kilometres – and in the right direction. On the third evening he stumbled upon a French patrol.

When challenged by the sentry, whom he could only just see, he answered in French that he was an English airman. He was told to advance with his hands above his head. This was very awkward, for he had lost his belt, and his braces were broken. He could only support his trousers by pressing his arms to his sides, so that when he walked towards the astonished sentry his trousers were around his ankles. He was taken to the patrol post and laid on a pile of coats. They gave him brandy. It was only then that he became fully aware of his exhaustion and the greatness of his pain. Eventually he was put in an ambulance and taken to hospital.

In the air attack he had shot down two enemy fighters – a difficult feat with a single machine gun. After the crash, although wounded in the leg, he tried to save the pilot, and was terribly burned. Then he evaded the Germans for three days and nights and returned to the French lines, although suffering great pain and nearly blind. I believe that he earned the Victoria Cross; but he was never decorated by the British. I hope that someday he will be.

Early one morning there was a great bustle in the Hôpital Militarie Carnot at Chalon-sur-Saône. After a while nurses and doctors came into our room. They quickly changed our bandages, dressed each of us in a rough shirt, and told us that in a few minutes we were leaving for the station to be evacuated further south. We asked them where we were going to. At first they answered with reserve, saying that casualties had been many in the recent fighting, and more wounded were coming down from the front. Later they admitted that the real reason for our evacuation was that the Germans had reached Rouen.

We were laid on stretchers and carried along the stone passage and out into a courtyard. It was like a barrack square. In all the long days we had lain in our little room we had never been able to look out of the window, for it was behind our heads, and we could not turn round. Occasionally we had heard birds singing outside. My imagination had conceived a view through that window of gardens filled with many coloured flowers; beyond, trees and fields, and far below, the wide River Saône. Outside our window there were none of these things – just a barren courtyard. I felt quite disappointed.

It was about half-past ten in the morning when we arrived by ambulance at the station. There we were taken into a long bare room, full of other wounded. About half of them were serious cases. They looked dejected and miserable. There were a few officers amongst them, but they stood aloof and took no notice of us. We were still there at midday, when Red Cross nurses – some of them looking very glamorous and amateur, but most charming – came round with ham, rolls and coffee. Both Alan and I had enormous appetites and had had nothing to eat – just our usual morning coffee to drink – before leaving the hospital. Now we both ate and drank as much as we could get – just as well, too, for we did not eat again that day.

When it became known that we were British airmen, the French soldiers crowded round us and were full of sympathy. They were anxious to know why they had seen so few British bombers and no French. We tried to explain, but it was difficult. They told us that France had been betrayed – most of their officers had deserted them. None of them spoke much about the fighting – just the interminable marching south away from the Germans. "And now," despairingly, "we shall be the slaves of the Boche."

Shortly after lunch we were taken out and along one of the platforms. Our "hospital" train was waiting for us. It was a short goods train made up of covered trucks, capacity "eight horses or forty men." The trucks were bare inside and had been swept out – but I think the last load had been horses, and there were many flies. Alan and I were carried into the guard's van, just behind the engine. We had with us a French lieutenant, also on a stretcher, and a nurse who turned out to be his sister. There was only just room to squeeze our three stretchers in together, and they were all touching. The nurse had to sit on the baggage, which filled up the remaining floor space of the van. Neither the French officer nor the nurse spoke any English, but by now we could speak enough French to get almost anything we wanted. The other wounded were huddled together in the goods trucks behind. Those who were not on stretchers had either to stand or squat on the floor.

It was a glorious day – bright sunshine, clear sky, and very hot. There was no wind. The heat encouraged hordes of flies, which settled on our stinking bodies. We could not ward them off. They settled on our faces and got in our eyes. My left eye was still almost closed by swelling, although the lids had been burned off; the swelling around the right one had gone down and it was stuck permanently open – a trap for flies and sunlight. Some of the time I had my head covered up completely to keep out the sunlight and protect me from the flies, but it was most uncomfortable in the sweltering heat, and I had had enough of blindness.

The train steamed slowly out of the station at about two o'clock. Although the train was short the engine was large and powerful. It was fitted with very efficient brakes. Every time we stopped the driver put on his brakes with a jerk, sending a shock through the buffers right down to the last truck and causing each one to crash violently against its neighbour. The wounded inside were thrown backwards and forwards, and we on our stretchers were badly jarred. The French lieutenant suffered most, for he had a number of compound fractures in splints.

We seemed to be by-passing all the big stations. At each of the small stations through which we passed crowds of refugees stood on the platforms and sat on the embankments beyond. The numbers of refugees on the roads and railways of France must have been enormous that day, for we were well off the main routes. Most of the refugees were old men, women and children. Here and there in the crowd, however, were scattered a few soldiers – ragged, dirty and dishevelled, without their arms or any of their equipment.

Alan and I were both badly disfigured. This was accentuated by the mixture of red mercurochrome and black scab which covered our faces. Often as we passed slowly through the stations we would see through the open door women covering their eyes and stifling a cry of horror at the sight of us. My face was particularly ugly, for while I was being burned it had screwed itself up into an expression of mixed fear and horror. I was reminded of my mother telling me when as a child I had made an ugly or disgruntled face: "One of these days you'll make a face like that, and it will stick to you." How right she had been, for my expression stayed as it was for months after I had been burned.

Eventually we arrived at Paray-le-Monial, which is a picturesque little town almost in the centre of France. It lies now just inside the occupied zone, near the line of demarcation.

It was pitch dark and very late at night when we arrived in the station. Although the real destination was further on it was decided that Alan and I should stay here while the other poor devils continued their miserable journey for several more hours.

We lay on our stretchers side by side on the platform, which was deserted. Our train steamed away, and we waited for a long time before we were put in an ambulance and driven to hospital. We were cold now and completely exhausted, and far too weak to talk. On the journey we had had nothing to eat and only a little water to alleviate our agonising thirst.

The ambulance ride was very short. In a few minutes time we found ourselves out in the cool night air again, being carried up steep steps leading into what appeared to be an imposing building. This was the fourth hospital I had been inside in five weeks. I hoped it was to be the last. I had no complaints. All things considered, I had been very well looked after and kept as comfortable as possible in all the other three hospitals. This new hospital, however, was a model.

The stretcher-bearers carried us through the entrance hall. A military doctor and a quiet nun with gentle eyes bent over us and asked all the usual questions. When they heard that I was an officer they wanted to separate us and put me in a room by myself. Naturally I did not want to leave Alan, so they agreed to keep us together and put us in a big, airy room containing four beds. Between the beds there was plenty of room to spare. This was a great luxury, for always before we had been tightly packed together. After they had put us into bed they gave us both infiltrations of scrum – or it may have been plasma. We needed it to keep us alive, for we were nearly gone. They also gave us bowls of hot milk flavoured with coffee. Soon we had sunk into the deep sleep of complete exhaustion.

When I woke in the morning the sun was shining through the large plate glass windows that took up nearly all the wall space on one side of our little ward. One of the beds opposite was empty; in the other lay a French soldier. He was sitting up and smoking. He wore his khaki shirt and a forage cap. He looked quite out of place, like a dirty mark on a clean white sheet. The fourth bed was empty.

The atmosphere of peace which had impressed me the night before still continued. A middle-aged novice pattered in and out. She made our beds, turned out the dirty soldier, and cleaned the room. She hardly spoke a word. When she had finished, the dressing trolley was wheeled in, and for the next two and a half hours two doctors and three nuns were busy dressing our burns. For the first time since we had been in hospital hot water was used for soaking off our dressings, and we suffered hardly any pain. For once we did not have to grit our teeth, nor did sweat stand out in beads on our brows.

The quiet efficiency and unemotional compassion of those nuns – compassion which could never be confused with the sentimentality that one meets so often inside hospitals, particularly with nurses – created so strong an impression on me that I believe that if I had stayed there long I should have become a Catholic. Here was one of the finest examples of true practical Christianity I had ever seen. It would have been perfect to have stayed in this hospital, but it was not to be.

After lunch we lay back peacefully against our pillows and gazed out of the window. I was watching the trees swaying gently to and fro and listening to the birds – enjoying my new-found peace – when I was wrenched back rudely into the reality of the war again by the hum of aircraft engines.

At first it was faint, but it soon increased in volume, until we realised that they were nearly overhead. We wondered, at first vaguely, whether they were French or German. We could not tell by the sound. Suddenly we heard the evil whistle of falling bombs, quickly followed by loud reports. We were very frightened – we felt so helpless, shut in and unable to move – for the bombs were dropping very close to us. It was a horrible sensation, lying in bed wondering where the next bomb would drop and knowing that there was not the slightest chance of moving. However, it was soon over, and the aircraft flew away. We were told afterwards that they were Italians.

Nuns rushed into the room. They lifted us out of bed and laid us on stretchers again. We had only been twelve hours inside this hospital, but we were leaving again on our travels. We asked why we were being moved, but they did not answer. However, we soon found out. This was a civilian hospital, and we were only admitted as emergency cases. We had to give up our beds to make room for the civilians injured in the air-raid. They were mostly women and children, and we passed them in the hall as we were being carried out.

We were taken back to the station. The bombers' target was drawn up alongside one of the platforms. It was a hospital train. The roofs and sides of each compartment were marked clearly with huge red crosses against a white background. It had not received a direct hit, but the blast from several near misses had broken most of the windows. It had been full of refugee women and babies at the time of the attack. They had thrown themselves on the floor, but many had been injured by flying glass. This same train was now going to carry us to our next and fifth hospital, in the town of Roanne. Our stretchers were strapped into place. There were rows three deep along each side of the compartment. I was in the middle row on one side and Alan not far away on the other. Above me was a young French airman, and below a soldier, both badly wounded.

When the train was full it started, with the usual series of jerks, and we were off on yet one more slow and tedious journey. However, this time we were given a meal, and at one of the stations on the way a party of well-dressed French women brought us champagne, fruit and cakes. I could eat nothing, for my right hand was causing me agony. At Paray-le-Monial it had been placed in a splint, but was not ready for such treatment, as all the fingers were soft and decaying rapidly. The pain was so intense that one of the doctors on board decided to remove the splint and give me a clean dressing.

There were only a few small blue lights flush with the ceiling to illuminate the whole compartment. Bowls, instruments, dressings, etc., were brought alongside my stretcher, and the doctor worked at my hand while an orderly held a torch beside him. It was a long time before he had finished. My hands were now in such a mess that it was difficult to distinguish between my flesh and the blood-soaked gauze which stuck to it. When he had finished he cleaned all the scab off my face. This was almost as bad as my hand. At least after it was over I could see clearly out of my left eye for a short while – the first time in five weeks.

The doctor's work was made exasperatingly difficult by the sudden jolts and jars that passed down the train from the engine every time we stopped and started. Once he slipped and fell on the floor, knocking all the sterile instruments out of the tray held by the orderly. This caused pandemonium. New sterile gauze and instruments had to be found. The doctor was very patient, but by the time he had finished with me he was almost crazy with irritation.

To add to the discomfort of this journey the sheet which they had wrapped around me in Paray-le-Monial when they put me on the stretcher was soaking wet. Once in the train, it was impossible to change it, so they covered me with army blankets instead. On top of this all my kit had been left behind, and I never saw any of it again. For months my sole possessions were the old flannel shirt they had given me at Chalon to which was pinned an envelope containing my fortune of 900 francs. The only other thing that travelled with me was my "fiche" – an envelope containing my medical history and temperature charts. I was annoyed to think that soon a German officer would be reading my personal letters, pocketing my Colt automatic pistol, and gloating over a lovely photograph of my wife (which was irreplaceable), for later, after the Armistice had been signed, my baggage stayed in the occupied zone while I was in unoccupied or Vichy France.

In the early hours of the next morning, we arrived at Roanne. Once more we were driven by ambulance from the station to the hospital, and so ended the last of a series of journeys on stretchers which kept me out of the clutches of the Germans but caused the loss of my fingers.

Chapter 4

Back to Life at Roanne

At the outbreak of war, the French military authorities took over a large number of buildings and converted them into reserve military hospitals. One of the best of these reserve hospitals had been established in a girls' boarding school in the town of Roanne in the department of Loire. This school was supposed to be the last word in luxury. Certainly, it was new and well-appointed for a French school, but I could find nothing there which justified the description "luxurious." It was, however, clean and reasonably comfortable. Above all, it was run as efficiently as the French Military Bureau's red tape would allow, by a *Colonel Médécin* and a matron, neither of whom were anti-British. It was to be my home for thirteen months.

Alan and I arrived at the hospital by ambulance early on the morning of June 17, 1940 – the day before it was announced to the French nation by Marshal Pétain that he had asked Hitler for an Armistice. The war in France was still going on; in fact, fighting continued in several places for some days after the Armistice was signed on June 21st. On our way from the station, we saw nothing of the town, for, as usual, we were inside a closed ambulance, and, anyway, it was pitch black outside. This was one of the most irritating features of the various journeys by train and ambulance we had made. Either it was dark, or we were shut up inside trains and ambulances out of which we could see nothing, the only exception being the train ride from Chalon-sur-Saône to Paray-le-Monial. It is difficult to express fully the depressing effect of spending weeks in bed in hospital and then seeing nothing on the only occasions when one is passing through the outside world.

As at Paray-le-Monial, they wanted to separate us, but in the end we were both admitted to a ward full of French soldiers and N.C.O.s, where for a few months we received the same treatment as the others. The authorities agreed to forget that I was an officer for the time being.

On arrival we were carried upstairs and along a passage with a tiled floor, until we reached the door of one of the original classrooms, which had been converted into a ward. The windows were heavily curtained for the blackout, and the only light came from two blued electric globes hanging from the middle of the ceiling, one at either end of the room. In the dim light I counted fourteen beds, all placed very close together. In each I could just make out the blurred outline of the occupant. In one corner the glow of a cigarette told me that at least one of the other wounded was passing a sleepless night in company with me. I had plenty of pain – too much to give me sufficient physical and mental composure for sleep.

At about six o'clock the black-out curtains were drawn back by an orderly, whose dirty uniform was half covered by an apology for a surgical over-all, which was equally dirty, and the sunshine streamed in to light up the bare little close-packed ward. At last, I had a chance to satisfy the curiosity which had irritated me all night and study my surroundings.

The backs of the beds on my side were touching a light wood and glass partition which separated the ward from the corridor outside. On the opposite side the rows of beds were backed by a wall which was almost entirely given over to window space. There was a narrow space up the centre of the room between the rows of beds on either side. The beds were all very close together and separated only by the width of a small bedside table.

I studied such parts of the other patients as were protruding from the bedclothes. With the exception of one Polish miner, they were all French soldiers – N.C.O.s and men. Most of them had several weeks' growth of beard, and the others several days', for, as I later discovered, it was not the habit here to shave more than once a week, if at all. Each of them wore a rough-looking, un-ironed flannel or cotton shirt, each one a different drab colour. On the top of the small plywood table painted white, which stood between each bed and its neighbour, lay a glass urine bottle surrounded by the few small personal possessions of each soldier.

At the end of the room there were two or three chairs placed around a plain deal table. In the corner nearest the door stood a varnished cupboard. Under the table stood a pail into which the orderlies and nurses emptied the contents of all the urine bottles when full. The floor, strangely enough, was parquet, and kept fairly clean. In between two of the windows and directly opposite my bed was a large notice saying: "Don't smoke, don't spit," but neither of these injunctions was taken very seriously by the patients.

All the cases here were serious, and I found out later that three-quarters of the hospital's five hundred beds were filled with wounded who could not get up at all. The soldier next to me had been run over by a tank and had got off with a broken pelvis and some punctures in his back and sides. He spent months lying on his stomach, smoking cigarettes and reading cheap paper novelettes. A little further down the ward lay another in a similar state with wounds in his back caused by shell splinters. A sergeant, only twenty years old, and by far the youngest of the French soldiers there, was recovering from a pierced intestine. All the other cases, except the Polish miner, had been hit by bomb and shell splinters. The Pole, however, had been injured while attempting to put a French mine out of use with explosives. They were a quiet crowd, especially early in the morning. When they did speak they used army slang, and argot – neither of which was intelligible to us at first.

At seven o'clock another orderly, as dirty as the first, arrived with an enamel jug full of steaming hot coffee and a number of bowls, one for each of us. While he was pouring out the coffee a nurse came in with a tray covered with hunks of army bread. French army bread is baked in flat round loaves with a very hard crust, which only the toughest teeth and the sharpest knives can penetrate. It was still white inside, but soon afterwards was to turn a nasty dull grey as flour grew scarcer month by month, the result of the German occupation and shortage of labour.

The soldiers brought out their pocket knives, cut up their bread, dipped the pieces in their coffee, drank the coffee, and when they had finished, lit up their cigarettes. The orderly swept most of the dirt and cigarette ends off the floor; and a nurse began to bring round to each patient in turn one of the two enamel washing basins, which she filled from a jug of hot water. Then with the assistance of another nurse she gave Alan and me a bed-bath. This did not take long in my case, as only my right foot, right buttock and the top of my right arm were outside the bandages. For a bed-bath in a French military hospital the patient lies naked and unashamed. Screens are never used and would look quite out of place. There was always something rather attractive about the simplicity of everything in this hospital, the directness of the nurses and the complete lack of prudishness and hypocrisy. All this grew on me, and the longer I was there the more I appreciated its worth.

At about nine o'clock there was a jingling sound out in the corridor, which grew gradually louder until it stopped at our door. Then in came doctors and nurses and an orderly. One of the nurses was pushing the dressing trolley, on the top of which danced rows of little bottles filled with different coloured solutions; round tins holding sterile gauze, rolls of bandages; cotton wool, rubber gloves, etc., all the usual paraphernalia necessary for doing dressings. Most of the equipment was old and chipped. Some of it did not look very clean. It had; however, all been sterilized, and dressings were always done by the doctors and nurses with a pair of forceps in each hand. No gauze, solution or cotton wool was touched by hand, as so often happens in English hospitals, where the outward appearance gives an impression of impeccable sterility.

At last, our turn arrived, and we discovered that here again, our dressings were to be removed more or less dry. That was to say, the old dressings pulled off – sometimes with the help of a little peroxide of hydrogen poured between the wounds and the sticking, dirty gauze – the wounds when exposed washed with ether, and finally covered with new gauze compresses, soaked with mercurochrome (when it was available, which was seldom).

It would be a good thing for some of the less well-informed and more outspoken English people who like to criticise the French since the collapse of France for their cowardice and lack of guts, to have seen how those French soldiers stood up to the rough treatment they received from their doctors and nurses. There is nothing effeminate or easy about life inside a French hospital. Anaesthetics are rare, work is done quickly, and dope of any kind hardly ever given. The patient has the full use of his senses throughout all the most disagreeable of his experiences during his term in hospital.

Next door to our ward there was a small room equipped for emergency operations. Here major dressings were carried out on all patients who could walk there from their beds. From seven in the morning until about ten or eleven at night doctors and nurses were busy. The whole day was punctuated by the groans and occasional screams of the greatest sufferers. It is perhaps worth noting that the loudest complainers were a number of German and Austrian soldiers who had been wounded near the hospital. Yet I am sure they were treated exactly as the other patients.

The doctor who did my dressings for the first two or three months was a *Médécin Lieutenant* – and a Jew. He was one of the most patient, hard-working men I have ever met. I both liked and respected him very much. He managed to cut down pain to a minimum, and, although busy from early morning until late at night, he still spent three hours over Alan and myself. There were only three other doctors working in the hospital. The head surgeon was a lieutenant colonel, the others were lieutenants, and when we first arrived they were all wearing uniform. After the Armistice, when the French standing army had been cut down to about 100,000 men, the uniform disappeared, and the doctors carried on with their work as civilians.

The hospital staff consisted of about hundred persons. They included doctors, nurses, orderlies, manager, secretaries, typists, etc., and five cooks. There were only seventeen nurses, and out of them only about six could be considered fully trained. The others were all young girls who were learning their job largely by trial and error. Some of them were, nevertheless, in charge of complete wards full of serious surgical cases. They may not have had much technical knowledge or experience, but they certainly knew how to get down to hard work.

Lunch was served at eleven. Each of us received a hunk of bread, a spoon, a fork and a porcelain bowl. We were supposed to use our own pocket knives as table knives. Our small drinking glasses – about half the size of an English tumbler – were filled with *pinard*. The ration was one glass only, but sometimes if one was lucky one might be given a little more after all the others had been served. The first course consisted of a few pieces of sliced tomato and lettuce dressed with pepper, salt, oil and vinegar. Next followed a small chunk of meat – roast veal today, boiled beef tomorrow. When that was finished our bowls were filled with hot vegetables. There were two for each lunch, and they were served one after the other from large aluminium containers.

Even as early as June 17th – the day before Pétain asked for an Armistice – potatoes were very scarce. However, other vegetables were still plentiful in the hospitals; beans, dried and fresh peas, turnips of various kinds – in fact, everything that was in season. Then the same bowl which had been used in turn for salad, meat and vegetables was cleaned by wiping a piece of bread round the inside and we were given a little jam to be eaten with any scraps of bread that were left over.

The nurse who looked after the ward was a great character. She was one of the few who had seen a lot of service in the nursing profession. Short, square and plain, she was extremely devoted to all her patients, who in turn worshipped her, and was most efficient. Quiet and unobtrusive in manner, she had nevertheless a dry wit that expressed itself in a few short words and was always mercilessly to the point. Hardly a patient knew her surname, for she was always called "Madame Marie" – even by the colonel. She spoke no English, but that did not matter, for between us Alan and I could now scrape up enough of those expressions peculiar to hospitals which we needed to make her understand our wants. As time passed we rapidly improved.

There was a loudspeaker fitted above the door and out of it came strident noises from worn gramophone records over-amplified and badly reproduced.

From lunch time until about two in the afternoon the whole hospital was filled with a bedlam of sound, as one popular song and jazz tune after another was played. There were only about a dozen records in all, and the repertoire was monotonous, to say the least. So strident, so continuous, and so disturbing was all this raucous row, that I used to lie back and pray for the time when the one peaceful record they possessed was put on. This was Handel's "Largo." It alone could bring comfort to my troubled mind.

The first few days after our arrival there were even more distressing sounds in the vicinity. An Italian aircraft machine-gunned the outskirts of the town; often there was the harsh racketing of machine-gun fire not far away, and occasionally the reports of big guns. At night there was a continuous rumbling over the cobbled street in front of the hospital and behind my head. First it came from French Army lorries retreating south; later heavy German trucks speeding both ways.

The Germans caught up with us, and Roanne was occupied for a few days before and after the Armistice was signed by German motorised units. Most of the soldiers were Austrians. It was reported to me with reluctance that their conduct was always correct. However, this apparently did not prevent the little *gamins* from running after them in the streets, spitting on their legs and shouting out: "*Sâles Boches! Sâles Boches!*"

This continued until the mayor was obliged to post notices to the effect that the German soldiers were only doing their duty and must be treated with the respect due to their good behaviour. Needless to say, many of the notices were defaced and covered with obscenities shortly after they appeared. When the Germans arrived, they found no opposition whatsoever. In a nearby town, they were even welcomed by the mayor and presented with flowers by the women. This, however, was an exceptional incident. So confused were the people of France by the sudden success of the Germans that they did not know what to do or think. They were completely at a loss for want of direction and leadership. This was Marshal Pétain's cue, and accounts for a great deal of his early popularity – particularly with the unintelligent masses, who did not at first realise that they were being offered nothing better than a dictatorship and Fascism.

While the German Army was in Roanne, Alan and I were extremely anxious. We were afraid that the French military medical authorities would be forced to hand us over to the Germans. However, although German officers frequently visited the hospital, partly to inspect it and partly to see that their own wounded were being properly treated, we were never disturbed. I had no doubt that our presence was known, but as I was expected to die and Alan was still very low, they probably did not consider it worthwhile to take us as prisoners back with them to Germany.

"Condition on arrival, very grave. For many months he lay between life and death" – this was part of the colonel's report when thirteen months later I was moved to Marseilles.

During the ten months that I lay immobile on my back in bed I was never more than half alive. As time passed I grew thinner and thinner, until soon all my bones stood out beneath the tightly drawn skin. Ribs, spine and shoulder-blades stuck out in lines, knobs and points. My two hip-bones stood out like a cow's horns, and the skin that was tightly drawn over them was shiny. I lay flat on my back with just a low bolster under my head. I had not the strength to sit up at all. My two arms lay all the time down by my sides and were never moved except during bed-baths, dressings, etc. My hands were laid gently on large cushions made from piles of cotton wool, one on each side. I could only turn my head slightly from side to side, and always had to return it immediately to a central position afterwards, as both sides of my face were raw and painful.

Round my neck I wore a small face towel on to which dripped all day the pus – and sometimes blood – which oozed from beneath the thick black scabs which covered my eyes, cheeks, nose and lips, for they did not clean my face more often than once a week – having a theory, which may have been a good one, that it was best not to interfere with it. My mouth was too tender for it to be possible to clean my teeth. My hair was falling out rapidly. Around me clung a stench of pus and decaying flesh, sweat and filth. This attracted the flies. I never smelt antiseptic except in the vicinity of the operating theatre.

The whole hospital stank abominably of dirty lavatories, festering limbs and decaying flesh. The flies loved this. They were attracted in large numbers, stayed and multiplied. Often I counted at least sixty at a time sitting on the dressings covering my hands and on the bed. Many more buzzed round my head and settled on my eyes and nose. It was the flies above all other things that nearly robbed me of my sanity. An effort was made to keep them off my face by fixing a small tent of mosquito netting over my head. Inside this I later managed to smoke a pipe – much to the amusement of the colonel, who called me "Vesuvius"! Also, after a great deal of persuasion, Madame Marie produced some fly-papers. They were completely covered an hour or so after they had first been put up, and then the plague continued as before.

The day after we arrived in Roanne, Marshal Pétain had asked Hitler for an Armistice. After the first shock had passed, the news was received by most of Roanne with a fatalism and resignation that was almost oriental. A surprisingly large proportion of the people considered that Pétain's decision was a good one – in fact, the only one possible under the circumstances. They considered that the British had deserted them at Dunkirk, and that any attempt to carry on the struggle from North Africa, for instance, was impossible.

Certainly, there was terrible and widespread suffering all over France – roads, towns and countryside packed with homeless and half-starved refugees, two million of the French Army already prisoners, Paris occupied by the enemy, and many towns and villages of the north in ruins; everywhere complete turmoil, from which the Government stood aloof. In point of fact, the Government departments were thrown into utter confusion, due to a combination of inefficiency in the bureaux and disorganisation caused by four hurried moves in less than two months (Paris – Bordeaux – Clermont-Ferrand – Vichy).

Then there were the changes of Government and General Staff – Reynaud to Pétain, Gamelin to Weygand. I believe that things having gone so far wrong, politically and militarily, Pétain's decision to pull the best chestnut out of the fire was a good one. I believe also that it was useless to allow the massacre of a nation to continue – a great nation betrayed by its generals, politicians and Fifth Columnists; a nation that was already beaten long before the Germans arrived.

They accepted the Armistice at Roanne with resignation, but here, as all over France, was born a new hatred for the Boche that will burn in the hearts of nearly all of them, growing ever fiercer until the day that the last German leaves French soil. I had already suffered for the French people, and now I was suffering with them. In the worst moment of France's great history, I knew that a link had been forged, binding me to them – the simple, honest people – for ever. I knew also that it was my duty to them to try and understand them, so that later on when, if ever, I reached England again I could champion their cause and do something towards the rebirth of a new France – as free, but more conscientious, than the old.

As everyone now knows, after the Armistice had been signed the Germans occupied the greater part of France. A demarcation line was established to separate the two zones – occupied and unoccupied. German troops were then withdrawn from all regions contained in the zone which was in the main unoccupied. Roanne, being inside this unoccupied zone – Vichy France – was rid of its German garrison. However, the field-grey uniform of the German Army was still to be seen in the streets, for an Armistice commission remained in the town to supervise the work of an arsenal – one of the largest in France – which was on the outskirts of the town.

The officers commandeered the Grand Hotel and made it their headquarters. The hotel remained open to French visitors and residents, and life went on very much as usual. The portrait of Hitler that had been placed inside the entrance hall looked rather out of place, however. The town was administered, as before, by the *sous-préfet* and the *Maire*. Now they answered direct to Marshal Pétain and the Vichy Government. The military commander of the town remained, and the barracks was still occupied by a regiment of infantry and a company of engineers.

For months French soldiers were still wandering about the town waiting to be demobilised. On demobilisation they were given a "Pétain suit." This was made of army khaki. With it was worn a khaki shirt and tie, a black beret and boots. The demobilisation of the existing French Army was one of the conditions of the Armistice. However, Pétain was allowed to retain a force known as the Armistice Army and consisting of roughly 100,000 men for the defence of Vichy France. Of course, the German authorities made certain that this army could not lay its hands suddenly on sufficient supplies of arms, petrol or other stores to become at all dangerous.

The *Armée de l'Armistice* was, and is likely to remain, a skeleton force. Training of a sort is carried out, but it is so restricted by lack of essentials, such as ammunition, petrol and oil, guns, tanks, etc., as to be, in fact, ridiculous. Its morale is low, in spite of the frantic efforts made by Vichy propaganda to glamorize and encourage it.

Most of the soldiers in our ward were eventually demobilised. When they were fit to leave hospital, they drew their Pétain suits and departed as civilians. None of them looked at all sorry to be receiving their civilian clothes. They were, and looked, defeated, philosophers rather than patriots. This was only to be expected, for the army they were leaving was in disgrace, and they felt it keenly. Anyway, they felt that the war was over for them, and were anxious to get home – if their homes still existed or were accessible. They wanted to be back with their families if they could be found.

The refugee problem continued. It was aggravated by the arrival of Alsatians and Lorrains who had been turned out of what was now German territory with only 1,000 francs and a little light baggage, having been forced to leave their homes and the rest of their possessions behind. Roanne, like small towns in the centre and south of France, was packed out with refugees from Paris and almost every other town of any size in the north. They had left behind their homes, their jobs, and most of their possessions. Few of them had time or facilities even to collect their money.

Now that France had been split into two main parts – and the occupied part, re-divided into further forbidden zones – they found themselves cut off and helpless. Many of them returned, but there were great difficulties in obtaining permits to pass from one zone to another. At first inter-zone communication was altogether prohibited.

The French radio, broadcasting from Vichy Government stations, gave out, for about an hour two or three times each day, long lists of names of people and places where families could link up with their lost members. It was pathetic. One wondered how the country could ever return to a state of organisation again. Organisation has never been a strong point of the French character, but now with all the added confusion brought about by the collapse the muddle was complete. Two-thirds of the country were occupied by the Germans; Alsace and Lorraine were German territory; entry to certain districts in the north was forbidden; entry to the occupied zone was restricted; there was a shortage of food, clothing, transport and money; there were crowds of wandering refugees everywhere; there was a lack of sufficient accommodation and employment; above all, there was lack of faith and confidence.

On July 3rd occurred the first brush between the new Vichy Government and Britain. The occasion was the attack on the French fleet at anchor in Oran. The Vichy-controlled Press talked of a break in diplomatic relations (later confirmed) with Britain. They claimed a loss of some two thousand French sailors drowned. Hitler had given his word, and Vichy had accepted it, that he would not use the French fleet against Britain. Vichy said that the ships when attacked had no steam up, and that some of the guns had already been dismantled. They also maintained that British aircraft had machine-gunned lifeboats full of survivors from the sunk and damaged ships.

All this had a bad effect on the French. They wanted to trust Britain and believed in their hearts that only Britain and America could save France from falling any lower, and eventually assist her to revive. In the hospital some said that the British had done well to sink the ships. As if, they said, it was possible either for Hitler or for Vichy to be trusted! Many others, however, looked upon this attack as the beginning of an attempt by Britain to seize the spoils of a broken France – for instance, her Empire in North Africa. They treated this incident as the equal to the stab in the back delivered by the Italians when they declared war on France after Germany had begun to overrun the country. On that day, July 3rd, most Frenchmen hated in the following order: Britain, Italy, Germany.

The position for Alan and me was very delicate. This incident will never be forgotten in France. It may have been a necessary move which, taking a very long view, would benefit the French in the end, but it was difficult for a Frenchman to appreciate it as such.

On July 14th there was no celebration to commemorate the taking of the Bastille at the beginning of the French Republic. The French Republic had now been replaced by the French State of Pétain at Vichy. Pétain ordered a day of meditation and of mourning for the dead of two wars.

In our ward, however, we had bottles of champagne and quite a celebration of our own. The result of this, for me, was a high fever, followed by fits of depression and acute pain.

Médécin-Lieutenant-Colonel Barbe was a great surgeon. He was in charge of the hospital at Roanne. He was of medium height and well built, with straight shoulders, although over sixty years old. On his way to and from the hospital he wore a black suit with a white waistcoat. His gait was sprightly, and he carried either a cane or a rolled-up umbrella. His linen was impeccable – an unusual feature of men's attire for a small town in the interior of France. His long white beard and wavy moustache were kept well combed and trimmed. His features were heavy, and his pale blue eyes had a kindly expression and an occasional twinkle. In the hospital he wore a white surgical overall and a skull-cap at all times. He had perhaps the strongest pair of wrists and forearms that I had ever seen on any man, except an all-in wrestler. He was a reserve officer and was demobilised after the Armistice. He and his wife shared a flat with the matron – Mademoiselle le Falcon.

Mademoiselle le Falcon was a women of striking appearance and exceptional administrative ability. She was a Bretonne, and certainly not anti-British. She spoke good English. It was often rumoured that she was a countess in her own right. Her profile – her whole face even – was that of an eagle. Her eyes were large and grey; except when she smiled they were icy-cold. Thin, firm, bloodless lips, high cheekbones, hollow cheeks and a sallow complexion, were in perfect harmony with her cold eyes. I hardly ever saw her hair, which was grey and kept very short, for she covered it with a surgeon's skullcap. Instead of the usual nurse's uniform she wore a white overall like the doctor's, flesh-coloured silk stockings, and low-heeled brown brogues.

She had the leadership and organising qualities of a general. All the nurses were terrified of her, for she ruled them with a rod of iron. She knew how to scrounge to the best advantage; had ideas and imagination; worked harder than anyone else in the hospital; and was as generous and kind to all the patients as she was hard with the nurses. She was sympathetic towards those patients who survived and found jobs for many of them after they had been demobilised. She slept little and took hardly any time off. Even when she did take a free day she used it indirectly in the interests of the patients. She had very many fine qualities. I liked her and got on very well with her, and I shall always be very grateful for the many things she did to help me. There was, however, one ugly twist to her nature. I know this, for she did all my dressings over a period of several months. There was not a patient in all the hospital who did not shudder at the thought of Mademoiselle le Falcon changing his dressings.

Colonel Barbe and Mademoiselle le Falcon had worked together in an ambulance unit during the last war. Between the wars they had operated a clinic in a town near Roanne. Their team-work was perfect. He did all the surgery, and she managed the hospital.

There were only about seventeen nurses for all the five hundred beds. One or two were fully trained and had even between ten- and twenty-years' experience. These were women in their late thirties, or older. The others were the equivalent of V.A.D.s, who were receiving their training in the hospital while doing the work. They made up for their lack of knowledge by hard work and a strong sense of duty and sacrifice – far superior to that of the average soldier they were nursing.

It was absolutely forbidden for a nurse to go out with a patient. Even if they were found talking to soldiers or officers in the courtyard or the corridors it was extremely likely that Mademoiselle le Falcon, who was never far away, would come and split up the group by sending the nurse away under one pretext or another. Later the same nurse would be lectured. Apparently these girls were expected to live like nuns.

One of the most important duties they had to perform, to my way of thinking, was to cheer up the wounded and dispirited, give them courage and inspire hope; they were cheerful and possessed a rich fund of that kind of sympathy and understanding which is most women's birthright; it was within their power to do great things towards the psychological side of the badly-wounded men's recovery; in fact, they were far better equipped for the mental than the physical side of nursing. Yet their efforts were almost completely negatived by the restrictions imposed by Mademoiselle le Falcon. Here in the hospital was a good example of one of the contradictions in French character. In the wards there was a complete lack of false modesty and prudishness, while outside in the town it was considered indecent for a nurse to be seen with a patient.

In spite of the great disproportion in the numbers of nurses and patients no nurse except Mademoiselle le Falcon herself was allowed to change dressings. The Jewish doctor left at the beginning of July, and from then onwards at least half the patients' wounds were attended to by Mademoiselle le Falcon. I have already described the methods used – tearing off the hardened gauze that stuck to the flesh. Mademoiselle le Falcon made the pain far greater than did any man. When she washed wounds with ether she used to rub as hard as possible. The worst dressings seemed to be her favourites, and she tugged and wrenched until the sweat stood out on my brow and my teeth set together like concrete.

My burns were not improving. The dirty dressings were green and yellow with pus. Once three stumps of finger were found grown together as they had not been properly separated with gauze the time before. Mademoiselle le Falcon forced them apart again with her forceps. This was done so suddenly and without warning that I let out a piercing scream of pain. Afterwards she had said it had hurt her more than me – and she really did seem sorry. I was furious at letting her get the upper hand in the fight for control, and decided that this, my first scream, would also be the last. The sight of my hands – pink pulpy messes, with only a few stumps of soft finger still attached, and these soon to be lost in the rough handling – was so terrible at first that they used to hold a towel in front of my face during the dressings. However, I still managed to see through the thin material and watch the proceedings. Several times the dirty dressings, left unchanged for a week at a time, were crawling with maggots.

By the middle of each week my hands had bled and suppurated so much that the cotton wool became soaked and dull gummy patches appeared on the bandages. The stench of these patches particularly attracted the flies, which were all over my evil-smelling body. They settled on the patches and maggots would breed. I can't describe the horror I felt when I first saw these little white worms wriggling out of my dressings and over the bed. I shouted for a nurse. My dressings were removed and found to be a writhing mass of these foul little insects. However, as they quickly reassured me, maggots are good for wounds, as they actually cleanse them.

When I die I shall be cremated, for no more worms are going to crawl over my body, dead or alive.

From the first day of the maggots, I became rapidly toughened to the sights and sensations of hospitals. Perhaps those little white worms did me a great service really, but I still shudder when I think of them.

Mademoiselle le Falcon, who was always exceptionally kind and considerate to Alan and me – except during dressings – considered that her two lonely foreigners ought to have a special concession as regards visitors; and we were visited nearly every day. This in spite of the rule that no one in the soldiers' wards was allowed visitors except on Thursdays and Sundays.

Most of our visitors in those first few months were French. Most came out of sympathy, but a few were merely curious, for we were the first wounded British airmen the town of Roanne had ever seen. They never came empty-handed, and always spoke kindly of England, no matter what they thought.

First-hand news of the evacuation from Dunkirk came from the English professor at the Roanne Lycée.

He was a Frenchman who spoke perfect English and had married an English girl. During the months of the war preceding Dunkirk, he was French interpreter to a unit of the British Expeditionary Force. He retreated with the rest of the British Army to Dunkirk and was evacuated in a small boat to England. Then he was sent back to France with units of the French Army, which had also come over from Dunkirk.

Towards the end of July, it was decided that as I had made no apparent progress at all a little fresh air would do me good. Perhaps there was an ulterior motive behind it all, for the stench of my burns was unpleasant for everyone. Anyway, one day they put me on a stretcher and carried me downstairs and out into the courtyard.

The courtyard was a dirt-covered square, partly overgrown with grass, particularly under the tall cedar, surrounded by firs, which occupied the corner farthest from the hospital building. It was under the cedar that my stretcher was laid, well out of the sun. With my head propped up a little by a pillow, I could see fairly well all around me.

I saw the hospital for the first time. It was a white three-storied building with a gable roof, covered with red tiles. It was of modernistic design and had only been built a few years before. In the middle of a built-up area not far from the centre of the town, it was surrounded by buildings – two factories, a convent, a girls' school and a number of private houses; yet it seemed to me always to be cut off from the town, perhaps because I myself was confined there for such a long time.

Groups of soldiers were playing "boules," a crude form of bowls played on rough ground, which was very popular in France. There were men from Senegal, ones from Madagascar, Arabs from North Africa, and the little Annamites from Indo-China. No colour bar existed, and they were mixed up with Frenchmen from every department of France. It was only chance that in our ward there were no coloured troops. There was nothing to have prevented them putting a Senegalese in the bed next to mine; in fact, some time after I had been moved from the ward it was filled with a mixture of Frenchmen, Senegalese, Arabs and Annamites.

The most striking thing about the soldiers was their dirty and slovenly appearance. Few of them bothered to shave; many were growing beards to save themselves the trouble. Most of them were dejected and slouched about with nothing to do. They wore odd pieces of civilian clothing with the ragged remnants of their uniform. Few could boast a pair of socks, and their army boots were neither polished nor laced up. Many of them wore canvas slippers.

It was not surprising that they were bored and dispirited, for they were not often allowed to go out into the town, and there was nowhere for them to go to except their wards, the bare courtyard, or the equally bare refectory. Later on, Mademoiselle le Falcon started a canteen. It had a beer bar, games and sets of cards. This was considered quite a social reform – the provision of a few small comforts for the wounded. Mademoiselle le Falcon had to overcome all kinds of stupid obstacles before she could start the canteen and stock it with soap, razor blades, suitcases, combs, etc.; all articles which were expensive in the town and inaccessible to those of the wounded who could not go out.

My first day out in the courtyard was a great one. At last, I could breathe fresh air after two and a half months in hospital wards. My life was no longer bounded by the four walls of the room; I was relatively free and could enjoy the sight of healthy growing things – the trees, the grass and the vegetables in the garden beyond the courtyard. Unfortunately, it only lasted for three days, because the pain and strain of being moved about was too much for me. The sunshine was too strong for my weakened lidless eyes, and the flies in the courtyard were blue and green – even more unpleasant than the hordes of houseflies in the ward; and so once more I had to confine my whole life to within the walls of the ward, my only contact with nature outside being the view I had from the windows of the top of two pine trees.

Whereas I was, if anything, declining, Alan was rapidly getting better. His hands had improved tremendously, and he could use the fingers of his right hand sufficiently well to hold a spoon. Gone were the days when we used to lie side by side while Madame Marie, standing between our beds and armed with a fork in each hand, shovelled food into our ever-open mouths. Now, not only could Alan feed himself, he was even getting up.

For some reason a tall patient never quite looks his height in bed, and when Alan arose for the first time little Madame Marie was like a dwarf beside him, for he was at least six feet tall and had become so thin in bed that he looked even taller than that.

Once on his feet, there was no holding him. Soon he had scraped together some civilian clothes, and a week or two later disappeared on the first of many visits out into the town. He used to walk, holding his hands up in front of him, for they were still in bandages and throbbed when allowed to hang down. Nothing deterred him. He could open doors by twisting the handles, which he gripped between his forearms. With the only two fingers that were strong enough on his right hand he managed to handle his money, smoke cigarettes and read a book. All this encouraged me greatly, for I felt that I, too, with only a few pieces of finger on my right hand and none on my left, would find similar ways and means to recover the independence which is necessary to self-respect.

A few days before my first and memorable visit to the courtyard Alan and I were lying back after lunch, sweating, exhausted and plagued by flies, when we were treated to a very pleasant surprise.

This was a visit from two English soldiers, who had walked all the way from the fighting in the north and arrived in Roanne, where they were forced to stop and rest their lacerated feet. In Roanne they were befriended and well looked after; but that is another story which cannot be told here. They were the first fighting members of the British forces in France whom we had contacted since being wounded, and we plagued them for hours with questions about the fighting in the north.

They were both Londoners, one tall and the other short and stocky, and they wore the old clothes which had been given to them by French peasants in place of their uniform. Their army boots were worn right through the soles and stuffed with newspaper. Apart from their sore feet, they showed no other signs of physical distress; on the contrary, they were bronzed and fit after the hard exercise. Bill, the taller of the two, was a Territorial. On the outbreak of war, he was called up, and soon after arrived in France with the B.E.F. He left behind a good job as a senior clerk in a large chemical works. By nature, he was quiet and reserved; it was he who was suffering the more from sore feet. While he was the brains of the combine of two, Fred, the smaller, kept up the morale.

Fred was a real Cockney in every sense of the word. He was short and stocky, stubborn and outspoken, good-humoured, but rather aggressive in his manner. He was also just and generous, and always ready to sacrifice his own interests and possessions if he felt that the cause was just. Elementary school up to the age of thirteen had left him almost uneducated, and of this he was deeply conscious. He need not have been, for his character had developed the hard way during the seven years' struggle against poverty that had preceded his entry into the Army as a conscript just before the war, at the age of nineteen. His first job on leaving school had been milk-delivery boy, for which he received only five shillings a week. After that he was a grocer's assistant, who dreamed of having his own small general store one day. He was only twenty when he married and was very much in love.

Conscription had drawn him into the Army, and when war broke out he was trained as a machine-gunner and sent to France. In company with a number of Highland battalions, he was taken prisoner by the Germans on the coast. Then for five days and nights he was one of a party of seven thousand British Tommies who were marched to Germany. They were forced to march all day with few and very short pauses. Some of the older men, who were veterans of the Great War, could not stand the strain, and after the first two days many fell completely exhausted to the ground. They were kicked by the German guards, and if they then failed to get up were left lying on the road, to be picked up later on by passing lorries.

They were given only one meal a day and had to scramble for it like wolves. This meal consisted of beans and bread. The beans never went right round, and the bread was thrown into the crowd by German soldiers standing up in the back of a lorry full of loaves. The prisoners were so hungry that often as they passed through villages a few of the bolder spirits would break off and slip into houses in search of food and drinks, only to be dragged back by the German guards, who manhandled them severely. The two greatest hardships were the lack of sufficient drinking water and the discomfort at night, for the weather was hot and they were always thirsty, and at night the heavy dew soaked them as they lay out in the fields, few having as much as a greatcoat to cover them. Fred was used to hardship and suffered less than many of the others; he also possessed a greatcoat, which he shared with an older man who could only just manage to carry on.

From the first moment after his capture, he had decided to escape as soon as a favourable opportunity occurred. On the fifth day he slipped off the road into a wood, waited for the marching column to pass out of sight, and realised that he was free again. He stayed hidden in the woods until night fell, then started to walk in a southerly direction, with only one fixed idea – to put as great a distance as possible between himself and the Germans. French peasants gave him clothes on the first day after he had escaped and told him the right road to take for Paris, which was now his destination. About three days later he arrived in Paris and went straight to the British Embassy. The British staff had left, for the Germans were already in Paris, and the Embassy was in the hands of the Americans. He asked for help; he was given the advice to get out of Paris as quickly as possible. He spent a night with the Salvation

Army or the Y.M.C.A. (I forget which), and it was there he met Bill, and they decided to join forces.

They had only a few francs between them, and nothing to sell, so they had to walk. They hoped that further south they would find a British Consul who could help them to return to England. Neither of them spoke French. They were unlucky, for they were still on the road when the Armistice was signed, and the barriers set up by the Germans on the demarcation line separating the occupied from the unoccupied zones. This meant that they would have to bypass the German sentries to get into unoccupied territory; so, they walked on south until they arrived eventually at Chartres, where the line is marked by a river.

At Chartres the banks of the river and all the bridges were heavily guarded by German sentries, but eventually, after sitting patiently for hours on the north bank of the river at a certain secluded spot, they were helped across by an old Frenchman who thought that they were Belgian refugees. They continued their search for a British Consul in the unoccupied zone. Once more they were unlucky, for after the incident at Oran, when the British fleet attacked the French, diplomatic relations with Britain were broken off by Vichy, and the British Consul had already left France for England before Bill and Fred reached unoccupied territory. Then finally at Roanne, Bill's feet gave out, and they decided to stay there until they had recovered.

While on the road they had seen long columns of German vehicles and many troops in the villages, but always they passed unnoticed, for they had the same appearance as many of the refugees, and there were far too many refugees for the Germans to be able to check everyone, except at the inter-zone frontiers. Most nights they slept in fields, but occasionally they found barns, and sometimes they were given beds by the many friendly farmers and peasants, who fed and helped them on their way, in spite of the danger of being caught by the Germans assisting British soldiers to escape.

In Roanne they succeeded in passing unnoticed for two or three weeks and used to slip in every day to visit Alan and me. Fred used to read to me for hours, although for him it was really hard work. He brought me a pipe and tobacco; filled it and kept it alight. Many a time he lifted up the tent-shaped mosquito-net which covered my face and drove out the flies, which always seemed to succeed in getting inside one way or another.

As he sat by my bedside he warded off the flies which settled on my evil-smelling bandages; he did many things for me which could not be attended to by the over-worked nurses – lifted me up and dried the sweat off my back, scraped the crumbs from my bed; all little things in themselves, which became of immense importance to me, lying motionless and helpless on my bed. One day he even managed to smuggle in some tea, which he brought to us triumphantly, complete with milk and sugar.

At heart Fred was a pure communist. He had been forced to tackle the hard struggle of life badly equipped with a poor education. He was always on the verge of poverty; in close contact with so many others even poorer than himself, it was not surprising that he quickly realised the fundamental truth that an effort towards equality of rights and property was man's most important social aim.

Although he was often stubborn to the extent of stupidity, I admired the courage with which he stuck to the conclusions with which I could not always agree. All the time he was at Roanne he was impatient to get back to have another "crack at the Hun."

During his travels he had seen much of the sufferings of France. He was impressed by the kindness of the many people who helped Bill and himself and intended to tell everyone at home all about it. I hope that he has done so and that he has remained one of us – the few British subjects who having had the opportunity to see something of the sufferings of a great nation under the Nazis, feels, like the rest of us, that he had a duty to perform; to do everything in his power to fight complacency at home and to encourage the people of his own country to make the sacrifices necessary so that Britain's war effort could be as total as that of the Germans and Russians.

Early in September Alan and I were separated. Most of the original cases had either recovered and been discharged or else they had been transferred to other hospitals. This left half the beds in the hospital vacant for a while, and it was necessary to redistribute the remaining patients in such a way as to have whole wards empty and ready for any new batches of wounded that might arrive. There was one empty bed in a small officers' ward, so I was moved into it, and Alan, who was now up and about all the time, was transferred to another soldiers' ward.

My new ward was a small oblong room with four beds pushed against the walls, each with its head in a corner. There was a door in one of the smaller sides and a window opposite which opened out on to the courtyard, two stories below. Most of the floor space not filled by the beds was taken up by two tall cupboards and two plain wooden chairs. Inside the window there were thick blackout curtains, and usually these were half drawn, so that the room could be kept in semi-darkness.

The atmosphere was stifling, and as all four of us had septic dressings which were only changed about once a week, the stench was horrible. Here also were hordes of flies. However, this room had many advantages; it was more peaceful than the open wards, and one of the officers had a radio and liked good music. We received many visits; our visitors being allowed in to see us at almost any hour of the day. The food was a little better, and in addition we had many presents of fruit, chocolates, etc., and an occasional bottle of vintage wine. I missed Alan, of course, but he still could come in and talk and read to me.

One of the three French officers looked exactly like Hitler. He had fractured the tibia and fibula of each leg; but his most serious injury was a badly fractured skull, on account of which his head had been wrapped up in a sort of turban. His neck became so stiff that he could not turn his head in either direction. He sat up all day doing fancy embroidery with great skill and smoking cigars; this all added to the particularly comic appearance caused by the turban, his stiff neck and small Hitlerian moustache. Unlike Hitler, he appreciated to the full the good things of life, especially food and drink.

Lieutenant Hitler's temper was a little short and his language atrocious. He said the most revolting and outrageous things to the nurses, who never even turned a hair. He was a reserve officer and held an appointment in the *Intendance*, roughly equivalent to a combination of the R.A.S.C. and the R.A.O.C. and had met with an accident at a crossroads when his small staff car collided with a heavy lorry. No doubt both he and the lorry driver had been working on the principle that the faster they passed over a blind crossroads the less likely were the chances of hitting anything. Later on, after he had left the hospital, Lieutenant Hitler paid us a visit. On the left breast of his tunic, he wore the ribbons of three decorations – Chevalier of the Legion of Honour, *Croix de Guerre avec Palme*, and the "wounded" medal, presumably as a reward for this fine feat of military skill!

One of the other two was a regular cavalry officer whose regiment had been mechanised. He was polite and extremely pleasant in a superficial way. He made great efforts to produce enough English from his school days' vocabulary to talk to me in my own language. He also had a Croix de Guerre, which I have no doubt he earned, for I imagine he was a good and courageous officer, in spite of his effeminate appearance. His trouble was phlebitis. Most of his day was spent looking at his face in a mirror; combing and clipping the black moustache and black silky hair, which made him look more Spanish than French; washing and covering himself with expensive Eau de Cologne. He did not stay long, and soon after was replaced by a tank officer who had received burns.

The third officer – also a lieutenant – came from the south, somewhere near Marseilles, and spoke with a rich Midi accent. He was a fine figure of a man, a swarthy Latin who was well built and covered. Although not exactly handsome he had a magnificent pair of eyes. They were black and shining, capable of expressing to the full his moods – sometimes placid, sometimes fiery and always sentimental. It was he who owned the radio and liked good music.

He was thirty-six years old, and for the last thirteen years had been on the reserve of infantry officers. By profession he was a schoolmaster, and amongst other things managed a choir of boys and girls which had earned itself a considerable reputation in the south of France. Until he was wounded he had commanded a section of Senegalese troops. He had received eleven deep wounds caused by bomb splinters.

His regiment of Senegalese had seen much hard fighting when the Germans broke through near Sedan, and its losses had been very great. All the time they were short of ammunition and pitifully equipped, but his troops behaved magnificently, except under bombardment by dive bombers, when they were temporarily panic-stricken, having never seen or heard anything like it before. It was during one of these bombardments that he had been wounded, and, although in great pain and losing much blood, had gone on with his task of driving a German unit out of a village, mainly with hand grenades. Then he had to be carried into the village he had taken. For this he was later decorated with the Legion of Honour and the *Croix de Guerre avec Palme.*

When the rather pleasant young cavalry officer left us, his place was taken by a lieutenant from a combat tank regiment. While leading his section of four light tanks into battle his tank was hit and caught fire. He managed to escape with severe burns on his legs, complicated by a shell splinter wound in one knee and minor burns on his hands and face. His mechanic was less fortunate and was burned to death. He also received the Legion of Honour and *Croix de Guerre avec Palme.*

All these officers treated me with courtesy and kindness, but they were a little irritated to find that I was of senior rank, although much younger than any of them. I explained that in the British forces, particularly in war time, young men received rapid promotion to fill vacancies, and they agreed that our system was better than their own, where old men held down jobs which required youthful vigour and initiative.

We avoided politics, but I soon discovered that they were all very indignant over the attack made by British warships on the French fleet at Oran.

Madame Marie, the nurse who had looked after Alan and me in the soldiers' ward, was for a time put in charge of our little room and its four officers. She was popular with all of us; but none of the others could have appreciated her as much as I did. To them she was only an efficient and devoted nurse; but to me in my complete helplessness she was everything. My happiness depended on her, and without her care I know I should have died. She was very good to me, and a bond of affection grew between us. The other officers used to call her my "Maman française," and in many ways she was like a mother, for I had to depend on her as a child depends on its mother. I particularly admired the way she washed and fed me while I smelt worse than the north end of a polecat running south.

She was nursing in the last war, when she lost her husband; but she never married again, which, in a way, was tragic, for she would have made a wonderful mother, and had gone on nursing right through the years of peace until the present war began. Her work never changed, for she never bothered to sit for any of the examinations necessary to advancement in her profession. She believed that her duty lay in personal service. As she once said, "I don't want to give orders, I prefer to do the work."

Sometimes when she had nothing to do for a while she would sit down in a chair in the room and knit socks for the young nephew whom she adored.

For months she was present at all my dressings, and there was something about her stocky little figure and the example of the many years of devotion that she had given to the nursing profession which gave me the courage – the will even – to live and enabled me to put up with the mental and physical suffering which was my lot.

As the condition of the other three officers improved they used to be taken out into the courtyard or wheeled out in invalid chairs into the passage-way, and I was left alone. They did not risk carrying me out into the courtyard for months after the failure of the first attempt, and for my part I felt too ill and worn to wish to be moved at all.

At night when I could not sleep and throughout those lonely periods when I was left shut up in the empty room I lived in a world of dreams and intense thought. The thinking was spasmodic, and often disjointed, but I feel sure that in that period of ten months which I spent exclusively on my back I covered at least ten years of normal thought. Often depression would descend upon me for hours; so, to cheer myself up I used to hum every tune and air that I could remember. Within my head I could hear the most beautiful music, but the sound which escaped my lips caused much scathing comment.

For me the week started on the day when my dressings were done, when for hours after the painful process already described was over I used to lie and tremble with what, I suppose, was nervous shock and relief. As soon as this local pain had died down I knew that I could look forward to one complete day that would be painless, provided I did not try to move my limbs. But on the next day pain would start again and would increase progressively, until at the end of the week, on the day before the next dressings were due to take place, it would have reached an almost unendurable pitch. In the night, when there was neither sight nor sound to distract my senses, I felt the pain most of all and had to strain my mind to keep it on thoughts other than of itch, cramp and pain.

About six times during the night, I used to have to shout at the top of my voice, which had regained some of its power, for an orderly to come and give me a urine bottle. Often no one would arrive for a long time, and I would be forced to go through another form of pain which, although not as acute, nevertheless caused unpleasant nervous reactions and was the more irritating because it seemed so unnecessary. A new batch of orderlies had by now arrived; they were little Annamites from Indo-China, and knew nothing about hospitals, which was not surprising, as they arrived straight from the arsenal where they had been working on explosives. On top of this, few of them spoke even pidgin French. However, although naturally slow in their movements and rather lazy, they were exceedingly gentle, and soon picked up the rudiments of the work allotted to them. At first some of the things they did were most unusual.

Once in the night after I had shouted for an orderly an especially unintelligent little Annamite arrived. He had a round, yellow-brown face, big slanting eyes and a vacant expression, accentuated by a drooping lower lip. When I had succeeded in making him realise I wanted the urine bottle which lay on top of my bedside table, he picked it up, examined it curiously from all angles, and then held it to my ear. After listening to it for a moment like a small child who has been told he can hear the sound of the sea in a shell, I gave the matter up completely and sent him in search of the night nurse, who would understand. They were not all stupid, and one in particular was a great help to me and a good friend. One of them had been told that the correct way to address me was "Monsieur le capitaine anglais," and for ever after that they called me "M'sr cap-i-taine a-glais." Said like that it made a nice long title, and I felt quite proud of it.

Two French women from Roanne and an American from Vichy played a great part in my recovery.

Madame Gris had lost her husband during the Great War and had remained a widow ever since. Her life had been full of interest, for she had travelled extensively, although only inside France. She was both charming and handsome in a frail way. Though about fifty, she exploited to full advantage her wavy silver-grey hair and her neat, almost girlish figure. Her eyes were grey and soft and her small mouth sympathetic. Her sensitive nature was deeply touched by the sufferings brought on by the war, and sometimes she depressed me a little with her tales of woe. Twice a week she came to see me, and she brought with her pâté-de-foie-gras, eggs and sometimes butter, until all these things became unobtainable. They were great luxuries even at first, for the food situation deteriorated rapidly with the approach of winter.

Madame Sourire was quite a different person. She was the mother of a girl of seventeen and a boy of thirteen. Her husband was a Breton and never came to see me, for he was strangely shy and moody and hated the inside of any hospital, Madame Sourire had a sunny smile and a sunny disposition. She was short, plump and placid – a perfect mother and an excellent cook; but above all she had a heart big enough to take in not only her own family, but all the lame dogs, like myself, that she came across.

To her I owe a debt of gratitude that can never be repaid. At first when she came to see me she talked very little. I could not speak very much French, and it was a relief to have one visitor who just sat and beamed at me and to whom I could smile back without bothering to think out conversation. She never seemed to get bored with this, and neither did I, for she was a comfortable and reassuring person. On every visit she brought something good for me to eat. On my birthday she arrived with an enormous "baba" cake running with rum and other presents. It gave her great pleasure to watch me eat the things she had brought.

The first time I saw Mrs. Corrigan she burst into my room exuding personality and expensive perfume. She is an American widow who needs no introduction to the West End society of London of a few years ago. Having profited for years in Paris and the Riviera from the best of the facilities for good living and amusement which France offered to her rich visitors until the German occupation, she decided after the debacle to devote her large fortune to comforts for French and British prisoners and war wounded.

So, she sold her Rolls-Royces, her jewels and most of her other possessions and bought instead two motor vans and large quantities of foodstuffs, clothing and other comforts, which she stored in warehouse buildings in Vichy. Then, with her secretary, she set up the headquarters of her organisation, which she called "La bienvenue aux prisonniers et blessés" – in the Hotel Majestic, Vichy. When her stocks became very low, and she could no longer replace them in France she managed to arrange for a consignment to be sent from Portugal. Anyone who knows anything of the difficulties incurred will realise that she needed influence, personality and great drive to achieve this.

When she could no longer get what she wanted by any other means she thought nothing of going to Pétain himself, who saw her and later entertained her. Periodically she would load up her vans and set off for the concentration camps and hospitals and distribute her comforts wholesale. One of her helpers, the driver of one van, was the Comte Armand de Rochefoucauld. Mrs. Corrigan was one of the very few privileged persons in Vichy France who could obtain passes allowing her to cross the demarcation line which separates the two zones, and for hospitals and camps.

On one of her expeditions, she had a bad accident not far from Paris. When they got her to the American Hospital in Paris it was discovered that she had received several fractures. While she was lying on the stretcher inside the entrance hall a number of Canadian nurses of the hospital staff came along, looking very upset. She asked what was the matter, and they told her that they had just been given time to collect a change of linen and were on their way to a concentration camp (probably at Besançon). German soldiers were waiting to take them under custody to the railway station. Mrs. Corrigan pulled out all the money she was carrying and distributed it amongst them. Later she had news of one of the girls, and learned that the money had been most useful, since for twenty-four hours they were given neither food nor any other necessities by the Germans.

As soon as they had discharged her from hospital she returned to her good work. She was quite indefatigable and could get up early, drive for many hours in her van, distribute her loads and then in the evening return looking as fresh as ever. On the several occasions I saw her she looked as if she had just walked out of a Paris beauty parlour, for she was always well groomed and beautifully dressed. She wore a fur coat for driving; it was probably the last one she had left of the many her wardrobe must originally have contained.

To the hospital she brought thousands of French cigarettes; and to me personally a radio, a complete wardrobe of clothes, including a suit and a most expensive dressing-gown from Paris, chocolates, English books, cigarettes, money and flowers. She was like a fairy godmother.

Although her mission was quite unpolitical, sanctioned by the French Red Cross and concerned only with acts of mercy and humanity, she soon had trouble with the Germans. Her inter-zone travelling passes were cancelled, and she had to confine her visits to prisons and hospitals in unoccupied France. On top of this there was the difficulty of getting her money from America to France, and just before I left France in October 1941, I heard from her that her organisation would soon have to close down. Petrol was no longer available, she had run short of money, and difficulties of every kind had arisen. Had it not been for that combination of a fighting nature, an active imagination and tremendous drive – qualities derived, perhaps, from her Irish-American blood – she would have been forced to give up long before.

She will be remembered in France as one of the greatest of the Americans who gave up everything to help to relieve the sufferings of the French people both before and after the collapse. In company with the American ambulances, the American Red Cross and the Quakers, she was doing a great, humanitarian job, and sowing the seeds of that better understanding between Americans and Frenchmen which will be necessary in the years of reconstruction that must come after the war is over.

I saw very little of Alan after he had recovered sufficiently to slip out into the town. Usually, he would drop in to see me for a short time each morning, and sometimes in the evening he came back and read to me; but freedom called, and he was not deserting me, for I had a new friend. His name was David.

David was an Englishman who had lived for many years in Paris. He was a composer and had studied under Cortot, the well-known French pianist, who is now working for the Government at Vichy. The story of David's journey from Paris to Roanne with the refugees is an interesting one; full of pathos tempered with humour; but it can't be told in this book. He first came to see me in September 1940, and after that first visit there were only three days upon which he failed to turn up until I left Roanne on June 6, 1941.

He was altogether charming; but because he was the best of all my many friends in France, I find it difficult adequately to describe him. I shan't even try. He used to sit and talk to me for hours, and he was most interesting, for he had travelled extensively in Europe and America.

David, more than anyone else, was responsible for the maintenance of my sanity and the psychological side of my recovery.

By the middle of October my burns still showed very little signs of progress under the care of Mlle le Falcon. She had done her best, but certainly her rough handling was one of the main causes of the slow healing, and another was undoubtedly the lack of nourishing food. She cauterised my burns with silver nitrate and dressed them in many different ways – with cod-liver oil, palm balsam, salt, mercurochrome, Vaseline gauze and olive oil. However, the dressings were still torn off roughly and the newly formed granulations damaged and scraped off in the process. Now, however, that the rush of wounded was over, Colonel Barbe himself took control, and part, at any rate, of my hands were saved by him.

For a long time, he had examined my hands every fortnight or so to see whether it would be necessary to amputate them. Luckily for me he was very patient, and always prepared to wait yet another fortnight to see what new progress had been made. Then one day he noticed that my right arm had started to twist around in a most unsatisfactory manner, and he gave me an anaesthetic, manipulated my hand back into place and set it in a plaster cast. From that day on my dressings were done under an anaesthetic by the colonel himself, and signs of progress slowly but surely appeared.

Often when I was wheeled into the operating room I would find Mlle le Falcon already there and waiting for me. She would immediately start to tear off the dressings in her own particular way, thus subjecting me to a considerable amount of pain that was quite unnecessary, as I was about to have an anaesthetic. It was strange that this nurse, who was always so kind to me in every other way and seemed to like me a lot, should be so brutal whenever she touched my dressings. When the colonel arrived and saw all this going on, a pitched battle of words would take place over my prostrate body, the doctor shouting at Mlle le Falcon in a most alarming fashion for such a mild old gentleman. Luckily he always won the argument, for Mlle le Falcon both respected and feared him when he was riled, and at last I would be able to relax. Trembling with pain, I would wait for the anaesthetic.

Once a week for over forty weeks I was anaesthetised, but never once by a doctor. However, the young nurse who gave me gas was very efficient, and no harm was done. She would cover my eyes and nose with gauze, then break a small tube containing local anaesthetic and hold it in her warm hand, so causing the liquid to escape in the form of spray on to the gauze covering my nose. I can still see the reassuring smile she used to give me before she covered up my eyes; still smell the sickly odour of the choking gas; and still hear her voice saying, "Respirez bien, respirez bien."

I never quite got rid of the feeling of oppression that used to come over me before one of these anaesthetics, but I did appreciate them, for they saved me a great deal of unnecessary pain and nervous strain. Although the pain was acute sometime after the anaesthetic had worn off, and although it kept me awake for a whole night each time, my progress, even if still slow, was very marked, and new hope for the future was born.

In the middle of December, I was moved from the little room I had shared with the three French officers and taken over to another part of the hospital, which was divided up into cubicles and set apart for officers. It had been a dormitory for girls in the days before the war when the hospital had been a girls' school. Usually there were about fourteen officers there at a time, but when I arrived there were only four. One of them was the tank officer, who had been burned and who had already spent some time with me in the little ward.

At first confinement in my little cubicle made me feel very lonely; for I could see only a window in front of me, but no view beyond a piece of the wall of the room, a washbasin, cupboard and the partition of the cubicle. I was still too weak to sit up and was therefore forced to lie on my back. I could not bend either knee, and my hands ached badly when I moved my arms away from my sides, where they still lay. I had now spent seven whole months like this. There was still nothing I could do for myself until a few days before Christmas, when I discovered a practical, if exceedingly uncomfortable and awkward, way of reading books.

The book was propped against my left arm, and I turned slightly sideways to read it, looking down instead of along the line. At first, reading like this was very trying, and it took me a long time to turn over the pages with my right hand, which was completely covered up with a plaster cast. I could only use my right eye – both eyes were running all the time. I used the bandage around the plaster on my right hand with which to wipe them. With constant practice, however, I very soon became quite skilful, and oblivious to everything else while my thoughts were concentrated on the lives and adventures of the fictitious characters in the many good modern novels which Mrs. Corrigan had sent to me. I used to read till I was tired out, and then fall asleep, still half on my back and half on my side.

So engrossed did I become in my books that I used to resent most of my visitors for the interruption they caused in the story of the moment. Apart from this, some of my visitors were most unpleasant and others liable to cause me trouble.

For instance, there was a French military doctor from the garrison who paid me a visit for the express purpose of venting his spleen upon the British. He hates us as a nation and used to come to express his hate to me. At first I tried to get rid of him by saying that I was a Scot and therefore was not interested in his opinions regarding the English; but he took no notice and became instead so offensive that I lost my temper in defence of the country which had always given me a good home and told him to get to hell out of my cubicle. I am glad to say that he was one of the very few French who ever behaved badly towards me.

Then there was the middle-aged woman who burst into my cubicle without asking the nurse's permission, kissed me soundly on both cheeks, and left behind an odour of stale scent which rivalled the stench of my burns. Then she sat down very close to my bed and showed me a collection of photographs of herself as a young dancing girl, some nude and in most suggestive poses. Quite why she came to see me I was never able to decide. She was a large, blousy woman, in her early forties. Everything about her – face, figure and dress – seemed to be rapidly running to seed. The photographs bore evidence of past beauty, but it had long since disappeared.

Although I disliked intensely the manner of her visit, I could not help feeling sorry for her, for being unmarried and childless, it was clear she lived entirely in her memories of the past – in the days when she was young and beautiful and a great success in her own particular line, which I imagine included other activities as well as dancing. For me it was no pleasure to be kissed by her; but for her, kissing me may have been an even greater ordeal, for my face was still covered with sores, to which had been added a straggly and patchy growth of ginger beard!

Yet another affectionate visitor came from the railway. He was an engine-driver who did not live at Roanne. Nevertheless, he arrived to see me well covered with oil and grime and kissed me fondly and soundly on both cheeks, then on the centre of my brow. He carried on his breath a sickly mixture of garlic and alcohol. He had heard that there was a British officer at Roanne and he had come to see me on behalf of his fellow workers, to tell me that the railway workers as a whole believed in General de Gaulle and the British. He said that they all listened in regularly to the French broadcasts from London, had formed groups amongst themselves and had concealed arms. All they wanted now was the leadership of a British officer, and they would rise up against the Germans. I pointed out to him that I admired all that he was doing and hoped he would continue his underground workings, but a great deal more carefully, for to be seen with me compromised both of us in the most obvious manner and would endanger quite unnecessarily the lives of his fellow workers.

Anyway, I was not in a position to help him from my hospital bed. He was most disappointed and went away, assuring me as he went that the workers of

France were united now because of, rather than in spite of, the Germans, and that when the British came back, as he believed they would, Frenchmen would fight courageously to the death until the hated Boche had been kicked out.

He was not the only violent de Gaullist who visited me. There was a regular stream of visitors – mostly women whose husbands were prisoners of war in Germany. The presence of an Air Force officer attracted them like a magnet, for they all wanted to tell me how grateful they were to the R.A.F. for bombing their own home towns! They came from Paris and from the towns of Alsace Lorraine; from Lille, Douai and St. Omer; from Rheims and around Soissons; from Boulogne, Calais, Dieppe; from Chartres, Le Havre, Brest, Lorient, Nantes and Bordeaux. The most enthusiastic of all were the women from the towns which had been attacked the most by the R.A.F., and the others were jealous of them and asked when it would be their turn to have the privilege of British bombs dropping on their own towns to kill off a few more of the *doryphores* (a bug which eats up all the potato crops – otherwise, the Germans).

Many of them were mothers who had lost their husbands in the last war; and now their sons were prisoners of war. Many were homeless, like the women of Alsace Lorraine, who had been turned out of "German territory" after the annexation by Germany of Alsace Lorraine.

These women all showed a most admirable fighting spirit, and I could not help feeling that if it had been the women and not the men of France who had fought the war the *débâcle* would have been longer delayed, to say the least. Of course, it was easy for the women to talk – especially after everything had happened – but there was, nevertheless, a courage and defiance behind all they said which made me hopeful for the future of France. They had experienced enough at the hands of rogues and the weak politicians who obeyed their masters – the clique of parasites who control French capital and did not give a hoot for the working classes so long as money still had purchasing power on international markets. These women hoped for a new France after the war, run on socialistic lines.

When I asked if the British bombs damaged the houses and missed the military objectives I was always told it was very rare for bombs to fall on houses, and that, anyway, everyone knew that it could not be helped occasionally. It was even pointed out philosophically that bombs which fell on private houses often killed the German soldiers as well as the French people who were lodging them. Their faith in the integrity and goodwill of the Air Force air crews was touching.

Many strange stories were brought to me by men and women who had slipped out of the occupied zone. From all their various reports I managed to piece together the following picture of the preparations made by the Germans for the invasion of Britain, which would have taken place but for the defeat of the Luftwaffe by the R.A.F. in the Battle of Britain.

A few weeks after the Germans had taken over the occupation of French territory on the channel coast it was noticed by the local inhabitants that large barges were being massed on the canals and rivers and in the docks and harbours. They were rapidly converted for use as invasion craft and modified to carry tanks and other heavy war material. On the sides of many of the barges the Germans painted "Thos. Cook & Sons" and the names of other British transport firms! Reports of similar preparations came through from Holland and Belgium. Invasion exercises were carried out on shore and in barges at high pressure until one day, according to the reports, a large fleet of barges set out either on exercises or as part of the projected invasion. They were attacked by British aircraft, who "set light to the sea" and, as a result, badly burned the German soldiers. Into the interior of France for days after went special hospital trains full of burned Germans. For months afterwards the burned bodies of many others were washed up on the shores of the Pas de Calais.

The arrival of contingents of burned German soldiers in towns in the centre of France was confirmed by a reliable medical source. Orders were given to the French doctors at the time the incident took place to evacuate a proportion of the beds of all military hospitals in certain areas just north of the demarcation line between occupied and unoccupied territory.

The sequel to all this was that for months afterwards German units carried out special drill on a lake near Moulin, just north of the demarcation line and inside the occupied zone. Dressed in various different types of protective clothing, they were launched in invasion barges. Halfway across the lake, kerosine was thrown on to the water and ignited. The Germans were made to pass through the flames to test the quality of their equipment, which it was hoped would prove non-inflammable. Unfortunately for them, the experiments were never completely successful. Day after day the German guinea-pigs were pushed out on to the lake, and many of them were well burned in the process.

When I heard this story, which I believed, it used to occur to me that an ordeal by fire of this kind would be suitable retribution for Hitler, Mussolini and all those wrong-headed and stupid old men both in France and Britain who had combined to bring about the war. Though not normally sadistic by nature, it seemed to me that an occasional dip into burning oil followed by dressings à la Mlle Falcon, protracted over a period of a few years, would be a suitable punishment for past offences and would, at the same time, tend to discourage potential offenders in the future.

In spite of all the efforts of my many friends I cannot honestly say that Christmas 1940 was a happy one for me. I felt very homesick. I had received no letters from home since June, owing, as I later discovered, to well-meant but misguided advice given to my wife, who was told not to write to me, in case she gave away my whereabouts to the French and Germans! However, I did have a few telegrams which were sent to a friend of mine for me.

In my cubicle David and Madame Sourire had placed a small Christmas tree. Visitors came in to see me all day long, each one bringing a gift, in most cases some little luxury which was becoming almost unobtainable. Their Christmas greetings indicated the hope that I would soon be back with my family and that the war would soon be over. There was not one amongst them all who failed to assure me of the faith they had in England.

Madame Sourire brought champagne, and we drank to all the things we believed in and hoped for most. Alan and David lit the candles on the Christmas tree. I thought of all the other Christmas days I had spent – in Scotland, with the R.A.F., in Egypt, in England, in Paris, 1938, with Hope, and at Berry-au-Bac in 1939.

After the others had all left David stayed on, sitting on the side of my bed. It was nearly dark now, and the lights had not yet been lit. Most of the candles on the little Christmas tree had gone out. Abruptly the jazz music from the radio in the next cubicle stopped, and as if by magic came the beautiful strains of my favourite carol, "*Stille Nacht.*" It was sung in German by a children's choir, and I was listening to it in a French hospital. Oh God, why must men be so stupid – so greedy for the things that do not really count!

With the New Year there arrived back in unoccupied France many trainloads of wounded French prisoners of war from Germany. There were also other special classes of prisoners being released by the Germans, such as doctors, railway-men, and other persons whose work was indispensable to the exploitation of France by Hitler.

There were all kinds and conditions of men in those first trainloads of repatriated prisoners. The old and the young; the sick, debilitated and neurotic; the seriously wounded, and many others who appeared to be successful frauds. As the hospital at Roanne was one of the original receiving centres I must have seen many thousands of prisoners pass through between January and July 1941. Officers and men alike arrived in tattered uniforms, worn out, filthy, emaciated and ill, but, on the whole, not demoralised. They told me stories which could hardly be believed, even if it were possible for me to record them here.

For the most part they had received very few parcels from home, and all had suffered greatly from lack of food and the extreme cold during the early part of the winter. Generally, their morning meal had consisted of a small cup of black ersatz coffee and a lump of grey bread of suspicious content. The bread certainly contained a large proportion of potato, and possibly even sawdust. The small lump of bread issued was the ration for the whole day. Lunch consisted of a thin soup, in which were floating a few pieces of potato. This was sometimes augmented by a small piece of sausage. I was shown a piece of this sausage, which had been smuggled out by one of the prisoners. It had the appearance and resilience of a piece of rubber. It was black and spotted with little squares of white fat. In place of the usual skin there was thin but tough paper. It would almost bounce. The only other meal was supper, which was the same as lunch, with a little jam in the place of the sausage.

Without the assistance of parcels from home it was only just possible for a fit man to keep alive. Even inside the hospital it was rare for wounded prisoners to receive any better food. For washing they were each given a small square piece of soap once a month. The specimens of this soap which were shown to me were like small pieces of firm smooth clay. When wetted they produced a white slime – it could not be called lather. At first I was a little sceptical when I was told about these things, but I should not have been, for after one look at the thin grey skeleton-like men who came back on each train I might have known that the things they told me were true.

Elementary foodstuffs, such as milk, butter, cheese, eggs, sugar, jam, real coffee and tea were never seen; later on, it is true, the conditions in the camps for French prisoners improved, but not to any great extent. In his book, *A Thousand Shall Fall*, Hans Habe gives an account of his experiences as a French prisoner of war which corresponds very largely to all the accounts given to me.

It was pitiful to see the tubercular cases who arrived on the last ebb of their strength. They were all put into a special ward, where they were given oxygen; many of them had neither the strength nor the will to live. If only there had been supplies of body-building food available they might have had a chance; but by now food conditions were so hard in France that there was little advantage gained from that point of view in leaving Germany.

The first thing that every prisoner wanted to do was, of course, to resume contact with his family. This was not always easy, for even if they were in the unoccupied zone the chances of getting in touch with them were at first slight, for every corner of unoccupied France was filled with refugees, and chaos still reigned. Imagine the difficulty of a returning prisoner trying to find a family, the members of which were still scattered. As for a prisoner whose family had remained in or returned to the occupied zone, in the first place he had to be demobilised before he could even apply for a pass to take him into the occupied zone.

This took time, for with the French Army demobilisation took much longer than mobilisation; and even after being demobilised it would be weeks before he managed to get permission to travel into occupied France – if he got it at all. The confusion was tremendous, and sometimes a soldier who, although badly wounded, was fit to go home would spend months trying to contact the members of his family, only to find out in the end that they were in occupied territory and that he could not get permission to return to them.

Most officers and men who returned to France after being inside a German prison camp were strong de Gaullists when they arrived. They would have preferred to see the whole country occupied by the Germans. They could not tolerate the ideas of the Vichy Government. For them nothing could be worse than to return home to find their country split into two parts, with movement from one part to the other controlled by the Germans.

On their arrival in unoccupied France their trains were met by Pétain or one of his generals, and they were treated to a welcoming speech, which invariably finished with a plea to devote their energies to the reconstruction of a new France on military-Fascist lines. The speeches were worded in such a way that the National Revolution programme of Vichy sounded like something far bigger than it could ever hope to become. Their reactions were probably a little bit sentimental at first, but not sufficiently so to shake for an instant, their belief in de Gaulle, and the idea of reorganising themselves in preparation for the day when they would be strong enough to assist a British force to turn the Germans out of France. They well understood from the start that any reconstruction of France while Vichy was in power would only mean a compromise with the Germans at the best, and slavery for them at the worst. They had seen the Germans at home and wanted no pact with them either in the present or the near future.

However, in spite of everything it was a great thing for them to be back in France again, and no longer prisoners, although they had not returned to any real form of freedom. It was interesting to notice how, after a month or so at home, most of them would allow their de Gaullist sympathies to be put aside for the time being while they grudgingly accepted the conditions which were forced upon them. It was the only thing they could do, for the alternative of open revolution would have gained absolutely nothing at that time. While from all outward appearances they accepted the state of affairs in Vichy France in order to earn a living for themselves and their families, in reality they were only biding their time until the great opportunity arose for removing both the Vichy Government and the Germans.

It was just before the New Year that news came through from the American Consul at Lyons to the effect that there was a medical board sitting at Marseilles for the purpose of passing badly wounded British service men for repatriation to England. It was decided that Alan was fit to travel to Marseilles, but I had to wait, as they did not want to take the risk of sending me, even on a stretcher.

There was a last-minute rush to provide Alan with the necessary papers, and after a great deal of difficulty at one bureau after another Alan was ready to leave on New Year's Day. He left under the escort of a middle-aged policeman, who carried his suitcase, two bottles of wine, provided thoughtfully by David to assist diplomatic relations, a sausage, and other things to eat, provided by Madame Sourire, and more food provided by the hospital.

I missed him very much, for we had been together through months of discomfort and suffering and shared unforgettable experiences right up to the time when I was put in the officers' ward and after. He had become a well-known figure in the town. Physically he was very striking, being very tall and for a long time conspicuously battle-scarred. Sometimes he amused himself by walking along the pavement in such a manner that the German soldiers he passed had to step into the gutter to let him pass. His height was accentuated by the clothes he wore – second-hand French civilian's which only just fitted, for few Frenchmen in that part of France could equal him in height and length of leg.

The Board at Marseilles passed him as permanently unfit to bear arms again, and he prepared to leave. However, the hospital ships which had been passing between England and Marseilles could no longer run, for they had been permanently held up by the German Armistice commission at Marseilles harbour. Alan was not deterred and found other means of getting back to England. Several months later I heard that he had arrived safely home and was undergoing plastic surgical treatment.

During the winter of 1940 – the first winter after the collapse of France – the food situation deteriorated so badly that there were no special diets of any kind even in hospitals full of wounded and repatriated prisoners of war.

For the workers in the towns, conditions were terrible, and it was only in a few very isolated districts in the country that it was possible to find meals equal to those served at the beginning of the war. More serious still was the fact that no improvement could be expected on any large scale with the arrival of spring and summer – in fact, when the summer did arrive there was even less to eat.

In February 1941 the menus served in the hospital at Roanne were as follows:

7.30.   Breakfast: Ersatz coffee, slightly sweetened, and dry grey bread.
12.0.   Lunch: Small piece of meat and two vegetables; carrots, cabbage, rice, beans and occasionally potatoes; army wine.
6.0.   Supper: Soup, and one dried vegetable; army wine.

Now, for healthy people not engaged in manual labour or suffering extreme cold, these meals were sufficient, especially as there was the addition of an occasional sardine, piece of cheese or jam, but for wounded and sick men there was little in the diet to assist a return to health. Such small amounts of margarine and other fats as were issued with the rations were absorbed in the cooking, but they were in such small quantities that it was impossible to detect in the dishes the presence of any fat. Eggs, butter and milk were never served in any form; fish was rare and sugar scarce. Between six in the evening and seven-thirty the next morning we saw neither food nor drink, and I personally used to be hungry all the time.

Yet, I was far luckier than most of the other patients, for I had a fairy godmother, Madame Sourire, who for a long time brought me a meal cooked by herself at home to supplement my supper. Then there was Madame Gris, who brought me eggs and butter, and Mrs. Corrigan, who sent me French pâté and sardines. Without these extra things I am certain that I could not have recovered, for there is nothing which saps physical strength and mental morale more than lack of food. Also, with deep and extensive burns, it is necessary for the body to replace large areas of lost tissue.

It turned out one day in February that Colonel Barbe did not think that I would ever be able to walk again; but at least he now believed I would live, which was, at least, something! Certainly, I had started to make rapid progress, thanks to his care of my dressings and the food from my benefactors. My face had just healed up completely, but my arms and side, my hands and my legs still had large areas as yet unhealed. I could now bend my right knee a very little, but my left was solid, and my left foot still encased in a plastic cast. My back was so weak that I was incapable either of sitting up by myself or staying up after being put in the sitting position. Yet one day towards the end of the month Mlle le Falcon arrived and announced that I was to get up and walk!

She and Mlle Chenille, the nurse in charge of the officers' corridor, managed between them to turn my naked skeleton out of bed and got my feet on the floor. They pushed me up on to my feet. With a great deal of cajolery, I ventured one step, and promptly passed out in a pool of blood which had gushed out of my legs on to the floor. This did not deter either of them, for they were tough, and the next day they tried again. This time I stumbled almost two and a half steps with my arms round their necks before I fainted once more. Again, they lifted me back into bed, revived me with cold water and told me that I was making good progress.

I found it difficult to believe it myself, but on the third morning we got as far as the door of the cubicle, turned round and came back again. It was on our way back that I first caught sight of myself in the mirror above the washstand. I had already seen my face in a mirror, but this time I could see nearly the whole of my body, for the mirror was large and I was naked except for my bandages.

Looking back at me from the mirror I saw a grey ghost, whose disfigured face was drawn and twisted and covered with a scraggy growth of dirty ginger beard. I saw an emaciated body that was a greenish-grey in colour and on which all the bones were visible. Whether the green colour meant that I was about to pass out, anyway, or whether it was just the shock of seeing my whole horrible body at once, I do not know, but I fainted once more. The sight completely broke my morale, and I cried bitterly all day.

My life had always been an outdoor one, and I had always devoted a large proportion of my time to physical activities. At school I had played games and loved them. Afterwards, working in London for two years, I had kept up my standard of physical fitness with P.T., swimming and rugger. Since joining the Air Force I had had more time and opportunity for exercise than ever before. Now my body, which I had treated with care and respect for years, was emaciated, twisted and horribly disfigured.

As the days passed I progressed. My supporters were Mlle Chenille and Ki. Mlle Chenille was a country girl who lived near Roanne. She was narrow-minded in some respects, but had many very sterling qualities, not the least of which was courage. Ki. was an Annamite orderly who shared Mlle Chenille's responsibilities in looking after me, and, of course, the other officers. He probably had a little Japanese blood, for he looked more like a Japanese than an Annamite and was exceptionally intelligent. He even spoke quite passable French.

After about a fortnight they put me into a wheelchair instead of returning me to bed at the end of my "walk." My back was still too weak to allow me to sit up straight, and at first I could only stay in the chair for five minutes before being put back into bed. Meanwhile my legs started to heal up much more rapidly, and my right arm began to bend a little more. Within a month of my first sortie, I was able to walk a little way by myself, hanging on sometimes against the wall.

Mlle le Falcon had been hard and cruel in those first four days of walking. She and my own nurse had cursed me roundly; told me I had not the guts of a louse and would always stay a miserable cripple. They got on my nerves so badly that I made, in my annoyance at their taunts, efforts which would otherwise have been impossible. Yes, they were cruel, but it was well worth it. I could no longer resent the rough way Mlle le Falcon had handled my dressings; it was more than offset by the good she had done me in making me walk again.

From now on I never looked back. I used to walk down the corridors of the hospital, opening the doors with my elbows, leaning against the wall whenever I was tired, and visiting all the wards where I knew I would find friendly nurses and wounded soldiers that I had known before or heard about since I had been in the hospital. I was not a very pretty sight. My hair was thin and had fallen out in places. I had a queer, twisted expression on my face, and I was as thin as a skeleton. I hadn't been inside hot water for months, and in fact it was 16 months before I had my first bath after my injury. I had an old pair of slippers on my feet, a rough shirt and an old pair of trousers.

But I didn't worry much about that. I had a new-found freedom. At last, I could leave my bed and my little cubicle for a few hours, and although there was very little I could do by myself, at least I could watch other people busy at work. My hands were still very sore, and I had to wear dark glasses to keep the sun and even ordinary light out of my ever-running eyes. After half-an-hour or so's walking my legs would be swollen to gigantic proportions and I would have to go back to bed and lie down for a bit.

One Saturday afternoon in the middle of March they dressed me up in a borrowed suit, put me in an ambulance along with a number of French soldiers, and off we all went down to the centre of the town, where there was to be a *prise d'armes*, and where I was to receive the French *Croix de Guerre*. I was particularly curious to see the town and also to see French soldiers on parade again. I had already seen something of the French Army before I was wounded, during the first eight months of the war, and I was interested to see what effect the defeat had had upon their bearing and discipline.

The little town of Roanne had hardly any character at all, not even bad. It was small, dirty, old and ugly. Most of the streets were cobbled, and fierce-looking little trams, dug out since the shortage of petrol had limited the bus services, swayed and tilted with great noise down the lines which ran through nearly all the streets. Most of the buildings and shops were drab, and looked as if they hadn't been painted for years. In one place, where there was a patch of waste ground, air raid shelter trenches which had been dug – probably in a hurry during the German invasion – were falling in and had obviously been used for most insanitary purposes.

Roanne made me think of an old person who had undone her stays and allowed herself to sit down for a few easy moments in a dirty and untidy room. It was old enough to be ugly and out of date, yet not old enough to be picturesque. Even if it had been cleaned up, repaired and painted, the disorderliness of its planning and its bad architecture would have continued to show it up in its true colours as a drab and dreary little town. It has many factories, but since the Armistice most of these have been closed, for they specialised in the making of fabric, and raw material was now unobtainable. However, the people seemed quite cheerful, in spite of everything, and when we arrived at the open square in the centre of the town where the *prise d'armes* was to take place we found a huge crowd gathered all round its edges, bobbing with anticipation of the excitement to follow.

There were Tricolours all over the place, arranged in big groups all around the platform where the notabilities were to be seated, and hanging from the windows, well filled with spectators, of the houses overlooking the square. I had the impression that I was coming to witness a victory parade instead of to be decorated by the meagre remnants of the great nation for which I had been fighting.

On the side of the square opposite the platform were ranged strong detachments of regiments of infantry and engineers. They were separated by the band, which arrived later than the soldiers with a great flourish, only to find that the space left for them between the two armed detachments was not big enough. However, after much gesticulating by the band-leader and the officers commanding the two detachments, half of the engineers were ignominiously pushed out of sight and the band marched into its place.

The soldiers did not look very smart – not nearly as smart, in fact, as the black uniformed *gardes mobiles* mounted on their shining chestnut and black horses and ranged on a third side of the square. I was surprised, however, to hear all round me French people saying how much smarter the soldiers looked now than they had done before the Armistice. They seemed to take it as an omen for the revival of the France of the past, or perhaps it was just wishful thinking.

In due course the general arrived, and after many military formalities a number of officers and men were decorated, and we all went back again in the ambulance. At the last moment the general had come round and told me that he could not give me my decoration in public, but that I must wear it, nevertheless, and later, after I had arrived back in hospital the colonel in command of the town garrison came along and gave it to me, full of apologies for taking me out in my weak condition and making me sit in the sun all afternoon for nothing. They all hinted that I would soon be back at another *prise d'armes* to be decorated with the Legion of Honour, but this never came about.

Probably this was just tact; or perhaps the war which broke out in Syria later on stopped it. It was appropriate that I should have come back to life and movement again in the spring; and as the weeks went by and I became gradually stronger I used to go out into the hospital courtyard, where I would sit in my wheelchair for hours in the early spring sunshine. Green shoots were appearing all over the black earth of the hospital vegetable garden. Buds were breaking out on the trees, and new grass spreading in irregular patches on the beaten earth of the sheltered courtyard.

As day succeeded day and spring turned to summer my strength started rapidly to return. Although still a pretty helpless creature and a ghost of my former self, I felt, nevertheless, that I was taking on a new lease of life, and the re-birth of nature all around me stimulated that feeling. I felt and looked like an old man, even although the tufts of beard that had decorated my face in patches while I had been in bed were now shaved off. But surprisingly soon even that feeling disappeared, for by forcing myself to walk round and round the courtyard and up and down the many corridors of the hospital until I could hardly move one foot after another I very soon won back much of my former mobility. I observed with greater keenness those around me, taking particular interest in the returned prisoners.

The flow had increased. Sometimes two hundred would arrive at the hospital at a time, but by the end of about a fortnight they would nearly all have left, and the hospital would be comparatively quiet until a new batch arrived.

I was by now the proud possessor of a new pair of brown boots given to me by the hospital, and two complete suits provided by Mrs. Corrigan and David, cut down to my measure and fitted with zip-fasteners on the sleeves, so that I could put them on in spite of the big bandages over my arms and hands. As my strength returned I grew restless for the sights and sounds of the outside world again, and from the end of April through to about the middle of May I often used to go out with David to drink an aperitif in a café, wander around the streets, and visit some of my friends in their own homes.

Each time I went out the effect of the German victory became increasingly apparent to me. The shops were only half filled with goods, many of them of a very inferior quality. Wool, leather and silks were extremely rare, the quality of linen was poor and cotton almost unobtainable. There was no pure coffee, and sugar, flour, milk, butter, chocolate, meat, fish, cooking oils and fats, were very scarce. There were, however, plenty of vegetables and a fair amount of local fruit. In the cafés the consumption of strong alcoholic drink was prohibited to two days a week.

The country seemed to be living almost entirely upon its own resources, or rather, what was left of them after the Germans had taken their pick. Perhaps the *patisseries* were the most depressing sight of all. Instead of the rows of newly baked crisp white French loaves and the array of rolls and fancy cakes, in the making of which the French are such experts, one saw now a few loaves of grey bread, which could be bought only with coupons, and a few heaps of rather unpalatable looking rusks. There were certain days of the week upon which it was permitted to sell cakes, but these were poor and miserable things compared with the delicacies of the past. They mostly consisted of tarts made with cherries when in season, or a kind of fig jam when there were no cherries. The pastry was thin, grey and heavy. Yet Roanne had the reputation of being well provisioned in comparison with other and bigger towns in the vicinity.

Later, when I visited Marseilles and Lyons, this fact was borne out. In the streets few of the girls wore stockings, as stockings of any kind – silk, wool or artificial silk – were extremely rare. They clumped about in quite artistic fancy wooden shoes, with their legs dyed a suitable tan to replace the allure of silk. The scarcity of boot polish, added to an inborn reluctance of most of the inhabitants of Roanne to use it anyway, accentuated the shabbiness of men whose clothes were wearing out, but were irreplaceable.

The people grumbled a lot about conditions, but kept remarkably cheerful nevertheless, and there didn't seem to be very much danger of any kind of revolt. They were philosophical, with the exception of some of the older people, and always, after they had been grumbling for hours, finished with a shrug of the shoulders and a laugh at some trivial thing or incident which amused them. They were always kind to me, and generous to an embarrassing extent. I was never made to feel a foreigner, and they took a great interest in everything

I had to say about my own country; so much so that I could not help reflecting that in England, where we seem to have so little time for anyone but ourselves, their treatment would have been quite different if the case had been reversed.

The presence of the Germans in the town was not conspicuous, and in the course of my wanderings I never saw one in uniform. It is true I never went near the arsenal, which was probably their main source of interest, but in other parts of the town when I did see them they were always in plain clothes. In fact, contrary to the usual belief, they were rather difficult to distinguish from certain types of Frenchmen in the towns. They were undoubtedly picked men of considerable experience, and it is said that there are very few German officers and technicians in the Armistice Commission in the unoccupied part of France who do not speak almost perfect French.

Occasionally I would see big touring cars painted dark grey and marked W.H., with two civilians inside. They were German officers probably on their way back to their hotel after visiting the arsenal. As there were very few cars on the road, and those mostly official, they were easily distinguishable. In their manner the Germans were unobtrusive; they were perforce absorbed to some extent into the life of the town, but I don't think they were ever accepted, for any Frenchman showing marked friendliness towards the Germans would very soon have been ostracized by his friends, and probably have his name noted for retribution after the war was over.

Perhaps the happiest afternoons I spent in the town of Roanne were with David, when he would take me down a side street, across a dark and tiny open courtyard and into a ground floor room, furnished with an old piano, an old disused double-bed and an indescribable heap of junk of every sort and description. There were also two or three rickety chairs and that strange atmosphere and smell which hangs about old, abandoned rooms full of dirty household things. Here David used to play to me for hours, intermingling his repertoire of Chopin, Mozart and Mendelssohn with compositions of his own. Although he called himself a composer, not a pianist, he played with a richness of expression and a depth of feeling which made the music live for me as never before.

On our way back to the hospital after one of these afternoons of music we were stopped in the middle of the street by a woman wearing very conspicuously an emblem consisting of a gold Lorraine Cross, the insignia of the de Gaullists, combined with an arrangement of French and British flags. She wanted to know how her son could get over to England and join de Gaulle. It was a pity that she was so indiscreet, firstly because I could not help her, and secondly because the incident put an end to my liberty in the town, as the hospital authorities were afraid that a repetition might cause trouble with the Vichy Government.

And so, after a few weeks of comparative liberty, I had to go back into the hospital again and forget that I had ever been free. This new confinement, combined with the outbreak of war in Syria and my rapidly returning strength, made me decide that the time was ripe to make a move towards getting back to England again. This was about the beginning of May. After a month of concentrated effort by myself, the hospital, the military authorities in the town and the American Consul at Lyons, I was at last given permission to go down to Marseilles to pass before a board of mixed doctors with a view to being declared unfit to take any further part in the war and be given permission to be repatriated by way of Spain and Gibraltar to England.

Early on the morning of the 6th June 1941 I left the hospital with a French *Adjudant*, who had the dual responsibility of looking after me and seeing that I didn't escape. I was driven in an ambulance to the station, where I said good-bye to David and was soon in the train on my way to Lyons.

At Lyons we changed trains and travelled very comfortably down the Rhône Valley in the Marseilles Express, a first-class carriage having been reserved for us. It was a lovely summer day, and the bright sunshine lit up the beautiful valley in a blaze of colour. The hills which sheltered the valley were covered with green vineyards dotted with little whitewashed houses, and in the valley itself on either side of river and railway stretched a wealth of cultivation: ripening corn, huge peach orchards and gardens filled with every kind of vegetable. Here was food in abundance, but it was heartbreaking to know that in the big towns all over France many people were starving, and the rest hard put to it to find a square meal.

As we sped down to the mouth of the Rhône sometimes we would come across marshalling yards full of goods trucks, many of which were big brown wagons, both open and closed, marked *Deutche Reichsbahn*. German railway trucks, a countryside abounding in foodstuffs and Frenchmen starving in the big towns; here were three facts which fitted closely together.

In the late afternoon we arrived at Marseilles station. We were met by ambulance from the big military hospital called Michel Lévy, where the medical board which was to examine me were meeting in two days' time. It was Sunday and, apart from a few trams rumbling up and down the broad main tree-lined streets through which we passed on our way to the hospital in the centre of the town, Marseilles was practically deserted. There was again that noticeable absence of motor traffic which was by now a characteristic feature of French towns. I had called in at Marseilles six years ago on my way to Egypt and I was hoping that I would be given liberty to wander round and see what it was like now, with its restricted trade, and its wealth of international travellers and tourists replaced by the officers of the German and Italian Armistice Commissions. However, I was to be disappointed, for the only other glimpse I caught of Marseilles was on my way back to the station in the same ambulance some eight weeks afterwards.

Chapter 5

Prisoner at Marseilles

T he Michel Lévy Military Hospital was shut off from the outside world by a huge iron gate and a high wall. Behind this gate the sick and the wounded were confined in a vast grey stone prison-like building, some five stories high, built in the form of a hollow square, enclosing a dusty beaten earth courtyard filled with rows of large plane trees, the leaves and branches of which successfully eliminated most of the light and sunshine, but did not prevent the high *mistral* wind from raising the dust and scattering it over everything. In the middle of the courtyard stood a fountain that never played.

The first impression was a most unfriendly one, and it was soon intensified by the welcome I received at the hands of the young pupil doctor on duty, who, after looking me up and down in an insolent fashion, said that he was not sure whether I was to be shut up in the hospital prison straight away or confined in a room by myself in the officers' section. It turned out to be the lesser of the two evils.

The hospital was slumbering in the heat of the summer Sunday afternoon. The courtyard was empty as my *adjudant* escort, the reception clerk and I crossed it on our way to the officers' section. We mounted a flight of stairs and arrived on the first floor in a dark and dingy high-ceilinged corridor with a stone-tiled floor, down the middle of which was stretched a strip of rough carpet. Against the wall at the near end stood a polished wooden bench outside a door leading into the doctor's room. There were four other doors on each side of the corridor, enclosing six officers' rooms, a gloomy and dirty little kitchen, and an unattractive little dining-room, containing a long table and chairs for the twenty odd officer patients who were well enough to eat their meals there.

While we were waiting to see another doctor the reception clerk told me how he and all his friends had been very much pro-English until the war in Syria had started. "But" he said, "to attack the French in Syria was a dirty trick; I and my friend will never forgive England for it." He was beginning to get quite objectionable by the time the doctor arrived.

This new doctor was also very young, and a student, but charming, and spoke a few words of English. He told me he greatly regretted it, but that I was to be kept in a room by myself, where he assured me, I should receive the same treatment as all French officers. He then opened one of the doors in the corridor and ushered me into a large bare-looking apartment, which I afterwards discovered was normally reserved for French senior officers – colonels and higher ranks. I don't think a British colonel would have found it very comfortable.

In one corner there was an enormous cast-iron bed which had been painted some years before with a dull grey paint. Flat wooden shelves were attached to the ironwork at its head and foot, and these also were painted in the same dull grey colour. On the longitudinal iron springs lay a hard mattress covered with grey unbleached sheets of a rough un-ironed cloth which was as tough as curtain material. For my head to rest upon, there was a hard bolster and a flimsy little feather-filled pillow covered with the same curtain-like material as that used for the sheets. An antique dark wood bedside cabinet with an artificial marble top filled the space between the head of the bed and the window, which was open, but shuttered with big heavy wooden shutters of the Venetian blind type.

On the other side of the window an old-fashioned glass mirror in a heavy wooden frame leaned down precariously over a small and dirty washbasin equipped with un-polished taps, from the cold one of which flowed tepid water. An old and solid table covered with grey baize cloth, two old wooden chairs, a cumbrous imitation leather and horsehair armchair with a sticky back and a massive unpolished wooden wardrobe completed the drab and old-fashioned furnishings of the room. In the corner, on the stone-tiled floor, stood a big white enamelled bucket covered with a lid. Its uses were multitudinous and can be left to the imagination, for in this room I was to be confined during the whole of my stay at Marseilles.

The hospital had looked old and drab enough first from outside and then from the courtyard. The corridor of the officers' section was certainly not prepossessing; but this room, with its thick stone walls painted dark grey for the first five feet, then a lighter grey up to the whitewashed ceiling, with its old and dusty woodwork and its drab furnishings, had a dejected and forlorn air which depressed me beyond all description. When the shutters were open and the bright sunlight filtered in through the trees in the courtyard outside it didn't look quite so bad; but at night, when its grey drabness was lit only by the inadequate single electric bulb which hung from the ceiling, it was indeed miserable.

The doctor left with the *adjudant* who had accompanied me from Roanne, and a nurse arrived to clean me up after the journey and feed me my evening meal. She was a tall, slim, good-looking girl, more Spanish than French in appearance; but the clothes she was wearing, for I cannot call them "uniform," were extraordinary. The thin white un-ironed nurse's veil, which concealed most of her black hair, was pinned behind her head and hung down like a pigtail.

A loose overall with short, wide sleeves and an open neck without a collar, generously exposed her suntanned neck and throat. Her bronze legs were bare and on her feet she wore wooden-soled sandals with wrap-over uppers made from strips of red, white and blue leather, and cut away in front to show her bare toes. Her lips were painted, and her nails varnished a bright red. On one finger of her left hand, she was wearing a big, coloured stone ring. If she was wearing anything more than I could see I should be surprised. She didn't fit in at all with any of my preconceived ideas of a hospital nurse.

After a scratchy wash she fed me with my supper of army wine, soup, a small piece of sausage, some rice, a piece of bread and a small hard plum. The time was about six o'clock, and this was my last meal of the day. I don't think she liked me very much. Maybe it was the smell of the old dressings round my hands, or maybe I had stared at her rather rudely in surprise when she first came in. However, I only saw her once or twice again during the rest of my time in the hospital. I heard a few days later that she had been taken away to look after the prisoners in the steel-barred prison on the floor above, where French soldiers who happened to be sick and sinful at the same time were shut in. I have no doubt she added a little glamour to the terrible dreariness that their existence must otherwise have been, for the prison was certainly no palace.

Before she left me she filled and lit my pipe, and as the door had been left open I decided to wander around the courtyard for a while and have a look round. I was still very weak at the time and my legs used to swell a lot when I walked, so after a short time spent wandering about I sat down on one of the many benches set in the cloister-like passageway built into the ground floor of the four attached buildings which surrounded the courtyard.

A few French soldiers, mostly Senegalese troops, in a blue hospital uniform or their own khaki, were sitting down near me. So far I had been rather surprised that none of the French officers had come to see me to make me welcome, for up to date the outstanding feature of my dealings with French officers had been their courtesy and their efforts to make me feel at home as quickly as possible.

However, after I had been sitting down for a short while a tall, good-looking man dressed in a light grey suit came up, introduced himself, and after talking to me for a short time explained that Médécin-Colonel Crapaud, who was in charge of the hospital, had sent round a special message to all the French officer-patients forbidding them to speak to me or have any dealings with me. This automatically excluded me from the officers' dining-room and the little garden which was reserved for them in a corner behind one of the buildings outside the courtyard near the soldiers' canteen. He told me also that the majority of the officers at present in the hospital were strongly anti-British and would probably not have had anything to do with me, anyway. He himself was breaking orders and running a considerable risk talking to me on this one occasion. He was a most charming man and had served as a military doctor in Syria, where he had got to know many British officers in the three fighting services stationed in Palestine. He had that international tolerance for other nations which is the mark of the intelligent observant traveller. He said that he considered it disgusting and shameful that Colonel Crapaud and the other officers should treat me so badly after I had been fighting in the defence of their country.

When I told him that I had only come to Marseilles for two days to go before the mixed medical board, and that I carried orders, signed by the French military commander at Roanne, relating to my return to that town after I had been before the Board, he expressed grave misgivings and said that I should be very lucky if I got out of this hospital before the end of the war. He only stayed talking to me for a few minutes but told me he would try and slip in to see me some time in my room, although he would have to be careful, as he could not trust the other officers not to report him to Colonel Crapaud if they saw him.

As I climbed slowly back up the stairs to my room my heart was heavy. I had a horror of the idea of spending the rest of the war inside this miserable soul-destroying old building, where I was to be restricted at every turn, not allowed to talk to my fellow patients, not allowed exercise, and in fact to be treated as a political criminal of the worst type. Had I never come over to France to defend her I should not have ended up in Marseilles as a prisoner in a crippled condition. But then, as Marshal Pétain said in one of his greatest rallying speeches, "Frenchmen, your memories are short." That night as I lay between the rough sheets on my "prison" bed, after having been undressed by an old white-haired woman whose duty it was to attend to the officers' needs during the night, I swore to fight Colonel Crapaud until I was out of his hospital.

The next morning, after my bowl of coffee (ersatz, of course), followed by a wash, I persuaded the nurse to leave my door open; I then went out and sat down on the bench in front of the doctor's office ready for battle. As I sat there for hours on end the many officers who passed to and fro looked curiously at me, but none of them said a word. The doctor in charge of the officers' section, however, was very charming. He was a Jew and had been practising in Paris before the war. He promised me to ask Colonel Crapaud on my behalf if I could go out with an escort to see the American Consul in Marseilles.

The answer that came back was short and to the point. No. While wondering what to do next I was also waiting for the *adjudant* who had accompanied me from Roanne and who was supposed to come and see me in order to make arrangements for the trip back to Roanne. However, he never turned up again, and it was only just before I left France that I heard that he had paid a visit to the hospital, had been told by Colonel Crapaud that he could not see me and that he was to return to Roanne and consider his orders regarding the English officer as cancelled.

Next I asked if I could go and see Colonel Crapaud but was told that this would be of no use, as he would refuse to see me. Things were looking pretty bad. However, I decided to hang about the corridor outside my room until Colonel Crapaud passed, as he was bound to do sooner or later on his rounds. Sure enough, the next day round he came, and I stopped him in the passage, explained who I was, and asked him if it was true that he was going to hold me there in the hospital. He said that it was.

The instructions, according to him, no longer applied regarding my return to Roanne. As he put it, "You have come down here, therefore you must stay here." As regards the American Consul, I would not be allowed out to see him, but he could come and see me if he liked. I had been warned that this Colonel Crapaud was a hard and stern man, and it certainly seemed to be true. He was tall and well built; his white hair was thin on top and brushed straight back in a manner that accentuated his broad brow; his nose was straight, his lips thin and he looked down upon me unsympathetically out of his cold grey eyes. He had the reputation of sticking firmly and unrelentingly to the inhuman letter of the law. Imagination and sense of humour seemed to have no part in his makeup. His strength lay in his relentlessness, and certainly his hold over the hospital staff and the patients was a firm one. But he never looked me straight in the eye and kept appealing to my doctor for corroboration of his statements.

As a result of this first interview I was allowed to telephone the American Consulate to ask the consul to come round and see me. I felt that I had won a moral victory in my first encounter with this strange man, and as the medical board was meeting the next day I let the matter of my departure drop for the time being.

The medical board consisted of three: a Swedish doctor representing the Germans, a French doctor representing the French and an American representing the British. It was their duty to examine British subjects of military age desiring to be repatriated to England on medical grounds. They very soon declared me totally unfit, and I left them with the satisfaction of knowing that I had medical grounds justifying my repatriation. There were other British subjects there, a few civilians, and some soldiers brought over from the French concentration camp for British soldiers and airmen, near Nîmes. I managed to have a few words with the British lieutenant who had conducted his fellow prisoners over from the concentration camp. He seemed pretty well fed up. Conditions, he said, were not too bad, but they were all bored stiff with nothing to do.

A day or so later an American Consular official came round to see me and promised to do everything in his power to get me out of this hospital and back to Roanne, and to make arrangements for my repatriation when the results of the Board had come through. And so matters rested for the next few weeks. In the meantime, I had plenty of time and opportunity for studying the life going on inside the hospital.

According to the instructions I was to be confined at all times to my room, but in actual practice the door was very often left open, and I used to sneak out, go down into the courtyard and sit on a bench with my pipe and a book; and there I would stay for hours on end, a detached and distant figure, with my face badly mutilated, my hair untidy, my hands swathed in bandages, dressed in a half-washed flannel shirt with rolled up sleeves and open neck, an old pair of blue linen trousers and sandals. At first nobody used to speak to me, but after a time a few bolder spirits decided to risk the head doctor's displeasure, and from then on I talked to many interesting personalities of all colours, creeds and conditions.

There were a number of orderlies detailed to look after the officers, of which there were about forty, for most of the rooms similar to mine contained two or three beds, and the corridor I have described was only one of three. These orderlies were mostly untrained; some of them were soldiers who were waiting to be demobilised and sent away from the hospital, where they had been undergoing treatment. They were always very good to me and were very pro-British.

As tobacco was now rationed and very difficult to obtain they would often share their rations with me. They were untidy and not always too clean. For a while I was unlucky enough to be fed by the dirtiest and dumbest of them, who used to come straight from cleaning out the passages and the lavatories to feed me with his fingers. I put up with this for some time, but eventually complained, and from then onwards was fed by a nurse. Most of these orderlies were having a rough time. About half of them were from the occupied zone, had little or no news of their wives and families and poor prospects of finding work after they had been demobilised. Those who had already become civilians again, but were working on at the hospital, found it very difficult to get enough to eat, either for themselves or their families.

Prices were high and food was scarcer in Marseilles than at Roanne. Ironically enough, in this, the biggest French port on the Mediterranean, fish was almost unobtainable. I was told that the fishermen, who were given a small petrol ration, had discovered that it was more profitable to sell the petrol on the black market to car owners than to go out fishing for a meagre return. Even wine was rationed, and the poor people of Marseilles were living almost entirely on tomatoes, cabbage and other vegetables, bread, a little wine and ersatz coffee. The population was underfed and miserable in every way, and the morale was rapidly falling. It had been estimated that 80 per cent, of the produce arriving in Marseilles harbour went direct into Germany. Then victorious Italy had to have her share. The port and town was alive with German and Italian officers working on the Armistice Commissions.

One day I received a visit from a lady in the Polish Red Cross. She told me that before me there had been four British airmen shut up in the prison inside the hospital for several weeks, and that not only had they been confined there and not allowed exercise, but they had also been refused visits from outside; the hospital itself was bad enough, but the prison inside was grim indeed, and they must have had a very miserable time.

Another of my visitors – for I did have a few in the two months that I was there – was half English and half French. He had been an interpreter in a French infantry regiment, and his unit, finding itself one day short of food, arms and ammunition, and about to be attacked by heavy German forces, threw away their remaining arms and beat a hasty retreat on foot in a southerly direction.

In one village they found a lot of chickens, and, as they had not had anything to eat for twenty-four hours, decided to stop running for a bit, cook the chickens and have a big meal before continuing on the next lap. The chickens were cooked to a turn, and they were just sitting down to a fine meal when suddenly they saw Germans coming in to the north end of the village, and they had to drop everything and run as fast as they could again.

Sometimes they would find that the Germans were in front of them, and they would have to run off at a tangent before returning to their southerly course again. He said that he had never run so far and fast in his life as he had in the French Army. Their officers had been the first to leave, by car, and they never saw them again. He was stuck in Marseilles waiting for the French Government to decide whether he was English or French. With a Danish friend he used to bathe a lot in the same *plage* used by the German officers. He said they were mostly of very fine physique and good swimmers. Often the Dane borrowed their German newspapers, and he would study the war from Dr. Goebbels' angle.

Sometimes I would wander round and watch the cooks at work inside the enormous cook-house, where vast quantities of rice, beans, split peas and other vegetables were always cooking in pots so enormous that small cranes had to be used for lifting them off the ranges. As mealtimes approached one of the fat cooks would come out and toll the big iron bell, and male and female orderlies would arrive from all directions, carrying big baskets for the bread and metal dixies for the vegetables. The food ration was sufficient to keep a healthy man alive and reasonably fit, but no one could have got fat on it, and often I saw groups of patients waiting for the nurses to come out of their refectory, hoping to be given scraps of bread which the girls had saved from their meal to give to their pet patients.

In this strange existence of mine, approximating fairly closely to that of a sick Trappist monk, I was forced to resign myself to a great deal of reading, and used to study all the newspapers and periodicals that I could get hold of from cover to cover. These were, of course, all French, and were full of propaganda for the Vichy Government and Marshal Pétain. German, Italian and British communiqués were given daily, and after the outbreak of war in Russia the headlines of the papers were concerned with the German advances, quoting the German communiqués, Russian claims being given a very minor place in a much smaller type. The same relative treatment was used for German and Italian communiqués as compared with the British, so that any but a very careful reader had already absorbed the German and Italian claims before reaching those of the British. The reports on the Syrian campaign left the impression of a small French Army beating back with great resolution an overwhelming attack from the British.

De Gaulle and his followers were constantly denounced and proclaimed traitors, who were fighting against their countrymen to undermine the French Empire for the profit of the British. Once I read in a Marseilles paper the full account of a speech made by Paul Marion, the Vichy Propaganda Minister, in which he said that de Gaullism and Communism were the two greatest evils with which Marshal Pétain and his Government had to contend.

Topical articles on Spain were common, and the Spanish Blue Division, enlisted to fight with the Germans against the Russians and Communism was given a big write-up when it left Spain. The Press, which expressed itself in full on the subject of the dastardly attack by the British on French Syria, showed considerable reticence on the Indo-Chinese affair; the Japanese annexation of certain districts in the north of French Indo-China being passed over as a comparatively minor incident and placed in an inconspicuous part of the paper.

The weekly journals, particularly the illustrated ones, such as *Sept Jours*, *Dimanche Illustré* and *Alliance*, were now going ahead full steam on pro-Pétain, pro-German and anti-communist propaganda of every sort and kind. For a long time *Sept Jours* had been almost impartial and had contained many very interesting illustrated articles on the war in the Middle East and in other parts of the world, giving unbiased and well-balanced criticisms both from a British and a German point of view; but its policy had been checked and it was suspended for a month after one of its more impartial articles, and when it next appeared had thrown in its lot completely with the others, having found itself unequal to the task of printing the truth in a country in which journalism had sunk to the low level of a propaganda minister's echo.

I had my second encounter with Colonel Crapaud a week or so after the medical board had examined me. Once again I stopped him in the passage, and after he had told me that I could not be sent back to Roanne I asked him to forward a letter, dictated by me, requesting such a move from a higher authority. He agreed to do so; the letter was written, and I was forced to settle down while the wheels of French military bureaucracy turned slowly round.

As week succeeded week the war in Syria came to an end, and soon after hospital ships arrived in Marseilles with French soldiers wounded in Syria, who had been repatriated by the British authorities there. On arrival in the port the returning wounded received a civil and military reception, during which they were congratulated for having fought to save the honour of France and her Empire. Then they were driven in ambulances provided by the French and the American Red Cross to my hospital and another. There were one or two serious stretcher cases, but the majority were walking and had only minor injuries. About half of them were Senegalese from Africa.

On the whole they looked fed up and dispirited. I talked to many of them and found few Frenchmen who had any desire to fight, either against the British, or anyone else for that matter. The Senegalese, however, seemed to have enjoyed it, as they enjoy any good scrap, and were quite sorry it was all over. They were full of stories of the hard treatment they had received at the hands of the Australians and the Indians. They also bitterly resented the orders they had received to leave their *coupe-coupes* behind. The *coupe-coupe* is a villainous native knife used for cutting off the head, or perhaps only the ears in some cases, of the lawful war victims of the Senegalese.

Sometimes when it was exceptionally hot I used to slip out of the courtyard into the chapel, the entrance to which was very near the officers' section. Here it was always cool and quiet, and one could read in peace without being annoyed by flies. One day, as I was coming out of the chapel after a quiet afternoon's reading, I met a young military priest, who, with his black cap, cassock and military belt, pale face and dark beard, had an aesthetic appearance which was belied when he burst into laughter, as he very often did. He told me that he had been a prisoner of war in Germany and that he had escaped and arrived back in the unoccupied zone of France. He was full of admiration for British prisoners of war he had met in the early stages of his captivity before nationalities were separated in the German prison camps. On one occasion he saw a German soldier write up in English, "God will punish the English." He then pointed out his handiwork to a diminutive British soldier. The Tommy studied it carefully for a minute or so and replied, "Oh, yes, I dare say He will, but before He does, the English are going to punish the Germans."

As time passed I became accustomed to the simplicity of life and the lack of events caused by my confinement and disabilities, until I reached a state of mental peace and resignation which I would never have believed could have been possible for me to attain. My mind, unfettered by any kind of responsibility, roved unhampered from thought to thought as free as a butterfly in a flower garden.

By the clipping of my wings and the loss of physical freedom I had acquired a mental contentment which I would not have exchanged for any other gift, and I began to wonder why it was that there were so few hermits and monks in the world. It became really pleasant to sit for hours in the courtyard on a bench underneath the arches of the cloister like passage, immobile myself, but fascinated by the simple but ever-changing scene. Hour by hour, day by day,

I would sit there. Sometimes I would hear a rumbling outside the hospital; the gate would open and in would come two chestnut horses, rather thin and underfed, pulling a narrow high-wheeled brown army van full of the week's vegetables. The vegetables would be unloaded and afterwards the carter and the horses would have their lunch. How hungry they looked, the three of them, two horses and one man.

I grew very fond of those two horses; we had something in common. We were both slaves of some remote organization which held us prisoners in that courtyard, bound to a strange destiny. On two afternoons a week a gang of Indo-Chinese sweepers, some armed with brooms and the others manning a water-hose fixed to a hydrant, came into the courtyard, sprayed water over the cloister like passageway, and swept away the dust they had laid. On Thursdays and Sunday's visitors were allowed to come in to visit the soldiers between the hours of one and three. Then there were the neat-looking Red Cross nurses dressed and disciplined in very much the same way as the nurses at Roanne, contrasting strangely with the military nurses, who were dressed like the nurse whom I have already described, who looked after me when I first arrived at Marseilles.

For a while before I left Marseilles I was looked after by a very charming Parisian nurse, and while she was busy washing me and giving me my meals and at other times, I used to give her English lessons, in return for which she brought me French books to read. Jacqueline was very cheerful and interesting to talk to, and she spent most of her free time walking and camping by the sea. Her parents were in Paris, and to get to see them she had to pass across the heavily guarded demarcation line between the unoccupied and the occupied zones. Sometimes she told me about Paris and how it had changed since the German occupation.

The thing that disgusted her most of all was to see German soldiers photographing the Eternal Flame under the Arc de Triomphe, kept burning in honour of the Unknown Soldier of France, sacrificed in the last war against the Germans in the cause of everlasting peace. Another thing which disgusted her was the number of German propaganda posters stuck all over the town and in the Metro stations, by means of which, in a number of different ways, the Germans were trying to destroy pro-British sympathy. In her opinion they were failing miserably as far as the Parisians were concerned. She also talked of the low living conditions and the disappearance of that invigorating sparkle which had earned France's capital the reputation of being the gayest city of Europe.

I had my dressings done every three or four days, and on these occasions I had to pass some of the soldiers' wards to get to the little operating room where septic dressings were attended to. Big, dreary, undecorated rooms were cut up into a number of smaller rooms, separated by wood and glass partitions and shut off by doors from the corridors so formed down the middle of the main apartment. The first time I wandered down one of these corridors and, looking in through the glass partitions, saw in each a number of beds similar to mine, packed closely together, occupied by dirty and untidy patients, I realised how lucky I was to have a room to myself. The old building seemed to have accumulated a mixture of unpleasant smells, strongly reminiscent of the closed-in parts of a Zoo, such as the monkey house. Through the whole of the hospital padded dishevelled and dirty looking patients, a few nurses, slatternly ward maids and orderlies, and an occasional doctor, wearing a white coat over his military uniform.

The hospital was constantly being washed out, but the untidy and dirty habits of most of the patients combined with the age of the building made it impossible to keep it clean. The little operating room where my dressings were attended to had much the same air as the rest of the hospital. It was out of date, most of the equipment was worn and chipped, and it was not too clean. But there was one thing about it which was greatly to its credit: everything that had to be antiseptic – forceps, gauze, dressings, etc., – was particularly well looked after, and although the outsides of the drums which contained sterilized gauze were rusty, the lids were religiously kept shut and the compresses never touched by hand.

The nurses and doctors who did the dressings rubbed their hands with spirit before each one and with forceps in each hand removed the old dressings, cleaned the wounds and applied the new dressings without touching a thing, except, of course, the final bandage. In fact, the exterior air of dirtiness in the hospital was counter-balanced by this meticulous care in doing dressings in the most antiseptic way possible.

One day in the middle of August, after I had been in the hospital for two months, I was told that I was to be sent to another military hospital at Lyons. This was a great relief, as it seemed to indicate that soon I might be repatriated, and, anyway, although the simplicity of my almost vegetable life had had its advantages, Lyons offered the prospect of a return to civilization and even perhaps a little freedom. At the best I had been very lonely at Marseilles, and although it had not succeeded in wearing me down completely, there were many times when the bitter irony of being imprisoned and isolated by the country for which I had been fighting bore very heavily upon me.

I had a genuine liking and sympathy for the French people and felt very much the sufferings and degradations which the military defeat had brought upon them, and it seemed a great pity that my high opinion of them should be badly shaken by the indifference, lack of sympathy and unfriendliness of a small number of French officers, most of whom had suffered only indirectly from the war and certainly no more than the average French civilian. I knew that had I been in the occupied part of France, particularly in the north, in Brittany, Normandy, in the Pas de Calais or near Paris, I would not only have been well looked after, but would have been hidden from the Germans by people who would have been shot immediately by the German authorities if I had been discovered.

Yet here down in Marseilles, in unoccupied France, one French colonel was so mean or so jittery, or so anxious to please the Germans and the Vichy Government, that he had given orders for me to be segregated from French officers and deprived of all their privileges as officers, although God knows they were few enough in that wretched hospital. At this time, too, I was in great need of physical building up, of sunshine and exercise, and these were things that were all denied me. Although the food position was very severe there were a considerable number of officer cases in this hospital who were given special diets. Undoubtedly they were cases which needed this extra attention, but I doubt if they needed it any more than I did. No efforts were ever made by the authorities (who believed me to be shut up in my room all the time, for I only got out of it by breaking regulations) to make my life a little more bearable by the loan of a radio or a gramophone, or English books. In fact, the Michel Lévy Hospital at Marseilles left an indelible mark on my memory – a very bitter reminder of the fact that it is easy for a few individuals in a very short time, through their unsympathetic and hard treatment, to undermine the good impression created by their fellow-countrymen over a period of months or even years.

When I arrived at the Michel Lévy Hospital I was fairly strong, although thin and undernourished, but when I left, after two months without exercise, without sunshine and with very little to eat, I was very weak once more.

Early one hot sunny morning towards the end of August the big gates of the hospital were opened and an ambulance with myself and an orderly in the back drove out into the streets of Marseilles, bound for the station. There had been times when I had almost given up hope of ever getting out of this hospital before the end of the war, and now that I was actually on the other side of those vast iron gates I found it very difficult to make an analysis of my feelings. Inside the hospital I had been shut off from the outer world and had gradually adapted myself to the strange, restricted form of the daily routine that had been imposed upon me. Now that I was free again – assuming that in the new hospital I would not be treated in the same way – I found that I had almost forgotten, even in the short time of two months, the complications of normal life. It was strange enough to be wearing a suit again, but to be back in a world of people who were neither doctors, nurses, wounded nor sick, but were walking about bronzed, fit and to all appearances free from the worries of war, sickness and restriction, was refreshing, and a great relief.

On arrival at the station, we got out of the ambulance, and the orderly who was accompanying me went off to buy the tickets, leaving me to watch the animated scene inside the entrance to Marseilles main station. There was little evidence of war; uniforms were far scarcer than they had ever been before, and on the whole the crowd was healthy and looked quite happy. However, when I studied the train indicator the existence of the German occupation was soon brought back to me, for although trains were still running to Paris, Bordeaux and the other big towns in the occupied zone, I remembered immediately that German officials would be controlling those trains on their arrival at the demarcation line separating the unoccupied from the occupied zone.

Of course, if you looked closely, reminders of the war could easily be found. The girls, although smartly dressed, were mainly stockingless and were wearing fancy wooden-soled shoes; no women could be seen smoking, as they had no tobacco ration; and even the men were reserving their few cigarettes for smoking after meals. The tobacco kiosk was empty, and the newsagent was selling nothing but Vichy, German and Italian propaganda. Trains, although as yet unchanged in appearance, were few and far between. Our train, the Marseilles-Lyons express, was waiting in the station, and we made our way along to the first-class compartment which had been reserved for us. A few minutes after we had settled ourselves in the compartment the train started, and until late that afternoon we were en route for Lyons.

The Rhône Valley had changed since last I had seen it. The fruit and grain harvests were mostly completed. I wondered how much of the harvest would eventually find its way into the hands of the Germans as food for the armies of occupation and for German civilians in Germany; the wine would probably be taken, its alcohol extracted and used by the Germans for war purposes. At one of the stations at which we stopped on the way, the platform was crowded with French officers who had been prisoners in Germany and had just arrived back in France. From the ribbons on their tunics, it was evident that they were veterans of the last war. Two of the oldest and toughest of them got into our carriage and we were soon talking about the conditions in their Oflag, the war in general, and its effect on France.

As usual, they were both mainly concerned with contacting their families again as soon as possible, and seemed bewildered and unable to arrive at any concrete ideas on the political situation in France and its new leaders. They were both in their early fifties. One was a captain and the other a lieutenant. One had also been a prisoner in Germany during the last war. From their accounts it appeared that conditions for French prisoners were improving, and that more parcels were getting through, though their experiences for the first few months of captivity were terrible, and similar to those I have described earlier on.

In their Oflag they had been shown German propaganda films of raids over London and other similar subjects, presumably calculated to show them the folly of putting any faith in England, as she would soon be Germany's next victim. Like the majority of returned French prisoners of war, they showed no antagonism towards England, although they felt that we had let them down by not sending over as large an expeditionary force as had been expected.

Another fellow passenger in my carriage was an executive in the French Air Ministry, who had just returned to France that day after having been flown round the world on a tour of inspection of air lines. We talked about flying. He had been shot down and wounded in the last war while commanding a squadron of fighters in the *Armée de l'Air*. Here was no collaborator with the Germans at heart, at any rate. Undoubtedly like many men in positions similar to his in France at the present moment, it was necessary for him to compromise, but to me he represented a typical example of hundreds of the Frenchmen in high places who are only waiting for the opportunity to be rid of the Germans and to turn once more to their old allies, from whom they hope help will someday come.

When we arrived at Lyons station an ambulance was waiting for us, and we were taken along to the military hospital which was situated in the boulevard running along the embankment of the Rhône.

Chapter 6

Parole at Lyons

I n outward appearance the Hôpital Desgenettes was an old grey prison-like building constructed on lines almost identical to those of the hospital at Marseilles. However, as soon as I entered the building I realised that my treatment was to be kindness and consideration itself. After my particulars had been entered in a book and I had said good-bye to the charming orderly who had accompanied me from Marseilles I was taken by the duty medical officer to the officers' section.

It consisted of a dark corridor with windows overlooking the courtyard of the hospital, furnished with old-fashioned settees, armchairs, a radio, potted plants of the aspidistra variety, a few old-fashioned pictures and photographs, and a noticeboard. It had a fairly comfortable and homely air and resembled in many ways a room in an old-fashioned army officers' mess. A number of doors opened into this corridor, and behind them were rooms each containing half a dozen or so beds for the officer patients.

Supper was being served when I arrived, and some twenty-five officers were seated round a large oblong mahogany table set in the centre of the dining-room, which adjoined the corridor. A small table was set for me at the side of this room and an old, charming and motherly nurse, who had seen thirty years' continuous service in this one hospital, introduced me to everyone and sat down to feed me at the small table.

The officers gave me a great welcome. They were mostly ex-prisoners of war who had been repatriated for serious injuries. Some of them were regulars who had been through St. Cyr and had afterwards seen service in the French colonies and at home, and the others were reservists, several of whom were veterans of the last war. They were nearly all subalterns or captains.

They all hated the Germans like poison, and deplored the fact that they were now under a Government which was forced to collaborate with their victorious enemy. They criticised strongly the politicians and the generals who between them had been responsible for putting a French Army in the field hopelessly armed and badly led. Stories were common among them of generals and colonels who had disappeared mysteriously in their staff cars in a southerly direction as soon as the fighting started, never to be seen again, although the units under their command had been surrounded and taken prisoner. They deeply deplored finding themselves in a France which was not only defeated but forced to collaborate with her enemy against her original ally.

Many of them wished to join de Gaulle's forces and carry on with the struggle, but the majority were too firmly rooted to their native soil to make the great sacrifice of leaving it, their wives, their children and everything they possessed, in order to make the hazardous journey, full of dangers along the route, of detection and imprisonment for desertion, finally to arrive in a strange country, knowing that at home their Government would have disowned them and declared them traitors. And so, for the most part these French officers, who had suffered under the Germans in the prison camp and who lived only for the day when it would be possible to turn the Germans out of their beloved France, now resigned themselves to the task of getting work and of biding their time until the moment was ripe for a general revolt against the oppressors.

At first I shared a room with a captain in the *Armée de l'Air,* who, like myself, had been a bomber pilot. He also had been bombing German mechanised columns, but had not been wounded, and had come to hospital to have his appendix out. He was an Alsatian and could not therefore go back to his own country, which was now German property. Naturally he wasn't very fond of the Germans and found it difficult to appreciate their kindness in taking over and guarding his property for him. He had a very strong character, was extremely intelligent, and altogether very pleasant. There were only our two beds in this room, which was smaller than the others, and often when I was there he would receive visits from fellow Alsatians, some of whom spoke English.

They were a grand crowd. There was nothing weak about them. They were for the most part of heavy, rather Germanic, build and bi-lingual. Some of them spoke English, French and German, as well as their local patois. Once or twice, I was invited out to lunch by some of them, and altogether I learnt to understand much of their point of view about the war and their feelings for the Germans, who had robbed them of everything they held dear. By nature, they were tougher and more determined than most Frenchmen. This hard side of their character was offset by a great generosity towards their friends and a love of good living, of music, good food and wine.

After supper that first evening some of the officers who were in a mobile state invited me to accompany them into the town to drink a *digestif* in one of the cafés. I pointed out that before doing so I would have to get special

Eamonn Andrews presenting William with the 'Big Red Book' during the filming of *This is Your Life* on 9 January 1961. In the background are, from the left, Cliff Michelmore, Warrant Officer Edward Odell, and William's mother.

The finale of the live TV programme *This is Your Life* on 9 January 1961. In the front row, are, starting seventh from the left, William's mother, William himself, his sister Mary (a surprise guest flown over from Australia), and his daughter, Anne. Among those in the back row are his sister Nena (second from left), Cliff Michelmore (fifth from left, with glasses), Warrant Officer Edward Odell (next to Cliff Michelmore), the actor Stephen Murray (immediately behind William), and William's son, Robert (fourth from right).

Left: This memorial commemorating the work of Sir Archibald McIndoe can be seen by Sackville College in the High Street at East Grinstead. The work of sculptor Martin Jennings, the statue, depicting McIndoe with a convalescing serviceman, was unveiled by The Princess Royal in 2014. (*Courtesy of Sarah Mitchell*)

Below: William, second from the left, photographed on the occasion of his 90th birthday. Also with him are, on the left, his niece, Margaret, daughter, Anne, and son-in-law, Stewart.

permission from the colonel in charge of the hospital and told them how I had been kept a prisoner in Marseilles. They were horrified to hear this, and apologised profusely for what they considered scurrilous treatment by their fellow countrymen. The colonel was not in the hospital that evening, so I could not go out, but the next morning I met him when he made his rounds. He was a man of medium build, extremely good-looking, and obviously very intelligent in the broad sense of the word. What a contrast to Colonel Crapaud of Marseilles!

He proved also to be sympathetic and considerate, but he was a strong man, and I should imagine a very bad one to cross. When he saw how badly I was wounded, but that I could walk about quite well, he said that it would be quite all right for me to go out when I wanted to, provided that I did not go away from Lyons and its environs, and that I gave my parole not to try and escape from France. At first this seemed almost too good to be true. However, I gave my parole and decided to take full advantage of my new found liberty to improve my French, study Lyons, and the life of its people. I also wanted to visit the American Consul and see what could be done about being repatriated to England.

My first day of liberty at Lyons marked the beginning of a period of two months charged with interest and excitement. My strength was rapidly increasing, and I could now speak and understand French. I had soon many friends, and above all I enjoyed a great deal of freedom of movement in one of the biggest towns of the unoccupied zone, which was literally humming with intrigue of every kind. De Gaullism, Pétainism, Communism, all had their ardent supporters. The de Gaullists were mainly patriotic and courageous Frenchmen, most of whom did not accept Pétain's view that the Armistice when it was made was a necessity but believed that France should have gone on fighting in North Africa and elsewhere. It was the habit of these people to listen to the Free French broadcasts from London to "work slow" in the factories, workshops and the fields, to group themselves together, hide arms, and encourage the younger men and women to leave France and join de Gaulle's forces.

It appeared to be their own lot to have to wait for an Anglo-Saxon expeditionary force to invade France and start pushing the Germans back. Then they would organise a revolt, turn out the Vichy Government, and flock to the side of the British and Americans. It is probable that at least eighty-five per cent of the French people are still pro-British and pro-American, insomuch as they look to the British and Americans for salvation from the hated Boche. Apart from this, there is a great deal of sentiment, too, attaching the French to us. They feel they have an affinity with us as freedom-loving, democratic people. They are full of admiration for the Russians and the tremendous struggle they are putting up against the German hordes, but few of the upper and middle classes would like to see a complete Russian victory, as they are afraid of the spread of Communism to France.

This view is not shared by the majority of the workers, who cherish Communist sympathies. Above all things, the de Gaullists want France for the French, and although none of them wish to return to the evils that existed just before the war and were due to bad politicians, graft and internal dissension, they are all anxious to re-establish and maintain all that was best and most national in pre-war France. First and foremost, they are patriots who think nationally rather than internationally. They exist in every walk of life in France, and in great numbers. Many of them hold high rank in the fighting forces, and even in the Vichy Government itself. Outwardly they have to maintain an appearance of being pro-Vichy and sometimes even pro-German. They can do nothing openly.

Communism, which had a very large proportion of supporters before and at the beginning of the war, has undoubtedly found many new recruits. The exposure by Pétain of much of the rottenness of French politics right up until the Armistice and the stubborn resistance of the Russians to the Germans have probably brought in many more recruits to the Communist party, men who are searching for some concrete solution to the chaotic state of affairs existing in France, who find no hope of a satisfactory new order under Pétain and the Germans, and who look to Communism as the only existing solution to their problems. Communists, like de Gaullists, have much to fear from the Germans and the Vichy Government. After the Jews they are the people whom the Germans hate and fear most in France. The de Gaullists probably come a good third. A very large proportion of the German and Vichy propaganda in France is directed daily against Communists and de Gaullists.

Most mornings I used to leave the hospital fairly early and walk to the British Consulate to find out if there was any news about my repatriation. It was a delightful walk, particularly as the late summer weather was so good. My way took me along the tree-covered embankment of the Rhône, past the three big bridges, and across the fourth to the Consulate, which was on the embankment on the other side. The population has increased enormously since the collapse of France, and there are usually many people about in the streets. When the sun shines Lyons is very attractive. The sunlight sparkles on the water, filters through the trees on the embankment, and lights up the whole town, but when it rains – and the rainy season is a long one – the whole town seems to put on a mantle of gloom, which is reflected in the character of the Lyonnais, who have the reputation in France of being rather dull and reserved.

Before the war Lyons had a tremendous reputation for good food and drink and was visited by gourmets from all over France and the Continent. When the German soldiers arrived and saw in the shop windows the wonderful display of cakes that were then still on sale they could hardly believe their eyes. After years of guns instead of butter, they had probably forgotten what good food looked like. During their short stay they bought up nearly all the food in the towns. Even the Lyonnais – themselves great gluttons – were disgusted at the quantities of food consumed by the German officers and soldiers at one sitting. It was a common sight to see German soldiers striding into a shop, each buying large cakes and tarts meant for several people and gobbling them in the shop.

The British Consulate had been taken over by the American Vice-Consul ever since the French had broken off diplomatic relations with the British. The Vice-Consul and his staff had plenty of work to do looking after the interests of British subjects in unoccupied France, of whom there was still quite a number, mainly women and men over military age, who enjoyed a great deal of liberty within the confines of the various towns in which they lived, although they could not leave the towns without special permission. The American Vice-Consul was responsible for providing them with funds on a repayment system, renewing their passports and negotiating periodically for their repatriation, if desired. There was a refreshing atmosphere of American hospitality and friendliness in that Consulate. It was an oasis of freedom in an oppressed country.

On my way back to the hospital from the Consulate I used to cross over the bridge again to the other embankment of the Rhône, and then stroll through the centre of the town, gradually working my way back in time for lunch at the hospital. I took a particular interest in everything I saw and found myself drawing comparisons everywhere between the France of Vichy and France before the defeat. To a casual observer passing through the streets there were few signs to remind him that the standard of living was rapidly declining to a very low level. True, there were practically no cars to be seen, but people were still fairly well dressed, except for the absence of women's stockings and leather-soled shoes, to which I have alluded before. There was as yet little evidence of great poverty, except in the slum areas. But the signs were all there to be seen on close inspection.

Lyons, the greatest silk centre in Europe, has plenty of fine shops which in times of peace displayed and sold a rich variety of silks and other materials, but now, although the shops still had their, perhaps depleted, window displays, inside there were few things that could be bought without coupons. To buy a new suit or a pair of shoes it was necessary to have a signed certificate from the *Mairie*, which would only be given on proof of necessity. The patisseries, which a year ago had been the joy of the German soldiers, were now reduced to selling loaves of grey bread and a few rusks for most days of the week and very inferior and unappetising cakes two days a week. To obtain the bread and some of the cakes it was necessary to give up coupons.

The cafés were no better. Even an enterprising proprietor who could find an occasional special piece of meat or a good cheese, provided by friends in the country or bought in the black market, would only be able to serve it without coupons to his clients at grave risk of having his establishment shut down immediately upon discovery. Game, fish, vegetables, fruit, and bottled wine were practically the only things that could be served in the cafés without coupons, and both game and fish were difficult to obtain; and so even the best and most expensive cafes served little but vegetable dishes, followed by a little cheese or fruit. There was no pure coffee to be had. It is no exaggeration to say that the average Frenchman was living on vegetables, fruit, bread, macaroni, a little *vin ordinaire* and ersatz coffee. Lyons, the city of food, was now on a very thin diet, which reduced eating to an unpleasant necessity – whereas before it had been an art – and left everyone very hungry, particularly in the winter.

Outside the biggest and best hotels stood the dark grey staff cars of German Army and Air Force officers, working on the Armistice commissions. This served as an ever-present reminder of the presence of the hated Boche. Only the Germans had petrol to spare. There were a few taxis standing outside the police station, but these were only available to French civilians in cases of urgency; for instance, on application to the police by telephone an expectant mother could be transported to the maternity hospital.

The Germans were hardly ever seen walking about in uniform, but generally speaking could be distinguished by their straight carriage, the cut of their Homburg hats, their firm jaws, pale blue eyes and set expressions. Most of them spoke perfect French and were extremely polite and correct in their manner. They were, undoubtedly, specially picked men, who were well acquainted with French life and customs, and at the same time shrewd and thorough masters of their work.

I had friends in one of the biggest hotels, and occasionally sat with them in the hotel lounge, watching the German officers come and go. On one occasion I was introduced to one of them. He was in the Air Force and of the same rank as myself. We didn't talk.

Lyons was crowded right out. To get a room in an hotel or find an apartment was practically impossible. There were refugees from every part of occupied or annexed France, many Alsatians, Poles, Austrians and Jews. Many of the Jews, in particular, were by now international refugees, who had been chased out of more than one country by the oncoming Germans. Soon, it seemed, there would be no corner of Europe left free for them to fly to. How many of these people lived is a bit of a mystery, for a large proportion of them could not register for ration cards and must have been living on their wits and other people's money. However, possibly made more cunning by centuries of persecution, the Jew takes a lot of beating, and some of them in Lyons, far from being held down, had surmounted all their difficulties and were making money some way or other, particularly on the black market.

One beautiful Saturday afternoon a friend of mine, a French officer, asked me if I would like to take the Blue Express tram which ran from the centre of the town down the banks of the Saône and out into the country.

The tram was really an electric train with six carriages and was packed right out the whole of the way to Collonge, which we had decided to make our destination. Collonge, although just outside the outskirts of Lyons, might have been deep in the country. The river Saône flowed fast between heavily wooded banks, and around one or two islands in mid-stream.

We left our tram and walked down on to one of the many grass-covered clearings on the banks, where the youth of Lyons – bronzed, healthy and happy – were sunbathing, swimming, or chasing each other about. Here on this beach lay the future hope of France. It looked a good hope to me. Young French men and women, who in past generations had pored over their books and had concentrated on indoor rather than outdoor amusement, had little in common with these fit young men and laughing girls who had left Lyons on their cycles and sped down here to spend the afternoon in the sun by the side of the river.

Further up the river the flash of the sunlight on oars dipping in and out of the water marked the stretch where members of the rowing club were out at exercise, practising for their next match. I felt an ache of longing to be part of the happy scene and to run, swim and row with the rest of them. This, of course, was for me quite impossible. Still, I had much vicarious enjoyment, for although the sunlight could not tan my body a deep golden brown, nor could my arms and legs thresh through the cool, sparkling waters of the river, my eyes could still see the beauty of the scene and my heart find a link of happiness with the laughing bathers.

My friend, the French officer, himself a good athlete, told me how he hoped that those young men and women would lift France up out of the pit of degradation into which she had been thrust, largely as a result of the failings of the past and present generations. We felt together that Marshal Pétain, whatever other mistakes he may have made, had done well to choose the youth of the nation as his hope for the reconstruction of France. We only hoped that the veneer of Vichy propaganda which covered every youth organisation in France under Pétain would quickly wear off before permanent damage had been done to the ideas and the ideals of young men and women.

It had been a perfect afternoon, and that evening, after I had said good-bye to my friend at the station, I limped back to the hospital through the soft light and lengthening shadows of the summer evening, feeling that there was still some hope of a great future for France in which the best of my many friends would find a suitable place.

Once or twice, I had heard that there was an internment camp full of British women somewhere in the occupied zone of France. I knew that British women had been rounded up by the Germans in Paris and elsewhere in the occupied zone. It was not until I met Chris, however, that I realised what a ghastly place it was. Chris and I met at the Consulate, and I was immediately struck by her appearance. She was only twenty but had the assurance and bearing of a woman of at least thirty-five, combined with the physical perfection of youth. Tall, with a wealth of long, fair hair billowing around her shoulders, she was a perfect physical specimen of Scandinavian womanhood. Her father was English and her mother Lettish. Their home was normally in Riga, but she had escaped to England before the Germans had entered Latvia. A month before the full fury of war broke on France she came over to Paris to study at the Sorbonne, and she was still there when the Germans entered the French capital.

One day all the British women in Paris were rounded up by the Germans and put on a train bound for an unknown destination, which later turned out to be Besançon, in eastern France. On the way the women were not allowed out of the train, which had no corridors, although the journey lasted for many hours. Many of them were ill and weak, and a few died before reaching the destination. The internment camp turned out to be an old army barracks, falling rapidly into decay. The women were forced to sleep on the stone floors of the big cold barrack room. Their bedding consisted of straw-filled palliasses and dirty grey army blankets. There was no privacy of any kind. Nuns straight from a lifetime spent in the seclusion of a convent slept side by side with women of the streets. Old women were mixed with young girls in their teens. Mothers were there with their babies. The mixture of types of women there was as varied as the coloured patterns in a kaleidoscope.

The food was appalling. Potato soup, grey bread and ersatz coffee formed the basis of the diet. Sanitary arrangements were equally bad. The lavatory was outside, and there was never any hot water. Many of the women fell sick and some had died. Most of the windows of the barrack room were broken, and only a few of them had been boarded up. The building was infested with rats, and lice were everywhere. The monthly ration of a small square piece of soap of inferior quality was of very little use in the struggle for cleanliness. When their clothes had worn out the women were issued with disused stocks of the old blue uniforms worn by the French poilus. They were not even clean when issued, and Chris told me that her particular uniform had a huge bloodstain on the trousers.

In spite of all the horrors of the camp, the morale of the women was marvellous, and cases of complete breakdown – apart from physical illness – were few. She herself managed to escape after four months, and by the time I saw her she had completely recovered from all ill-effects. But she was exceptional, both physically and mentally.

This was only a part of the whole story that Chris told me herself one afternoon while we were sitting together on the side of the lake in the Parc du Lion d'Or. Rowing boats were out on the deep blue water, couples were *en promenade*, children were playing all round us, and away before us the bright sunlight lit up the white stone of the massive 1914-1918 war memorial which interrupted the tree-lined avenue on the opposite side of the lake. There was a terrible significance about this war memorial, inscribed all round with thousands of names of Frenchmen of the Rhône who had given their lives in the last war, believing no doubt that their sacrifice was made to end all wars, believing also that at the end of that war the obstacles set in the way of the development of civilisation would be removed and that any return to the medieval horrors of killing and destruction would for ever cease.

Yet in the living memory of the wives and mothers of many of those men another war was being waged, and already their beloved France had been defeated by the old enemy. French territory occupied by the enemy was now no fit place for the women either of France or Britain.

At that very moment British women who had not shared the energy and fortune of Chris and managed to escape were being subjected to a form of slow mental and physical torture under conditions shameful in a so-called civilised world. Would it soon be the turn of the happy people around us in the park to suffer directly under the weight of the Nazi boot? Would it later be the turn of British women in England and elsewhere in the Empire?

Time passed quickly at Lyons. There was so much to see and learn and I did not intend to let my crippled state and disfigurement interfere with the satisfaction of my curiosity. Sometimes Chris and I would wander round the markets in the morning. They were most depressing, as there was now so little of anything worthwhile to buy. Les Halles was a covered market crowded with the shop-like stalls of butchers, fishmongers and fruiterers, with here and there an oyster or *escargot* bar. Most of the oyster bars and many of the butchers' stalls had closed, and on the counters of the majority of the few remaining stalls open, were set cards marked *"Pas de merchandise"*, bearing testimony as early as half past nine in the morning to the fact that there would be nothing more for sale that day.

The fruit stalls were not quite so bad. Stocks of peaches and apricots were good, and when their season had passed there were plentiful stocks of grapes. We used to visualise the bustle and excitement that must have animated Les Halles in the good days before the robbery of the resources of the country by the Germans – stalls overloaded with varied stocks of foodstuffs of good quality.

France had lived too well. She had been like a spoilt child. There had been plenty of everything at a very cheap price. Now that she had been deprived of most of the good things of life to which she had become accustomed her suffering was more acute than would have been the case for a less self-indulgent country. Elsewhere in the greengrocers, grocers and dairies there was the same scene of deprivation even in the summer. Potatoes were very rare indeed, and although in the summer months there were good stocks of green vegetables, the variety was poor, and prices relatively high; the following winter would obviously be harder than the last, which had been quite hard enough, when the majority of the working classes had lived almost exclusively on bread, a few dried vegetables, turnips of various kinds, ersatz coffee and restricted quantities of *vin ordinaire*.

Sometimes before lunch Chris and I would sit at a table outside one or other of the many cafés, sipping an aperitif and watching the life of the town going on all around us. Usually we didn't smoke, as tobacco was rationed and scarce. Conversation in the cafés was still lively, but everyone was forced to take care not to discuss too loudly, political and social matters, as the self-appointed agents of *La légion* and the professional Gestapo – not to mention official Vichy spies – were everywhere, straining their ears for signs of any criticism of the Vichy Government and of the Germans, and waiting always to detect any signs of planned revolution and de Gaullist organisations.

It was interesting to notice how many Frenchmen had given up reading their own papers since the débâcle. Instead, they turned to the Swiss papers for true news of the war. I often wondered why the Swiss papers had never been suppressed in France, for their journalists made many thinly veiled attacks on the methods and deeds of the Axis Powers and the Vichy Government. Articles reporting unfavourable conditions in the countries occupied by Germans and Italians were common, and although these articles were to some extent counter-balanced by, for instance, a report of the Leipzig Fair, praising German craftsmanship and ingenuity, the reader was still left impressed by the horrors of Nazi oppression. One always felt that the few plums handed by Swiss journalists to the Germans and Italians were given with a very bad grace, merely to accord with the Swiss Government's policy of placating the Germans.

In the same way as they looked to the Swiss for their newspapers an even larger proportion of Frenchmen turned to the B.B.C. for their news. I seldom met a Frenchman who did not occasionally listen in to the English news in French and the de Gaullist programmes from London. Of course, it must be remembered that many who listened to the English radio also listened to the Vichy programmes.

Often in the evenings we went to one or other of the many cinemas in Lyons. Good French films were still in the majority, but there were also several German productions translated into French or with French captions. The news films concentrated on Vichy propaganda, showing Pétain on one or other of his many tours round the unoccupied towns of France, reviewing troops of the new army, decorating airmen from the squadrons that had fought against the British in Syria, or visiting athletic meetings, Youth Movement parades, and massed demonstrations of *La légion*. There would be shots of French wounded disembarking at Marseilles from the ships that had brought them back from the war in Syria, alternated with films showing the latest German successes in Russia, the first with an anti-British and the second with an anti-Communist running commentary. One newsreel showing Pétain in the company of German officers was booed by the audience, but on the whole the people of Lyons, undemonstrative as ever, accepted the news that they were given in an oppressive silence, in which inevitably one sensed strong disapproval and sometimes hate.

I spent many evenings in a certain restaurant with my various French friends. They would talk for hours of France before the war and of the grave political errors committed by French and British politicians who had failed so miserably to deal with the Germans in such a way as to prevent them again becoming an aggressive military Power. We would talk of French art and music and of Paris at the height of its gaiety. I would hear all the latest news and gossip from the occupied zone.

Yvonne, in particular, was full of information of interest, for she was one of the many French women who made a practice of crossing periodically from one zone to the other and back again, partly from desire to meet old friends, partly out of curiosity, but mainly for the sheer adventure of passing through the fields at night unseen by the German guard. It was surprising how many French people managed to pay regular visits to the occupied zone without the special permission of the German authorities, which used to take weeks and sometimes months to obtain.

Amongst other things I heard how the German Army officers were now comfortably installed in all the old haunts of the R.A.F. at Rheims, and it was strange to hear the names of Café de la Paix, Strasbourg, Coupole, Lion d'Or, Maréchal Foch and many other hotels and cafes in connection with the German Army. I asked Yvonne, who had always recent news from a big town in the north of France, how much change the German officers were getting out of the French girls. "They get some of the *petites poules* who know no better," she replied, "but the real women – ah non!" She, like many of the other girls, used to bait the Germans in every conceivable way. In some of the brothels Germans had been diseased on purpose by infected women – this in spite of very strict control.

Yvonne used to visit with another girl, cafés where she knew there would be German officers. She would select a table as near the Germans as possible and start talking of the terrible sufferings that the Germans would have to go through that winter in Russia – the cold, the cruelty of the Russians to their prisoners, and so on. She talked with such a carefully imposed air of sympathy that the German officers, although well aware that their legs were being pulled, could do nothing but sit and fume or get up and leave the café in disgust. Yvonne took me one night to a little restaurant tucked away in a back street of the town to have supper.

On the way I asked her if we were likely to see any Germans there. She just laughed, and I soon understood why. For when nearly everyone had finished eating the patron came in, looked round to see that there were no *sâles boches* present, and began to tell story after story, lashing at the Germans with the full force of his Gallic wit. There were roars of applause at the end of each story, and had I had any doubt of the fact, this incident would have assured me that the French had lost none of their sense of humour. Although they grumbled a great deal, they could still laugh at their own misfortune.

Before I left Lyons an exhibition was held and Marshal Pétain came to open it. So far I had missed seeing him, first at Roanne and then at Marseilles, when he had paid visits to those two towns. Now that I was free to go about as I pleased I determined not to miss seeing him for the third time. He was due to arrive by train from Vichy one Sunday morning. From the station he was going to drive in a procession of cars with his Ministers, staff officers and other Government officials, to the *Préfecture*. His route would take him along the Rhône embankment, past the hospital, and across the Pont Wilson to the *Préfecture* on the other side of the river. The way was bedecked with groups of national flags (for the French flag was still flying in unoccupied France) and lined with soldiers, police, Pétain Youth, Boy Scouts, Girl Guides, and behind, a fairly large but not enthusiastic crowd. By now Pétain had lost nearly all his popularity in most parts of the unoccupied zone.

Half an hour before the aged Marshal was due to arrive I left the hospital and walked along behind the crowd to the Pont Wilson. The soldiers lining the streets were not smart. Their uniforms fitted badly, their belts and equipment were left unpolished, and their boots unshined. The junior officers in charge of them were rather weedy-looking, and even they, although clean, had apparently not found time to have their belts and boots thoroughly polished.

But the most remarkable thing about the soldiers was their expression of complete and utter boredom. They were spaced at about five-yard intervals and had their backs to the crowd. Not so the police, of whom there were tremendous numbers. They looked smart enough, but there was something rather ominous in the way they were standing with their backs to the road, looking in towards the crowd. The children in their various uniforms added a slight sparkle to a very lifeless scene.

Soon a low rumble of distant applause was borne up to me where I stood on the Pont Wilson, and the procession appeared in the distance, getting closer and closer. Marshal Pétain and Admiral Darlan were sharing a car, a big open tourer surrounded by very thick, plated, bullet-proof glass. As further protection there was a diamond-shaped formation of mobile police on motorcycles. Judging from the thickness of their clothing and the weight of their crash helmets and the way each motorcycle overlapped its neighbour, they must have formed themselves into a bullet-proof screen for the Marshal and Darlan. The children shouted: "*Vive le Maréchal! Vive le Maréchal*" and the cry was taken up half-heartedly by the crowd. Officers saluted, soldiers presented arms, and Marshal Pétain passed, looking twenty years younger than his real age – a fine, dignified figure – calm, if not altogether confident, looking a little wistful, but leaving an impression of a good, a strong and just man, who had devoted himself to France at the worst moment of its long history.

I did not feel the same way about his satellites. First, there was Darlan, sitting at his side. He was short but well-built and was wearing the uniform of admiral of the fleet. He looked capable, tough and hard. The admiral, who had won his promotion in the *bureaux*, was undoubtedly a very nasty man to cross. He had not the same dignified bearing as Pétain. Rather was there an air of defiance about him, and as he looked from side to side one sensed that he was ever on the look-out for a would-be assassin. He did not look afraid; but neither did he look assured.

In the cars that followed staff officers and Government officials, ministers, prefects and mayors were huddled closely together. I have never seen so many prominent, responsible men out for a state airing in public looking so uncomfortable. They must have known that there were few people in the crowd who bore them any love and many who hated them. They must almost have felt the mutterings of the ordinary men and women in the crowd. Those of them – and perhaps they were few – who were a hundred per cent collaborationists, who had thrown in their lot with the hated enemy, must have had deeply troubled consciences.

And so, the procession moved on to the *Préfecture*. I had seen the head of the French State and many of its highest members. I felt – and I think most Frenchmen felt – that Marshal Pétain, a good man in himself, had a mixed and dangerous retinue. I hoped that the best of them would be strong enough to hold the worst in check. Had Napoleon seen that procession he would have wept.

After a great deal of work on the part of my friends of the American Consulate at Lyons and of the Americans in the American Embassy at Vichy, special permission was received from the Germans through the French Ministry of the Interior for me to leave France. When I first heard the news I could hardly believe that it was true, for it happened just after the arrangements for the exchange of the British and German prisoners of war in Germany and England respectively had broken down. Also, a few weeks before, the German authorities in France had decided that they would not allow any more British airmen and soldiers held as prisoners of war in unoccupied France to be repatriated.

Only a week or so before I had even been ordered to go to St. Hippolyte, near Nîmes, where there was a concentration camp, inside which the Vichy authorities had shut up British soldiers who, after having escaped from the Germans either in Germany or in occupied France, had been made prisoners of war on their arrival in unoccupied France. It was only at the last minute that the head doctor of the military hospital at Lyons had obtained special permission to keep me in his hospital on account of my disabled and infected condition.

My fortunes had been so varied and my position so insecure, and the efforts for my repatriation so long-drawn-out and so often set back, that now I felt that until the moment that I left France at the frontier and arrived in Spain I could not believe that at last, after two years in France, I was really going home again.

However, there were many preparations to be made, and many problems to be solved before I could in fact leave. Not the least of these was the necessity of a capable travelling companion to act as my nurse on the way, for obviously with one hand still in bandages and the other almost useless, there was little that I could do for myself, and alone the journey would have been impossible. Chris solved this problem by volunteering to come with me provided we could arrange for my departure to synchronise with the dates marked on her Spanish and Portuguese visas.

This was all arranged, after a great deal of running around between Consulates and *Préfectures*, and our last few days in France were devoted to packing, looking up railway timetables, buying tickets, and rushing from one end of the town to the other and back again, saying good-bye to all the friends we had made.

Saying good-bye was difficult. Our friends were of the very best kind. They had accepted us exactly as they had found us, had done a thousand and one things to help us, and had always made us feel at home – so much so that leaving would have been unbearable if our real homes had not been waiting for us. We had been overwhelmed with hospitality, even to an embarrassing extent. For instance, the barber who used to cut my hair had asked me out to dinner with him at a time when I knew it was very difficult for him to find enough to eat for himself. We had to admit to ourselves that in England under similar conditions, and as foreigners, although we might have found plenty of people who would have helped us, there would have been very few so interested in trying to understand the point of view of the foreigners in their midst.

On my last morning at Lyons I went for a long walk alone all round the centre of the town and along the banks of the two rivers; a soft morning mist still lay in the hollows and around the bridges, men with hoses were at work washing the streets with water from the roadside hydrants, the busy little trams were rattling along, carrying the late shoppers back to their homes with their meagre provisions for the day, and the workers to and from their work in offices, workshops and stores.

The hustle of everyday life went on as usual. France had fallen low and might fall even lower before the war was over, but men and women had still to work to keep themselves alive, even if most of their work profited themselves little and the hated Boche a lot.

Chapter 7

Journey Back

That evening, the 10th October 1941, Chris and I left by train for Grenoble on the first stage of our journey home. At the station we said good-bye once more to those of our friends who had come to see us off. In spite of all the difficulties involved in getting food for themselves they had managed to find us two chickens, thermos flasks full of hot chocolate and coffee, and a host of other things, in case we should have difficulty in getting food on the trains going through Spain. These were things that they seldom saw and probably wouldn't see again for a long time. In a very hungry country this last gesture of friendship was most touching.

The train drew slowly out of the station, and at last we were on our way home. For a long time, we sat and looked at each other, unable to express the sensation of knowing that at last we were actually going home. To the forced exile in wartime this sensation is something too big and exciting to be lightly discussed, and in our case our feelings were complicated by nostalgia for the France we were leaving behind and anxiety for the future of the many friends we had made there.

At Grenoble we changed into the wagon-lits train that was to take us down to the Spanish frontier, by way of the Rhône valley, Montpelier, Narbonne, Perpignan and Cerbère.

Sometime after we had started we suddenly began to talk and went on without a break well on into the night. We talked of our friends and our experiences and of France, of the journey before us and of the kind of England we expected to see when we eventually arrived there. While we were talking the train was speeding on towards the Franco-Spanish frontier. Eventually, tired out, we went to bed. We slept so soundly that we had only just reasonable time to get up, wash and dress, before we reached Perpignan.

All our movements were severely handicapped by the fact that Chris had the night before badly squashed one of her thumbs in the train door, leaving us with only one sound hand between two people. However, although this state continued right on to England, somehow we seemed to manage quite well. As we stood in the corridor the blue sea of the Mediterranean behind us sparkled and in the *midi* sunlight before us we could see through the window the golden-brown countryside stretching out for miles, cut up into hundreds of vineyards and crossed by long straight roads lined with plane trees, and we realised that we were taking our last good look at France. This fact was driven home to us by the distant Pyrenees outlined in a soft grey-blue, separating defeated France from ravaged Spain.

Before we reached Perpignan we met three Americans. Two of them were on their way back from the American Embassy in Berlin and the other was an Embassy courier travelling between Switzerland and Portugal with the diplomatic bags. Naturally we had a thousand questions to ask about Berlin – how had it been affected by the R.A.F. bombing, how were the people holding out against the food restrictions, what was the average German thinking about Hitler, how tight was the control of the Gestapo and the Nazis on the German people, and so on.

From the answers we were given I formed the impression that the German people had been no more demoralised by the R.A.F. bombings than the people of England by the bombings of the Luftwaffe. I was also surprised to learn that the Germans were no nearer to starvation than the French, although, of course, food restrictions were very much greater than I was to find we had in England. As for damage in Berlin, it appeared that the Germans constructed big hoardings round all damaged buildings with such rapidity after each bombing that the damage was soon out of sight, and so the more easily forgotten. There did not seem to have been any signs of panic. On the contrary, the German people, like the English, had been infuriated by the bombing, and this fury may even have mounted their morale. However, up till that date – October, 1941 – the bombing of Berlin by the Air Force had not reached its full force.

At Cerbère, the last French town on the Mediterranean coast before the Spanish frontier, we had to get out of the train with our baggage and go through the French Customs. There we had to give up all our French papers, ration cards and any unused coupons. Naturally, we had not kept our coupons, but had instead given them to friends who needed them, and we had a little bit of trouble about this and had to swear blind that we had used them all up.

This was not very convincing, as they were dated; and it was only the 11th of the month. However, eventually, after our bags had been examined and our papers checked, we were allowed to get back into the train again for the short train journey between Cerbère and Portbou, the nearest Spanish town on the other side of the frontier. And so the first lap of our journey was completed, and from now on we were not likely to strike any difficulties on our way home to England, as we would be under the care of the British Consulate as soon as we reached Barcelona.

The fact that we were in Spain, a country which has never recovered from its long civil war and has since been systematically robbed by the Italian and German Allies of Franco, under the excuse of payment for services rendered, was evidenced by a certain shabby meanness and an unspoken sense of desperation which seemed to hang over the people at the station, and even over the very countryside itself.

Unshaven, rather dirty and badly dressed men, ragged children, thin, unkempt and drably clad women (on the faces of whom no amount of cosmetics could hide the thinness of their cheeks and the bloodlessness of their lips) made up the majority of the crowd of people waiting for trains or hanging about the station aimlessly. The station itself was dirty, the buildings drab, and badly in need of a good coat of paint. The inside of the Customs House at the Port Bou station was, if possible, less prepossessing than the station itself. Passports were examined in a small, dirty little room by officials sitting behind a long counter.

On the walls directly behind the officials were pasted posters reminding Spaniards that Franco had promised bread for all. The fact that there wasn't bread for all, as I later found out, made the posters grimly incongruous. There were other posters showing, in good examples of modern commercial art, symbolical groups of workers superimposed on a background of factory chimneys with wording stressing the necessity of discipline. Behind one of the officials a large notice stated that "A good Spaniard gives the National salute." One corner of the room was partitioned off to form a little stone prison with a heavily barred door. This added to the misery of the scene.

I was glad my papers were in order, as I should have hated to spend any time in that little prison. A number of police were lounging about, smoking cigarettes. Perhaps the police get more cigarettes than the average Spaniard, for the latter has a very small ration and is seldom seen smoking. The police uniform was dark grey and of very thin cloth. Around their tunics they wore bright yellow belts, complete with a holster holding a Mauser revolver. They wore wide breeches and black calf boots, laced right up the front. In their hands they carried truncheons. They were mostly tall and gaunt and their legs thin and spindly. They moved around silently (for their boots were rubber-soled) and with the easy grace of carriage, common to most Spaniards.

When our papers had been examined and the officials had ensured that we carried no more than 500 French francs each, the limit of French money which might be taken into Spain, our disreputable baggage was examined. The Customs officers treated our parcels of food, which already looked a bit worn and were held together precariously by string, with considerable suspicion. However, after they had examined the chicken-bone contents of some grease-paper packages and looked into the thermos flasks, their disappointment was so acute that they didn't bother about our bags. Thanks to our American friends' knowledge of Spanish and experience of the Spanish Customs and railway authorities, we were soon free to go over and settle ourselves in the train which was to take us to Barcelona. We were travelling first-class and were thankful for it, as the second and third-class compartments were filthy and overcrowded. Soon our compartment was full, and we were on our way.

The country through which we were passing was not unpleasant and seemed fairly rich in agriculture. But the villages, and the villagers in them, were drab and poor. The houses were badly laid out, dirty, and rather ugly. No effort seemed to be made to keep them in good repair, and most of them looked as if they had not received a coat of paint anywhere for years.

The train stopped at Gerona, which was very picturesque and attractive, although it also had that same air of poverty and neglect. A fine church standing on one of the highest parts of the town attracted our attention, but we were told that it – like nearly all the churches in the towns in Spain which were under the control of the Reds at some time or another during the civil war – had been burnt out. The Reds had attempted to destroy the churches completely, but had only succeeded in gutting them, and the work of restoration had already begun. However, in spite of the large sums of money more or less forcibly collected from the people, little progress had been made. The town had also been badly bombed, but this was not apparent from the train.

After we had left Gerona the country became more wooded and hilly. On one side a brilliant fiery sunset gradually faded out as the sun sank down behind the hills separating us from the distant Mediterranean, while on the other side, blue wooded mountains were softly outlined against a paling violet sky. Dusk turned slowly to darkness, and we were surprised to notice how little illumination there was in the villages through or near which we passed. Spain, a neutral country, had no other reason for blacking out at night than shortage of electricity, gas and oil; we had the impression of a country "blacked out" but having no efficient air-raid wardens to control the few delinquents who were showing lights. Often the only light in a village came from the open door of some small, bare café.

So far, even in the few short hours that I had been in Spain, I had been ever conscious of an atmosphere of poverty and despair, reminding me all the time of how Spain had been ravaged by civil war and afterwards held down in a state of poverty and misery by the greedy insistent demands of her two Axis partners. Later, in Barcelona and Madrid this feeling increased, and did not leave me until I reached Portugal.

After a comfortable and reasonably fast journey, we arrived about nine o'clock in the evening in Barcelona station. Here one of our American friends suggested that we should go and have dinner as his guests at his hotel, which was one of the biggest and best in Barcelona, as its name – the Ritz – implied. We pointed out that as we had no Spanish money and could not change the 500 French francs which we had each been allowed to bring into Spain, we ought really to be looking for the British Consul. However, he insisted, and as the British Consulate would undoubtedly be closed, anyway, we decided to leave it until the morning. And so, we pushed our way through the crowds of ragged beggars who haunted the station entrance, got into the hotel bus, and were soon rolling through the streets of Barcelona to the Ritz.

It seemed very incongruous to Chris and me to be going to a large expensive hotel after our experiences in France, and we enjoyed it to the full, like two excited children. When we arrived at the entrance to the Ritz hotel, after having been shepherded through the big swing doors by a uniformed commissionaire, we must have seemed quite out of place.

Neither of us looked very pretty by this time. Chris had her thumb bound up; we were both dirty after the long journey. I had no hat or coat and was wearing one of my borrowed suits, which didn't fit very well; added to this, my hands were all bound up and my face badly disfigured. However, we managed to get rooms, and after a bath and a shave and a general sprucing up I felt fit to face the sophisticated world again. One sign of the times in our rooms was the fact that there was no soap. However, we were used to that, as in France it was impossible to buy soap without coupons, and the quantity was always so small that it was necessary to use it with care.

Luckily we had both managed to get some soap before leaving France, which was just as well, as otherwise we might well have stayed dirty for a long time. I particularly enjoyed my bath, as it was only the second I had had in seventeen months, the first being at Lyons after sixteen months of bed-baths only. It was nice also to be in an hotel that was properly heated, for in France few hotels except those inhabited by the Germans were heated. Of course, here in Spain, too, the situation must have been generally the same, for coal was particularly scarce – so much so that Barcelona, which is normally lit half by gas and half by electric lamps in the streets, had had to abandon gas-lighting completely.

There were many Germans' staying in the hotel, but I did not notice them particularly until the morning we left. We met our friend and went into the dining-room, where once more we felt very much like two country cousins. It was all very magnificent and rather fun. The menu was a revelation. There seemed to be plenty of everything to eat; varied hors d'oeuvres, many kinds of sea-foods, meat, vegetables, Spanish melons, omelettes, ice creams made of real cream, fruit, butter, and excellent Spanish wine. There was only one small thing which reminded us that the majority of Spaniards were starving, and that was the fact that we had only two very small grey rolls each.

Chris and I made complete pigs of ourselves, and conversation was almost impossible until we had eaten our way through the menu. In France the country as a whole was suffering severely from the shortage of food, but here in Spain it seemed that money could still buy practically anything except bread. It was such a long time since either Chris or I had seen any quantity of really good food that we forgot to be ashamed of the fact that, while we were glutting ourselves, outside the hotel hungry beggars were wandering the streets of Barcelona, desperately begging for a few coppers with which to buy a scanty, insufficient and unpalatable meal, probably their only one for days. Certainly, there was no sign of shame on the complacent faces of wealthy Spaniards and foreigners, as guilty as ourselves, seated at their gluttonous repasts all round us, and who, like ourselves, were profiting fully from the excellent service of the polite Spanish waiters, whose own relations may well have been starving in their homes.

Spain was indeed a land of contrasts, and unpleasant contrasts at that. In France, except for the "black market" there had been at least some measure of equality between rich and poor, for the rationing system was thorough and all-embracing. There was practically no commodity in France which was not rationed, but here in Spain it appeared that with a sufficiently large sum of money it was possible to buy almost anything. In France ration tickets had to be surrendered in shops, restaurants and hotels, in fact, anywhere where a commodity could be publicly purchased. But in Spain ration cards seemed unnecessary in the hotels. Later, when I arrived in England, I was shocked to find the same system to a great extent here in this country.

As we shamelessly enjoyed our coffee – which was real – and liqueurs, I noticed that excellent cigars were still plentiful for those rich enough to pay for them, whereas cigarettes were severely rationed. Strangely enough, it appeared that there was one thing money could not buy in Spain, in addition to unlimited quantities of bread, and that was matches. Even in the luxury of the Barcelona Ritz matches were quite unobtainable, and in fact the only time I bought matches in Spain was from beggars in the streets, which was even more incongruous and confusing.

After dinner was over our friend wanted us to go dancing. In Spain, night life, including theatres and cinemas, starts much later than in most other countries, and dancing went on in the hotel ballroom, which was one of the best places to dance in Barcelona, until two a.m. Dancing was in full swing when we arrived, and we found a table with difficulty in a secluded corner near the band. We ordered a bottle of sparkling wine, not unlike champagne, and after talking for a little the others joined the couples on the crowded floor and left me content with my pipe to enjoy the dancing vicariously.

The next morning, I woke up to hear the sound of children's voices singing marching songs in the streets below my bedroom window. I got up, pushed open the blind, and looked out. There, down below me, just disappearing out of sight along the wide tree-lined boulevard was the tail-end of a short crocodile of little girls in white blouses and navy-blue skirts, with their blonde hair gathered tightly together in two little pigtails. They were too far away for me to hear what they were singing, but it didn't sound like Spanish.

Anyway, I could not imagine little Spanish girls regimented and marching about so neatly dressed, working up appetites which they would not be able to satisfy and singing when they had so little to sing about. Least of all could I imagine them with little blonde pigtails. However, I thought no more about them, and it was only later on in the day that I found out who they were.

After Chris had helped me to wash and dress and we had finished our coffee and rolls we set out for the British Consulate. It was Sunday morning; the sun was shining brightly down on the broad tree-lined boulevards, which were thronged with people enjoying their routine Sunday morning walk. The Consulate was not far from the hotel, but our route took us through part of the most beautifully built section of the town.

The British Consulate General in Barcelona is situated in one of the busiest streets in the city, on the third floor of one of the large but rather inconspicuous buildings, screened by the tall trees lining the side of the boulevard; in fact, the Consulate would have been quite inconspicuous if it had not been for the large Union Jack floating out over the street, hanging from the end of a flagstaff leaning out from the balcony of a bay window.

Inside the Consulate one of the consular officials, after having decided whether we were P.O.W.s (prisoners of war) or D.B.S.s (distressed British subjects), gave us some money and cigarettes and promised to try and fix up a place in a plane to our next destination – Madrid. There were three air lines – German, Italian and Spanish. The best was the German, but it did not take British subjects.

All three were booked up well in advance, so that we should be lucky if we managed to get a plane before the police forced us to move on, for it was forbidden for people like ourselves to stay any longer than was absolutely necessary in Spain. In the meantime, we could stay on at our hotel and wait for developments.

We decided to go that afternoon to see one of the last bullfights of the season, which was taking place at the big arena, and places had already been booked for us all. And so, after lunch, we left the hotel and followed the stream of people making their way along the wide boulevard leading in the direction of the ring, which stood on the other side of a palm-covered open space.

It was a tall, perfectly circular, red stone stadium of fairly recent construction. The architecture was a rather attractive mixture of Moorish and modern styles. Inside, the round sandy arena was surrounded by tiers of narrow stone benches, forming concentric circles which spread out up the sloping auditorium until they reached a ring of boxes at the very summit. One half of the ring and the auditorium was in the sun and the other half in the shade.

The president of the bullring – in this case the governor of Barcelona – had already arrived in his box, which was just above and behind our places in the middle of the shady side of the arena. He was surrounded by a number of senoritas wearing the mantillas of tradition and looking very picturesque and beautiful. Behind the governor I was surprised to see a group of Nazi officials, complete with their high-fronted peaked caps, brown tunics, Sam Browne belts and swastika armbands.

I had not expected to see any Germans in uniform here, but they were all part of the show, for after the classic ceremony of the keys, when the president threw down the keys of the ring to two horsemen waiting there below, there was a sudden burst of military music, and the band of the Spanish Foreign Legion marched into and around the arena, followed by detachments of cavalry and infantry of the famous Spanish-Moroccan regiment which corresponds to the French Foreign Legion and is very popular in Spain. Behind the Spaniards there followed a long crocodile of boys and girls of the Hitler Youth, led by brown-tunicked black-booted men leaders, each with his Sam Browne belt, swastika armband, and little dagger. There in the procession were the little girls with their blonde pigtails bobbing up and down against the back of their clean white blouses, looking very neat and innocent in their navy-blue skirts, white socks and black shoes, the same little girls that I had seen from my bedroom window that morning. In front of them marched the boys; some dressed very like the girls, with blue shorts instead of skirts, and others in navy-blue ski suits, with swastika bands on their left arms and long-peaked caps on their heads.

After this strange-looking parade had made several circuits of the arena, in the middle of which was a circular arrangement of the words *"Arriba Espana"* (Spain Arise!) they all filed out through the tunnel leading out of the arena under the spectators, and there was a pause until the band reappeared again amongst the spectators, where, after settling itself, it stood up and struck up a few warning notes.

Immediately the whole crowd – and the auditorium of the bullring was filled to capacity – stood up at attention, with their right arms stretched out stiffly in the Axis salute, while the band played *"Deutschland Uber Alles"* followed by the Spanish national anthem. Looking around at that multitude of outstretched arms everywhere, I found it difficult to believe that the Spanish people were not a hundred per cent pro-Axis, but I was assured then and many times afterwards by the most reliable people that underneath this show of approval for all things Falangist and Nazi at least 80 per cent of the Spanish people were pro-American and pro-British. Every bullfight in Barcelona has a parade of some kind or another before it begins, and this time it happened to be in honour of the Hitler Youth, a detachment of which was paying a visit to Spain at the time.

Now that the propaganda was over the bullfight could begin. There is so much ritual and tradition involved in a bullfight that it has an almost mystic significance. That afternoon we were to see eight bulls killed, one after the other, until towards the end a distinct pungent odour of blood rose from the sandy arena. For my part, I was too much interested in the novelty of the scene, the ancient ritual and the graceful movements of the *toreros*, to feel squeamish about the bull.

Perhaps I was becoming too familiar with the sight of human blood to bother much about the blood of a bull. The red cloak and medieval costumes of the men, the dart, lance and sword with which the bull was enraged and finally killed, the graceful attitudes and lightning movements of the toreros, and the immense powerful figure of the huge black bull careering about the ring – all these things were sufficiently exciting to obliterate the feelings of pity I had expected with regard to the bull's sufferings.

During the ceremony of the keys and before each fight, when the president chose one or other of the notables about him to enjoy the honour of holding the torero's hat while the latter was despatching the bull, I had noticed that the governor of Barcelona seemed very popular with the crowd. Later I was told that he had earned his popularity by refusing on one occasion to allow two ships loaded with olive oil and rice (two of the basic foods of the Spanish diet, when available) to leave the port of Barcelona for their Italian destination. Instead, he had ordered the distribution of the cargoes amongst the poorest people in the city, saying that he could not allow food to leave Barcelona while Spaniards in this city were starving. Of course, Spaniards were starving all the time, and many other ships must have left before and since for Italian and German destinations, but the gesture was a great one, the more so as he was reported to have told Franco over the telephone that he did not care if he was shot for it; he would not change his mind or alter the orders he had given.

We stayed on in Barcelona for three days, waiting in vain for seats on a Spanish plane bound for Madrid.

In the end we had to go by train. There were only two running each day to Madrid for passenger traffic, one leaving very early in the morning and the other late at night; this in spite of the fact that the railway linked the capital of Spain with Barcelona, the centre of most of the country's trade and the port for France and Italy. Naturally the competition for seats and even standing room was tremendous; so much so that some short while before we arrived in Barcelona a new regulation had been made, stopping all reservation of seats and controlling the number of tickets sold for each train. It had therefore become necessary to queue up outside the booking office for several hours before the train was due to leave even to be sure of having a ticket, not to mention a seat.

This regulation had produced the most ludicrous results, for on the morning upon which our police permits to remain in Barcelona expired Chris had got up before dawn and waited many hours for a ticket. She had just received one of the last by the time I arrived in the hotel bus half an hour before the train was due to start, yet when we had squeezed our way through the crowd that swarmed all over the dirty station we had no difficulty at all in finding a first-class carriage with only two other occupants in it, and this after the last tickets had been sold, and the train officially declared full.

While waiting in the hotel entrance for the bus to take me and our luggage to the station a number of Germans in civilian clothes booked out at the reception desk and left by car to catch the Lufthansa plane, which flies daily non-stop between Barcelona and Berlin. They had the air of typical German business executives. Each carried a briefcase. They had that usual air of quiet efficiency and concentration on the job in hand that, coupled with complete self-assurance, characterised their colleagues in unoccupied France. The train was filthy, and even the first-class carriage in which we were travelling was full of dust. Our two fellow travellers, a man and a woman, regarded us with great curiosity and a little suspicion.

At first I think they took us for Germans. Chris would pass as a German anywhere, with her long fair hair and bright blue eyes and Germanic build, and I was carrying a copy of the German paper *Signal*. When they found out later that we were English they seemed quite disappointed. For most of the first half hour they discussed us together in Spanish. They were a very ordinary looking couple, both in their late thirties. The man didn't look particularly intelligent, or what the Spaniards would call *sympatico*. His wife was plain almost to the point of ugliness. She was tall and dark. Her heavy woollen clothes were ill-fitting, dull and unattractive. When their curiosity could be contained no longer the man turned to us and asked in French, "Are you German?"

"No."

"English?"

"Yes."

Then followed a string of similar questions. Why were we in Spain? Where had we come from? Were we brother and sister? Were we married? Where was I wounded? What was France like? And so on interminably for about an hour. We didn't like them very much, least of all after they had finished interrogating us. They showed the bad manners, too, most unusual with Spanish people, of talking about us in their own language with many obvious signs referring to my injuries that were almost offensive in their directness.

After we were clear of the suburbs of Barcelona the train followed the coast for some time. We passed through tunnels cut in the cliffs and in the rocky brown hills; we crossed high viaducts spanning dried up river-beds, weaving in and out, up and down, through the hills and valleys, getting farther and farther away from the belt of cultivation.

Chris and I had still stuck to the two big packages of provisions given to us at Lyons before we left France, and about midday she took down one of the packages and we started to make our lunch of tinned sardines, paté and stale rolls. This caused great interest to our travelling companions, who accepted, after some pressing, a little chocolate. The man also accepted several of the few precious Chesterfield cigarettes that had been given to us by the Americans.

There followed more questions, and the man volunteered the information that he was employed by a cigarette paper company. Business was not good, as tobacco was scarce and rationed as strictly as in France. After a while the conversation turned to politics. We were told of the fine qualities of the Germans and Italians. This was too much for both of us, and we gave vent to our own opinions on the matter. The whole episode was childish. What annoyed Chris and me most was the obstinacy of these stupid people, fed on Axis propaganda, and their point-blank refusal to believe facts that we were able to put before them. For the rest of the journey, from early afternoon until midnight, the atmosphere in the confining space of the compartment was considerably strained.

For hours we rumbled on over the arid yellow-brown countryside, deserted except for an occasional village or solitary peasant walking alongside his panniered mule or black donkey. After we had passed through Zaragoza late on in the afternoon the scene changed. The barren plain merged into rich cultivated land; a gloriously fiery sunset glowed in the sky, its burning reds and golds blending perfectly with the brilliantly variegated rich greens of the cultivation. Before the sunset had burnt itself out we were making our way through fertile little valleys bounded by bare rocky hills rising up sheer in all directions.

Here was the Spain of which I had always dreamed: simple little stone houses, vineyards sloping up the hills, fields of crops and vegetables lying in the hollows of the valleys along the banks of the little mountain rivers; winding roads and tracks along which black-haired, sunburned peasants, the women in sombre black dresses, were leading strings of well-laden mules on their way home from the fields over the narrow stone bridges. For a long time, the railway line followed the tortuous path of one of the largest of these rivers, confined in a narrow valley by rocky hills, the summits of which were silhouetted against the darkening indigo sky.

Soon night began to fall. The scene faded slowly out, and the last few hours of the journey passed in darkness. Once more I noticed particularly the lack of light in the villages and small towns through which we passed. Even neutral Europe was living in semi-darkness, as if becoming accustomed to the total black-out which invasion would bring.

I was glad when we reached Madrid at last. The journey had been long and uncomfortable. Sun, smoke and dust had combined to make my lidless left eye sore and bloodshot. The compartment was uncomfortable and our fellow travellers not at all congenial. My finger-less left hand, as yet unhealed, was hurting me and I was still weak in the legs and back. A feeling of moving like a detached ghost through an impoverished and miserable people in whose lives little colour had been left and who were struggling against heavy odds for their very existence, came over me. In this strange frame of mind, I was ill-prepared for the sight that greeted us when we got out of the train in Madrid.

For sheer abject misery I have never seen its equal. The smoke-filled ill-lit station was crowded with ragged, drably clad civilians and a few disreputable Spanish soldiers, dirty and untidy in their ill-fitting uniforms and worn boots. Most of the crowd were wandering aimlessly about, as if searching for something that was not there. Men, women and children alike were pale and drawn about the eyes and cheekbones. On the faces of many there was a half-crazed hopeless look that completely defeats my powers of description.

Chris and I pushed our way as quickly as possible through the dense crowd and scrambled into the dirty little hotel bus that was to take us to the Hotel Mora, where accommodation was booked for all British refugees. Ragged beggars pressed all around us, frenziedly beseeching us to give them money or food. Many peered closely at me, apparently fascinated by my disfigurement, although they must have seen many a face like mine during the civil war. Inside the ramshackle little bus, we were huddled together in the dark with a crowd of other people and soon covered the short distance between the station and the hotel.

The Hotel Mora was small but clean, and we managed to get a bath before going to bed. This removed the grime from our bodies, and the next day we tried to beat some of the dust out of our clothes. In the morning, we went out into the bright sunshine and saw quite a different side of Madrid on our way to report at the British Embassy. We walked along a beautiful broad avenue separated on either side from fine white buildings by wide strips of tree-shaded gardens. Here the hired nursemaids of the well-to-do were out with their prams, smart white-gloved and helmeted policemen were standing at the crossings, directing a traffic of large expensive cars and a few taxis.

There seemed to be no connection here with the scene of breadless and wretched beggars which had greeted us the night before at the station. Spain was certainly a land of great inequality and violent contradictions. The British Embassy, with its air of unshakable solidity and calm dignified detachment reminded me that I belonged to a great nation which seemed still able to hold its head high in a few corners of Europe in defiance of the *fait accompli* of the

German military conquests elsewhere. There it stood, secluded in a side street, like a fortress as yet unshaken by the sabre-rattling of Hitler or the perpetual infiltration of his agents into everything Spanish. I very much hoped that behind its camouflage of complacency a great deal of far-reaching and subtle diplomacy was taking place.

In the Embassy I reported to the Air Attaché, and it was now brought back to me that not only was I British, but also still belonged to the R.A.F. He invited Chris and me to stay with him at his home that night, as we could not leave for Lisbon until the next evening. His house was in the outskirts of Madrid, and he took us there in his official car. That evening we came back to the Embassy to see the film "Target for Tonight." What a strange sensation it was to be back again in the midst of English-speaking people and to smoke English cigarettes.

We, who had been pitying the ragged beggars, now began to feel pretty ragged ourselves. It was now two years since the declaration of war, and a year and a half since I had been amongst English people. Somehow the atmosphere was wrong. To me there was a strong feeling of "business as usual." I had been hoping against hope to find evidence of that intensity of effort which characterised the Germans in neutral countries, but I saw only the unmistakable signs of die-hard British optimism: let us hope that I was wrong. We saw very little of Madrid, for we left the next evening for Lisbon, after getting up late and taking full advantage of the hospitality of the Air Attaché, Wing Commander Dickson, and his wife, a particularly charming couple, who made us feel very much at home. For me, living even for only one night in a real home after so many months in hospital was most enjoyable.

The train pulled slowly out of the station, we waved good-bye to Wing Commander Dickson, and once more were en route, this time for Portugal. We were both reluctant to leave Spain so soon, for there was so much that we wanted to see, but at the same time it was good to feel that we were once more on our way home and getting nearer all the time. In the sleeping cars there was a great mixture of nationalities, Spaniards, Portuguese, Americans, Germans, British, French and Italians, to mention a few only. The British courier was there looking after the diplomatic bags he was carrying from the Embassy in Madrid to the Legation in Lisbon. The Gestapo, too, had undoubtedly a representative. Chris was put in with a middle-aged English spinster and I with a Frenchman.

The next morning, we soon arrived at the Spanish frontier station of Valencia de Alcántara, where we had to show our papers, pass through the

Customs, and deposit our Spanish money, which we could not take out of Spain. The station was unimpressive, rather characterless, not particularly clean and not very dirty.

After our bags had been inspected we had to pass one by one into a little room where a final personal check was made, and our personal papers and possessions examined. This was done by an embittered looking little middle-aged woman dressed in a shapeless grey uniform. She had the appearance and the manner of a wardress. Her gloved hands seemed to be itching to strip any well-dressed and arrogant woman who crossed her path or was suspected of hiding anything about her person. She was brusque and ill-mannered, but fortunately did not worry very much about us.

The male officials were no more genial and seemed completely devoid of a sense of humour, and to relish the opportunity of wielding power over the nationals of more powerful and better organised countries than their own. In fact, the atmosphere of this little Customs House was, to say the least, hostile. There was no sensation of "welcome tourist." The whole procedure took a long time, but eventually all the passengers who were going on to Portugal had been checked; and the train crossed over the few miles of no-man's-land which separates Spain and Portugal and pulled up in the Portuguese station of Marvão.

I cannot hope to convey more than a very sketchy impression of my feelings as the train drew into Marvão station; with a sudden rush of relief, I realised that at long last I had left the Nazi, Fascist, Falangist, Vichy idea and influence behind and was amongst a friendly, honest and peace-loving people who enjoyed freedom and contentment under a *benevolent* dictatorship. At last, it was possible to talk openly, to express one's ideas freely, without having to lower the voice or look around carefully to see who might be listening.

At last, I was in a country which was happy, well fed and well organised, a country which was Britain's oldest ally, where the life of the people was simple and satisfying. And yet before, in my ignorance, I had believed that Portugal was dirty, disorganised, and demoralised.

Marvão, the first railway station on the Portuguese side of the frontier, was not only clean and neat, it was really beautiful, and fitted perfectly into its surroundings – a rich and lovely countryside. Flowers were everywhere. The station buildings were cool and clean. Railway and Customs officials were not only neatly dressed and efficient, they were even friendly and polite, and very quickly carried out their duty of examining passport visas and checking the baggage. To save trouble to all concerned this was done in the train.

A British Consular official was waiting at the platform to meet all British travellers, and he told Chris and me that we were not allowed to go direct to Lisbon but must go to a little town called Caldas da Sunha and wait for further orders. This meant that we would go on in the train along the Tagus Valley until we were only a few miles from Lisbon and would then have to change trains twice before reaching Caldas late that night. It turned out that no refugees were allowed to go and stay in Lisbon, which was by now full up, and that the Portuguese authorities had made arrangements for all refugees of all nationalities who were passing through Portugal to be accommodated in hotels at Caldas.

Of course, in my case, a returning prisoner of war, travelling under special arrangements made by the Air Attaché at Madrid, this regulation should not have applied, but it was impossible to go against the Consular agent, particularly as he was providing the Portuguese money and tickets necessary for the rest of the journey. After a while the train started again and carried us swiftly through the rich undulating countryside, abundant in vineyards, crops and orchards, in the direction of the Tagus Valley and Lisbon.

A restaurant car had been attached and we had plenty of time to take lunch before we changed trains. We were soon seated at a table, making our first contact with Portuguese food. The Portuguese believe in five full meals a day, and this was one of them. The first thing we noticed was the white rolls on our plates. After the grey adulterated bread of France and Spain we had forgotten what white bread looked like.

Refugees from all parts of Europe who did not enjoy the same advantages as we did in Spain almost invariably over-ate to the extent of making themselves ill when they first arrived in Portugal. Thin and undernourished, after many months of privation, their systems were unable to cope with the rich food of Portugal, which had not been changed by war conditions. White rolls, plenty of butter, an omelette, fish, chicken, vegetables, cheese, fruit, wine, coffee and liqueurs – all these the restaurant car offered us for lunch, and we ate it, every bit, half afraid that if we left anything we would regret it later on.

Sitting with us at our table there was a well-dressed and obviously quite wealthy French lady who was on her way to America. Like us, she could not get used to the idea of so much good food. "C'est formidable. J'ai bien oublié l'existence de choses pareilles! Ah! La pauvre France!" For the rest of the meal, or rather in the short pauses between wolfed mouthfuls, we compared the conditions of food in France and Spain and Portugal "Of course," she said, "before the war we never talked of food in France, but now it has become so scarce that we talk of it all the time." Chris and I smiled, remembering well how the French had always talked about their food. The French *cuisine* had been such a rich and worthy subject for conversation. How we all three wished we could have sent some of the food before us to our hungry friends in France.

The sun was near its zenith as we sped along the Tagus Valley and stopped at the junction station at which we had to change trains. We climbed down on the scorched platform and stood watching a porter collecting our strange baggage. This consisted of four suitcases and two large dilapidated paper parcels holding the remains of the food we had brought with us from France. There was a wait of two hours in front of us before our next train arrived, and as the heat was terrific (we felt it the more after over-eating at lunch) and the sun too strong for my sore eyes, we went into the cool of the refreshment room and ordered iced beer.

The refreshment room, with its spotlessly clean floor, neat curtains drawn back from the windows, and fresh checked linen clothes on the tables, was typical of the simplicity and comfort of Portugal. At one end of the room stood a polished counter with a glass case full of packets of cigarettes and cigars. Most of the packets were Portuguese, but there were a few American and English brands too. We bought a stock of cigarettes, being unable to resist the temptation of buying tobacco without coupons. While we were there a newsboy brought in copies of recent London newspapers. This added a particularly friendly touch to a most welcome atmosphere.

It turned out that instead of one we had two more changes to make before we were finally installed in the train for Caldas. The first train was very modern and consisted of comfortable all-metal carriages, probably built in Germany. The next two were old-fashioned, but equally clean and fairly comfortable. In the last train we were sitting in a carriage by ourselves when we suddenly remembered that it was getting late, and we had not eaten anything since lunch.

Chris had been asleep, and I completely fascinated for hours watching the sun setting over the lovely richly cultivated well-wooded countryside, the clean white cottages, the picturesque peasants and their donkeys, little towns, villages and an occasional old castle. But now it was dark and there was nothing more to see. Chris pulled down one of the paper parcels. She had given most of the remains of our supply of food to a group of barefooted little urchins at the station of the Spanish frontier who had been scrounging around the train, clambering up on the steps and looking through the windows and begging for food. They had fought for the paté and stale rolls, and gulped them down like starving young animals, which they resembled both in appearance and habits.

However, we still had a couple of stale rolls and a tin of sardines left. With the help of my pocket knife and Chris's fingers we soon had the tin open and were in the middle of a messy but satisfying meal when the train stopped at a station and the carriage door was opened to disclose the kindly and rotund features of the Spanish wine merchant's traveller who had helped us with our luggage at the last change. He looked a little surprised to see us eating oily sardines with the aid of Chris's fingers and surrounded by the greasy contents of an open brown paper parcel. He would probably have been even more surprised if he had known that the Portuguese sardines Chris was popping into my mouth had come all the way with us from famished France.

Bringing sardines to Portugal was about as incongruous as taking coal to Newcastle. He came in and sat down, after asking our pardon in French for his intrusion. From his attaché case he produced a carton of Chelsea buns and a bottle of white wine, which he insisted on adding to our feast. He was most charming and told us how much he hoped we would be happy in Portugal, but to be careful not to shock the people in any way, as they were very old fashioned, particularly in the small towns and villages. He told us that the Portuguese people were mostly poor, but all contented. Dr. Salazar was a dictator, but a very homely one, who lived humbly and without luxury, was frugal and honest; wore no uniform, seldom spoke in public, and had no fancy statue. Obviously to a man like that the bombastic methods of the other European dictators must have been very distasteful.

Portugal was rich, partly as a result of the wonderful work of national reconstruction carried out by Salazar ever since he came to power, and partly as a result of the war. Lisbon was the clearing house for British, German and American affairs in Europe and America. Some people in Portugal hoped that the value to Hitler of a neutral country with an Atlantic port would deter him from a direct invasion of Portugal. Portugal was carrying out – and would continue to carry out – a policy of strict neutrality. As for the sympathies of the Portuguese themselves, they were whole heartedly pro-British and -American. They had a particular admiration for Roosevelt, and great confidence in Churchill. He asked many questions about our adventures in France, and in return told us a little about himself.

He left us before we reached Caldas, and we missed him. He was cultured, polite and altogether charming. His large face radiated good nature and an innate honesty. He was bubbling over with good spirits, and from his figure it looked as if he did full justice to the huge meals of his country. To me he was a typical example of many Portuguese that we met. Of course, it is true that it is easy to be happy and cheerful and kind when everything is going well and there is an abundance of all the necessities of life. The Spaniards – with the possible exception of Customs officials and other Government agents – had managed to be very polite, if not particularly gay on a starvation diet. Most French men and nearly all French women managed to find something to laugh about – usually themselves – even in their worst privations. But I felt that in the Portuguese there was an inherent honesty, kindness and friendliness that would have survived all tragedies.

It was late when we arrived at the little station of Caldas da Sunha, but the friendly hotel porter was there to meet us and lead us up to one of the little hotels where the refugees were staying. It was too dark for us to gain anything but a fleeting impression of quiet and cleanliness. The hotel was simple and charming; everyone in it, from the hotel manager down to the lowest member of his small staff, radiated a kindliness and friendliness which would have been embarrassing had it not been so wholeheartedly genuine.

By some misunderstanding a double room had been ordered for me and Chris. After we had extricated ourselves from this matrimonial tangle they gave us little rooms up at the top of the hotel, looking down into the yard. Down in the sitting-room we met refugees of all nationalities, with English predominating; there was also a piano and some English periodicals. Amongst the refugees there were men over military age and many women and children. Everyone had exactly the same treatment. The possession of private means in England made absolutely no difference.

By an arrangement between the hotel and the British repatriation officer at Lisbon full board and lodging was provided, and in addition each adult was given a sum of money equal to ten shillings in Portuguese currency each week for cigarettes and other little necessities or luxuries. With such a small sum of money in their pockets and no means of getting any more, their lives were very simple and somewhat restricted, but no one could possibly have had any grounds of complaint, for the Portuguese people went out of their way by gifts of clothing, invitations to the cinema, and a thousand other small kindnesses, to make sure that the international refugees were made to feel at home and really happy.

Most refugees had to wait several weeks before getting a place on a boat and had to be ready to leave at very short notice. One of the last ships had been torpedoed and many of the Caldas contingent lost. A retired naval commander, who lived nearby, came in every day to answer any queries and generally look after the interests of the refugees. On arrival it was necessary to register, and the registrations were controlled by the police.

No one could leave Caldas without special police permission, and the town was situated far enough away from Lisbon to make it inaccessible. Now, this was the Portuguese way of handling the problem of refugees. This was a Portuguese concentration camp, believe it or not. To me it was a model for all nations. I had seen concentration camps in France for Spanish refugees, camps that had been built during the civil war and are still going to this day. These camps were bad enough, but even they did not compare with the German, Italian and Spanish concentration camps.

Portugal was giving the world a lesson in good manners and ordinary humanity, for Caldas was a spa with beautiful air, a lovely little town, within reach of the sea, with clean and comfortable hotel accommodation, delightful people, unlimited leisure, freedom of speech, and within reason, freedom of action; no wonder the refugees, arriving in a low physical and often nervous condition, soon were carefree, bronzed, fat and happy. Portugal should be proud of Caldas. It will be remembered with gratitude by all British and other refugees who were forced to stay there by circumstances.

The sun was slanting in through my window when I woke up the next morning and the air was alive with domestic noises; voices from the kitchen below and the clatter of saucepans mingled with the clucking of hens in the yard. They were peaceful, happy sounds. Here was sanity at last. After breakfast and a bath Chris and I wandered out through the front door of the hotel, which opened straight on to the street. The hotel stood near the top of the little town.

Although it was Sunday I heard no church bells, but instead the mixed sounds of a country market, for Sunday at Caldas was market-day, and a cavalcade of gaily dressed peasants was making its way into the town past the hotel and down the road to the market. There was no sound to jar the nerves and no sight that wasn't pleasing. There was an incessant soft pattering of unshod hooves, donkeys heavily laden with panniers and bundles, led by women with pitchers on their heads, children driving the sheep and goats, and the men walking leisurely. I needed a shave, so we followed the crowd down into the oblong market square, surrounded by shops, where the crowded market was already in full swing and would be going on for the rest of the day.

We found a little barber's shop opening up in the square. The door was kept open, and while the barber was scraping gingerly round my scarred face I could hear all the sounds of the market outside. In the evening, after the market was finished, the men would foregather and drink together. Meanwhile the women, mounted on the donkeys, would set off for home, followed by the children herding the sheep and goats. Later that night the men would start tottering home themselves, bringing with them such remains of the cash proceeds of the day which had not been spent on drink. Some of the more drunken might perhaps end up in the town jail which we had passed on our way to the market. They would be quite comfortable there, for prisoners were allowed to receive visitors in the afternoon and could enjoy a smoke and a chat in their cells. There appeared to be no real crime in Caldas.

Back in the hotel lunch was served in a large room crammed with well-to-do Portuguese and groups of refugees of mixed nationalities. The refugees were very cliquey. We felt that the gossip and scandal of the English boarding-house kind must be thriving and wondered just what relationship they had fixed between us. I hoped we were let off fairly lightly on account of my condition.

Shortly after lunch a big dark saloon drew up outside the hotel, and Don Darling, the British repatriation officer, got out of it and said he was going to take us to Lisbon, as air passages had been provisionally arranged for Chris and myself. I had to be hurried back to England for an operation on my left eye, which was by now very uncomfortable. We said good-bye to the other refugees, and they gave me a large bunch of chrysanthemums. We felt rather badly leaving them like that, for many had been waiting for weeks for the chance of a passage on a boat. The Dodge, driven by a Portuguese, set off at breakneck speed, and to me it was a miracle that we did not kill any of the peasants and domestic animals strewn all over the road as we rushed on to Lisbon. On the way I discovered, much to my embarrassment, that Don and I had met before, and that I had been very rude to him. However, the whole incident was explained and forgotten, and we were soon the best of pals.

The next day we collected our tickets from the British Overseas Airways office and were told that reservations had been made for us on the plane leaving for England at dawn the day after. That night we were too excited to go to bed, and instead visited a night club with Don and a friend. The company was good, and it was a grand evening, but the night club was pretty poor. A few hours before dawn we set out – all four of us – in a taxi. Once more we experienced Portuguese motoring at its fastest. Home was getting so near now that I had a queer excited feeling in the pit of my stomach which never completely left me from then on until we arrived in England. In spite of great efforts in self-control, I felt that if anything was to stop us getting home now, it would be too much for me. We arrived at the airport with plenty of time to spare. It was still dark.

We came blinking into the lighted airport building and left our bags on the Customs benches. In the caféteria bar we ate sandwiches and drank whiskey while waiting. While we were there our captain and crew came in. They were tall, blond Dutchmen, with pale-blue eyes and that particular kind of cheery disposition that seems to be the prerogative of merchant seamen and long-range airline pilots. They were flying us home in a K.L.M. Douglas airliner under charter to British Overseas Airways.

The seven and a half hours flight from Portugal to the west of England was child's play to these men, who were accustomed to the long routes between Holland and her East Indian Empire. In the airport building stood cheek by jowl the officers of four national airlines, the British, the German, the Italian and the Spanish. We were told that sometimes the airliners of all four nations would arrive within a minute of each other, and the harassed Portuguese authorities were faced with the difficult problem of coping with the diplomats and emissaries of three hostile and one neutral nation at the same time. True to the Portuguese policy of strict neutrality, the rule was first come, first served.

Soon it was time to leave. Dawn was breaking cold and grey as we walked out on to the aerodrome. Against the pale sky the brown hills that surrounded us at some distance from the edge of the landing field were darkly outlined in silhouette. Mechanics were moving like shadows around our camouflaged Douglas DC-3 airliner.

We said good-bye to Don, climbed through the door in the fuselage, and settled ourselves in the comfortable high-backed seats reserved for us. The pilots walked past us into the control cabin, closing the door behind them. The engines started up one after another with a roar and a splutter. We taxied over the aerodrome, turned into the wind and took off. We were on our last lap home. Europe, with all its distress, lay below us and soon would be behind us. We were leaving behind us events and people that we could never forget.

As we flew up the coast to Oporto, Portugal lay below us, a patchwork of green fields, golden-brown hills and yellow sands, lighting up in the early sunlight. At Oporto we landed and refuelled, then we took off and climbed high up on our course, until soon the coast of Portugal was out of sight. It was fair weather; cumulus clouds began to form like flat puffs of steam, and the silver-blue sea lay below. And so, the scene remained as we flew on to England and home. Chris closed her eyes and was soon fast asleep, her head lolling and her mouth open, tired out with the excitement and lack of sleep. I was left to my own thoughts.

As the hours passed and the distance separating us from the English coast steadily diminished I saw vividly in retrospect each event that had taken place since that fateful day just over two years before when I had flown over to France with my squadron. First I saw those eight irritating months of comparative inactivity, when boredom and frustration were broken only by a few reconnaissance flights, night leaflet raids, and two short periods of leave. Next the suddenness of the expected German attack on the Low Countries, followed immediately by my own ordeal by fire.

The next five weeks, when I could hardly be said to be fully alive, the five weeks in which France was collapsing, the catastrophe of Dunkirk was taking place, and I was being evacuated from one hospital to another – five weeks of nightmare, in which stretchers, trains, refugees, hospitals, bombs and the sound of shell-fire all had their place. Then a year in hospital in a France broken and suffering – the first ten months, helpless and immobile on my back, followed by my miraculous return to some shadow of my former mobility, despite all doctors' prophecies. After that the relentless confinement in the heat of a Marseilles hospital and the sudden change of being on parole in a friendly Lyons. Then, after many repatriation disappointments, the unexpected permission to leave, and finally the interesting fortnight travelling through Spain and Portugal.

It didn't seem possible that so much could have happened in so short a time. What an enormous difference there was between those two flights, one from England and the other back. I had left England and my wife in the height of my physical prime. Now, two years later, I was returning a physical wreck, crippled and disfigured. The most painful reunion in my life lay before me. Yet I had felt and seen so much suffering that I no longer had the same capacity as before to feel pain, mental or physical.

I had become toughened and had developed a detachment so complete that my mind stood ever outside my proper self, watching and criticising even the deepest emotions that were affecting my heart and body. During the past month there had often been times when I had convinced myself that my home-coming would be so painful to those I loved that it would be better for me not to return until my disfigurement had been patched up, and I would not have tried to come home, had it not been for the fact that in France I could have had neither the benefit of the finest plastic surgeons nor the nursing and nourishment necessary to bring me back to some semblance of a normal human being.

Just before the English coast came in sight of the pilot in front the steward came aft into the passenger compartment and fixed little wooden shutters over the windows. This denied us the privilege of seeing England at all from the air, for the shutters were still in place when we landed at a West Country aerodrome. As we climbed stiffly out on to the aerodrome we looked round to see if anyone of our friends or relations had come to meet us but saw no one. In fact, our arrival in England turned out to be a complete anti-climax, and we felt decidedly flat. However, the airport authorities had provided tea for the passengers. There were twelve altogether, and while the Customs were clearing our baggage we drank our tea and wondered what would happen next.

After a while I was given a message which had been waiting for me and had come from the Air Ministry. Eventually an R.A.F. ambulance arrived to take me to a nearby hospital. Chris, feeling the anti-climax of our arrival even more than I, wished me "Bonne chance" and disappeared.

Chapter 8

Looking Back

Four months have now passed since my arrival in England. Reunions have taken place. The long period of mental and physical reconstruction has begun. My first ambition – to be in the hands of one of the world's finest plastic surgeons – has been realised. Already two operations are over. For the last three months I have been recovering strength for the next of many more complicated operations in an R.A.F. convalescent hospital in the West of England.

This hospital was a luxury hotel in peacetime. It has an indoor swimming pool, covered tennis and squash courts, a modern gymnasium, a private cinema, and many other amenities calculated to restore physical and mental health in the most agreeable manner possible. Much of the privacy and all the advantages of the luxury hotel are combined with those of a modern hospital. As I dictate this story, sitting beside the open window of my little room, I can see the sea – a triangle of silver water filling in the gap between the wood-covered slopes bordering the hotel's grounds. There are fishing boats out there on the silver waters. Gannets are soaring and wheeling overhead, their plaintive cries mingling with those of smaller birds in the woods and the sound of voices from the hotel's golf course. There is an atmosphere of peace and sanity.

One thing above all others is impressed upon me. In England, and wherever the English language is spoken throughout the world, there is still a large measure of freedom, for complete freedom of action is impossible in any ordered civilisation, even in peacetime. I take it that we are fighting, not for complete freedom of action, but for the measure of it which we already know to be practicable. But we are fighting for complete freedom of thoughts and opinion, and the right to express it.

While the war is on we are obliged, in our own interests, to sacrifice much of our freedom, strictly on the understanding that it will be restored to us if and when we win the war. Sometimes I wonder whether or not it will be necessary for us as a nation to lose all our freedom before we appreciate to the full how much it means to us, and just how debased life can be without it. It is my belief that the French people as a whole realise now, as never before, since the French Revolution, how much freedom matters to them, and that they have learnt this lesson only by the loss of their freedom since the German occupation.

I sincerely hope that this book, with its exposure of some of the conditions I myself saw and experienced in France, may help to impress the value of freedom on anyone who may doubt it, and that we as a nation may be forced by our Government now to give up more of the freedom and many of the comforts that prevent the organisation of our war effort from approaching the 100 per cent mark. For we must sacrifice freedom to gain freedom.

Looking back over the ever-changing months of the first two years of the war in France, I feel it is my duty to try as far as I am able from my personal experience and observation to answer here in print some of the questions I am repeatedly asked by people who are anxious to find out the views and reactions of the French people and find it difficult to get in touch with anyone who has lived recently in close contact with the French.

The French people, for the most part, admit freely that their lives were too pleasant and irresponsible before the war and for the first eight months after war had been declared, when the French Army was sitting in the Maginot Line. They bitterly regret now their indifference to the way the country was misgoverned by one bad Government after another, while they themselves were concentrating solely on making money and having a good time spending it. They realise that their army was good and bad in some respects, and that it was extremely badly officered and equipped; they are deeply conscious of the shame attached to their inglorious military defeat; they are bitterly resentful of the break in relations between themselves and the British Empire; they are a little anxious, now that Britain has taken over Syria and attacked Dakar, and wonder whether their Empire will be returned to them in the event of a British and American victory.

Every Frenchman worth the name, hates the Germans with a hate developed through three major invasions in the last seventy years. To live they are forced to work for the Germans, and although there are undoubtedly Frenchmen of the big industrial class who are profiting from the Germans, the average Frenchman, particularly the working Frenchman in the occupied zone, works only for the Germans because he cannot make a living any other way. The spirit of the people in the occupied zone is best illustrated by the jealousy felt in Channel towns which have not been bombed by the R.A.F. as much as have their neighbours. It is also well demonstrated by the fact that

R.A.F. personnel brought down in France have invariably been well looked after by the French, in spite of the fact that the Germans would shoot any Frenchman helping a British pilot. The morale of the women is particularly high, both in the occupied zone and the unoccupied zone; but in the south of France, where the people have not suffered directly from the German invasion, except in so far as their rations have been cut down and the produce of their parts of the country robbed, the morale is not as high as in the occupied zone.

All over France the Italians are hated at present even more than the Germans. The French resent the way the Italians stabbed them in the back at a moment when their armies were being driven back by the Germans, and afterwards, when the Armistice had been signed, claimed a glorious victory over the French Armies, when in actual fact a very small number of French divisions had kept the whole of the Italian Army at bay. Marshal Pétain and the Vichy Government have few followers in occupied France, but quite a large number in unoccupied France. Darlan and Laval are the two most hated men in France. Nearly all the French people are pro-British in so far as they look to Britain and America to help them out of their present predicament. In the occupied zone the people are almost universally pro-British. Almost every man or woman to whom I talked in France listened in regularly to the B.B.C. programme in French. These are the facts very briefly.

One day, perhaps, it will be possible to write the real story of the French people during this present war. It will show examples of individual courage that will surprise critics in this country. It will also show how the French people, in spite of everything, are still working through underground channels in the interests of the *Entente Cordiale.*

PART 2

The Way of Recovery

Dedicated to my Mother

Chapter 9

Two New Eyelids

Briefly, the treatment of burns almost invariably employed in France while I was there, was as follows. First, the burnt areas were cleaned with liquid ether and peroxide of hydrogen. Then they were wiped over with scarlet mercurochrome, covered with dry sterilised gauze and finally enclosed in cotton wool and bandages. Sometimes the gauze was soaked with Peruvian balsam or cod liver oil. Occasionally it was covered with Vaseline. So short were stocks of medical stores, however, that the gauze was nearly always left dry. Dressings were left unchanged for at least four days, and often for a week. It is easy to imagine the pain caused by the rough removal of the dressings, for no anaesthetics were given to me for months, and the dressings, hardened by mercurochrome, were wrenched from the raw flesh. Apart from causing exquisite pain and profuse bleeding huge areas of new pink tissue were destroyed each time this was done.

By October 1941 I had recovered sufficiently to be repatriated by way of Spain and Portugal to England. My legs were still stiff, and heavily scarred from below each knee to the groin. My eyelids had been burned off along with the wing of the left nostril of my nose. My mouth, cheeks and forehead were ribbed with keloid scars. But worst of all were my hands. No fingers remained on the left hand – they had rotted and had then been torn off during dressings. A few short stumps remained on the right, but I had not yet learned to use them, and they were a mass of nervous reactions. The outlook for my future life seemed very black. I was entirely dependent on other people. I could not even feed myself. At times it seemed to me that I had lost everything – my health, youth and career. Added to all this came the complete collapse of a marriage that had seemed ideal and had been very happy before the war.

Yet in the midst of all this wreckage burned a virile spark of hope and faith, for I had heard something of the wonders of British plastic surgery, and at least I was home again.

My hope and faith were soon transformed into realisation; and the writing of this book was made possible.

For months I have wanted to write this book but have shirked it until now. It is difficult to write about myself, and anyway I do not like doing it, yet I do not know of any other way of assuring the reader that the complete recovery of a full life is possible for someone who has in effect lost both hands. So, risking an accusation of priggishness and egocentricity, I have written the following account of two years spent in and out of English hospitals.

Here in this book, I have tried to give the reader a message of hope and faith. I have tried to explain something of the wonderful work being done in this country in the treatment of burns, with their accompanying disfigurement and deformities – treatment which makes my experiences in French hospitals seem to belong to the Middle Ages. I have tried to show you how ordinary people like myself can, with the care and attention of surgeons, nurses and friends, completely overcome the worst calamities that war can bring to one, so that if any one of you who reads this book should go through experiences such as mine, and those of some of the other characters in this book, you may know right from the start that all is not lost. Quite the contrary. One's life can be enriched beyond all measure, and it can take on a completely new lease, as mine has done.

If you are a mother or a wife you will, I hope, learn through the pages that follow, that whatever may happen, or may have happened, to anyone you love, he can overcome almost anything through his own faith and spirit, strengthened by your love and understanding, here in England where surgeons and nurses give freely of their qualities of skill and devotion – qualities not to be excelled in any other part of the world.

***

The Douglas transport plane that in eight hours flying time had carried me from Portugal to England circled a west country aerodrome and landed. When the door was opened we, the passengers, got our first glimpse of England; for in the interests of security blinds had been fitted to all the windows in our compartment some time before we arrived within sight of the English coast. The first sight of the green grass of the aerodrome and the camouflaged buildings beyond filled me with deep emotion. Yet I cannot pretend that I was altogether happy to be home again.

Doubt troubled my mind. For some months I had been aware of a premonition that my marriage would collapse upon my return home; in fact for many reasons, I had not wanted to come home, and would have far preferred to remain in France. I knew that my mother had been very ill, and I believed that the sight of her war-battered son would cause her a severe shock. I felt that I ought not to visit her until my face and hands had been patched up.

To all my friends in France I felt a traitor; for living conditions were terrible when I left there, and many of them, too, were in danger. Yet in my heart I realised that by staying in France I could serve no useful purpose. It was much better for me to return to England – and to a new life. It had to be a new life, for the old one had been destroyed. Having left England in the prime of my youth it was painful to return conscious of the fact that I had changed mentally and become rather hard. Actually, that hardness had helped me to withstand pain and disappointment, and it continues to help me now.

There was no desire left to go back along the paths I had covered in England, and elsewhere, before I had been wounded. It was not surprising, therefore, that I had already guessed that my marriage was about to break up. When during my first few days back in England the cornerstone of its structure was removed, I found it difficult to feel any strong emotion, and watched with a terrible detachment the whole affair crumble into ruins.

Tragedy and ruin, physical and emotional, faced me: but somewhere beneath the ruin a spark of hope burned brightly. That spark was going to be fanned into a strong flame of resolution. Physically, I was about to be reborn. My eyesight would soon be saved by the grafting of new eyelids. My hands too would serve me again after the surgeons had begun to work on them. I was back in a land where hospitals were good and surgeons magnificent. I was going to have the best surgical treatment in the world.

An R.A.F. ambulance carried me and my crude "refugee" baggage through the streets of the nearby town, out into the country again and on to an R.A.F. hospital. I began to take stock of the England I had not seen for nearly two years. As we passed through the outskirts of the town I saw for the first time some of the damage caused by the *blitz* bombings. It surprised me to see how extensive it was, for in France I had been unable to visualise the sufferings of the English people under bombardment.

Apart from this evidence of suffering, England looked incredibly peaceful, and the people placid and contented. Their faces had changed a little, perhaps. Their expressions after two years of war seemed more purposeful, and they wore their uniforms more naturally than when last I had seen them in 1939. Military cars and vans that we passed had a satisfactory used appearance. The barrage balloons were greyer – two years had dulled their former bright silver finish.

Out in the country beyond the town the pale afternoon sun brought out all the mellowness of autumn. Trees were brown and gold and the hills were neatly patched with buff ploughland and dark green fields. Behind me in Portugal I had left summer heat; here in England it was cool, almost cold; and the year, sad and graceful, was slowly dying. There is usually something about the mellowness of autumn that invades my current mood, and conquering it, transforms it from whatever it may have been to a state of faintly regretful reminiscence. This time my mood was already in harmony with the season. It seemed impossible to me that only twenty-seven years of my life were behind me. I felt old and found myself more easily in sympathy with old people than with those of my own age.

This feeling was no doubt the product of months of brooding and of concentrated thought, and a certain temporary ageing of my body. I wondered whether my mind would recover the lost enthusiasm of its youth while my body was being repaired. Now that seems almost to have happened, and yet I have lost something – just what I cannot say – that I do not seem able to recover. Blind faith, perhaps, and a certain gullibility; these have been replaced by disillusion, scepticism, and a firmer grip on my impulses. In other things I had, however, become enriched. I felt that my mind was more open than it had been before – I was no longer anxious to lay down the law and was interested now far more in the points of view of others than in my own.

Before, I had been self-conscious; but the months of disfigurement had cured me of that. One thing in particular troubled me. I felt completely detached from everyone and everything. My emotions, long over-exercised, had lost their keen edge and their responsiveness. I had to be subjected to great misery before I felt sad, and to experience great pleasure before I felt happy. To be conscious of a feeling of detachment is, no doubt, the lot of all those of us who feel that we have been jolted out of a definite place in the community of men.

The R.A.F. hospital to which I went was part of a hutted camp. The whole place was heavily camouflaged, and a barrage balloon wallowed unconcernedly above it. It differed little in outward appearance from the thousands of little groups of hutments scattered over the country which provide temporary shelter for soldiers and civilians, airmen and prisoners of war. Inside, the linoleum-covered floors were polished and shining, the paintwork in the wards was clean, and the nurses and doctors were fresher in appearance and better dressed than those I had become accustomed to in France.

I was told that the officer who commanded the squadron in which I had served in France was in the officer's mess. I went along to meet him. He had changed little. He was still heavy in build and hearty in manner. He was obviously embarrassed when he saw coming towards him a strange apparition of grotesque humanity – only faintly reminiscent of one of his flight commanders. He gave me a tankard of beer and good tobacco for my pipe. Then he told me what had happened to other members of the squadron.

Of the flying crews few were still flying; some were prisoners of war; many others had been killed in action. Among the names of the lost were many of the best; but it was good to hear that at least some of them had escaped. This meeting provided the first link with a past that I wanted badly to forget, and for months afterwards I contrived to avoid reunions of this kind. It was too painful then – but that feeling has passed with time.

Two days later, after arrangements had been completed for my transfer to a plastic surgical unit, I was taken by car to a southern town. We left in the early afternoon and arrived in the pitch darkness of the blackout.

England looked strangely placid and unconcerned. Although the soldiers looked purposeful, the civilians appeared to be carrying on their ordinary way of life, very much as if the war had never begun. Did anyone realise that just across the English Channel crouched an army of gangsters, armed to the teeth and waiting only for the fall of Russia before springing on us? Apparently there were a few who did, for all the signposts had been removed and here and there along the side of the roads lay rough anti-invasion barricades made from tree trunks and barbed wire.

Apart, however, from these small signs of preparation, England seemed strangely unmoved by the threat of invasion. At first this apparent apathy, all the more obvious to me because of my recent contact with defeated France, astounded me. In Russia, Moscow was still threatened, and Kharkov, with its five aircraft works and its great tractor factory, had been captured. Although Stalin still remained in the Kremlin as the supreme military commander, the Russian Government had been evacuated to Kuybyshev. In France fifty hostages had just been shot at Bordeaux. The execution of a hundred others had been postponed as the result of an appeal made by Pétain and Darlan to the German authorities.

These facts, and the many other reverses and miseries suffered by the Russians and by the peoples of all occupied countries, were uppermost in my mind. It was therefore not surprising that I felt strongly resentful of the seeming indifference of Englishmen. At the time it seemed to me outrageous. Yet as the months passed I began to realise that this apparent apathy was to a large extent an illusion, and that in reality there was a wide consciousness of the gravity of the situation alive in English hearts. People did realise, even if they did not show it or say anything about it, that with vast areas of Russia in the hands of the Germans, we were in dire peril. I have learned now to appreciate the fact that often beneath the guise of our national outward unconcern lies an inner greatness. Then, looking through the eyes of an exile, who for two years during the war had been out of the country, I was constantly amazed at the way the English people refused to believe that either Russia or England could fall. This faith, which I could not then bring myself to share, is now being justified.

Arriving at my destination[2] in the blackout I was conscious of the Plastic Unit[3] only as a modern brick building surrounded by a conglomeration of wooden huts. I was taken into one of the huts and found myself in a brightly lit ward. In the sister's office I was received by an Air Force doctor who examined my papers and passed me on to the sister in charge. She showed me my bed. Most of the other beds were filled with patients who were almost completely obscured by bandages. The ward was clean, bright and cheerful. From a radio a voice crooned: *Kiss the Boys Goodbye*. This tune, which was repeated almost hourly, as popular jazz always seems to be for months on end, haunted me for a long time; it irritated me, but I could not get it out of my mind. I will always associate it with that first night in Ward 3.

One of the nurses fed me with supper, undressed me, and tucked me up in bed. I do not think that I fell asleep that night; but the night nurse, who was Irish, came periodically to chat with me, and this made the night seem shorter. I could have asked for a sleeping draught but was then rather prejudiced against even the mildest of drugs. During those long sleepless hours, I thought of many things, and by morning had decided that I was very lucky to be back in England again.

A complete new life was opening out before me. It was going to be a great adventure. The foundations of a new mental and physical structure were

---

[2]   The Queen Victoria Hospital in East Grinstead, also referred to as the QVH or the Cottage Hospital.

[3]   In the late 1930s the British government was making plans on how to deal with casualties from the increasingly inevitable war. They were particularly concerned that there would be large numbers of burns casualties from aerial combat and air raids. The Queen Victoria Hospital in East Grinstead was to become one of four specialist Emergency Medical Service units to deal with the casualties. The new hospital site had space to build extra wooden army huts' to accommodate its growth. Under the inspired leadership of Sir Archibald McIndoe, the 'Plastic Unit' became world-famous for its pioneering treatment of Allied personnel, particularly aircrew, who had been badly burned or crushed and required reconstructive plastic surgery.

about to be laid. My old life was already a thing of the past and I did not regret its passing. The rich experience I had gained, directly through my own suffering and vicariously through the suffering of others, had, I felt, equipped me better for life than normally would have been the case for many more years. I had gained something of patience and something of assurance that I had not possessed before – something too of an increased appreciation for simple and fundamental things.

Ward 3 came to life early in the morning.[4] First of all, the patients were washed by busy nurses. Then the beds were made, and light green covers tucked in – the inexorable sign that the day had begun. Soon breakfast appeared. I ate heartily for I was still thin and weak. I remember that they gave us eggs sent from Ireland. After the ward had been cleaned and tidied, one of the nurses brought in vases full of flowers and placed one on each patient's bed table, and on the tables in the centre of the ward. Someone switched on a radio, and it remained on all day. So far the radio was the only irritating element for me in the life of the ward.

I began to take stock of the other patients for the first time, for I had been unable to muster up any interest the night before, having been exhausted by the series of tiring journeys that I had made since saying goodbye to France a fortnight before. Most of the patients were R.A.F. flying crews. I cannot now remember all the names of those who came and went, but from time to time many nations were represented. There were Irishmen, Englishmen and Scots; New Zealanders, Australians and Canadians; Dutchmen and Frenchmen; Poles and Czechs. Most of them had been badly burned; others suffered from serious jaw injuries. Several of the pilots had been shot down in flames during the Battle of Britain many months before. Others had never known the satisfaction of getting to grips with the enemy for they had been burned during training nights, which infuriated them.

In one of the end beds lay Peter.[5] His face was scarred, and his legs were still unhealed. His hands had been set in plaster before he reached this

---

[4] As the East Grinstead Museum website also points out, three new wards were established in the army huts erected in the hospital grounds: 'Ward I [was] for dental and jaw injuries with a separate Dental hut as a base for surgery and treatment; Ward II for women and children, most of whom were air raid casualties or who had inherited conditions that the London hospitals did not have capacity to deal with; Ward III for officers and the most severely burned and injured service personnel.'

[5] This is believed to be Pilot Officer Peter Clarkson Weeks. Weeks suffered burns to his face, arms, hands and legs when his Hawker Hurricane, N2586 of 607 (County of Durham) Squadron, crashed at RAF Usworth, due to engine failure, on 1 September 1940.

hospital, with the result that his fingers had become webbed together and only his thumbs were left free. He had been burned in his Hurricane before he had had a chance to contact a Hun.[6]

Somewhere near the middle was Geoffrey's bed.[7] He was up now, but his hands were in bandages. His face and hands had been burned during a dog fight in the Battle of Britain. Already he had been given new eyelids and his twisted and curled fingers had been grafted with new skin and partially straightened. One eyebrow had gone, but since then, that too has been replaced. Now as I write he is back on operations in the R.A.F. Fighter Command and commands a Spitfire squadron. Many operations have been done on his hands, and his fingers have been straightened considerably. Since his return to operations against the enemy he has distinguished himself and won the D.F.C. He has now certainly destroyed at least five enemy aircraft, and probably several more.

Some of the other patients had lost their ears and eyelids, hair and noses, and even their lips. It would be many months before their new faces would be completed, but they all looked quite cheerful, and behind what at first appeared to be expressionless red masks, their individual characters were soon apparent. One of the most remarkable things about a face that has been mutilated by fire is that the power of expression lives on in whatever remains. A look in the eyes, a tilt of the head, or some movement of what remains of the mouth, provides the clue to a man's nature, no matter how complete may be his disfigurement. Burns often twist a face into a false expression of misery, but one twinkle from a roguish eye is enough to dispel that myth.

Whereas most of the patients were grotesque in appearance, the nurses were nearly all very pretty. There is no doubt in my mind that a pretty nurse is a tremendous inspiration to a disfigured patient, particularly in the first few self-conscious months when each glimpse at his reflection in a mirror gives him hell, and often causes him acute embarrassment. These pretty, cheerful girls played a large part in the promotion of that spirit of cheerfulness which existed in this particular ward, and throughout the whole hospital.

---

[6] Initially admitted to Sunderland Hospital, Weeks was moved to RAF Hospital Halton on 22 November 1940. He arrived at East Grinstead on 15 January 1941, and went on to endure a total of seventeen operations there.

[7] Pilot Officer Alan Geoffrey Page. Serving in 66 Squadron, Page was badly burned when his Hawker Hurricane, P2970, was shot down north of Margate, Kent, on 12 August 1940. Having baled out, Page was rescued by a passing boat, before being transferred to the Margate Lifeboat. He arrived at East Grinstead on 29 November 1940.

After more than two years of observation and experience of the life of Ward 3, I am convinced that four main things are responsible for the cheerfulness which, in time, invades the consciousness of even the most unreceptive of patients. The first is simple. We are a community of people who have shared a misfortune which, with variations, is common to us all. For the type of misfortune is the same, and the variations of it are only in degree. We are all disfigured, therefore disfigurement is not unusual.

We are quite unaware of it for most of the time that we are there – in fact we can even temporarily forget it. As brothers in misfortune, we have the collective strength to overcome more easily our individual troubles. Of course, the struggle becomes much harder when we leave Ward 3, alone, to go on leave or for convalescence, and return to the outside world. The second thing is the way the nurses have come to accept us automatically as quite normal human beings – as indeed we are behind our forbidding exteriors. They have taught us to laugh at each other and at ourselves. They are cheerful when we are fed up and gentle when we are in pain.

They understand us, and they turn this understanding to practical and comforting ends. The third thing is the atmosphere brought in from outside by the many friendly people who visit us. Most of them are people we have grown to know and like. They take us out of the ward when we are fit and entertain us in their homes or elsewhere. They bring us flowers and books, ideas and occupations. Above all they make us realise that in the world outside Ward 3 we shall not be without friends.

Our own parents and individual friends have an even greater power to help us, but they cannot all be with us very often. The fourth and last thing is the greatest of all. It is the atmosphere of hope and encouragement which emanates from the man who has made this hospital what it is today. He, supported by a team of crack surgeons, has just the right mentality and character necessary to inspire hope and confidence in his patients.

There are many great surgeons in the world, but I wonder if there is another who combines the qualities of great skill and great human understanding to such a degree as Archibald McIndoe[8]. He is frank and open with his patients,

---

[8] Sir Archibald Hector McIndoe CBE, FRCS was a New Zealand civilian plastic surgeon who worked for the RAF during the Second World War. He arrived at East Grinstead on 4 September 1939. McIndoe and his team treated thousands of men, women and children who suffered burns and similar injuries. He pioneered medical techniques which went on to underpin the future treatment of burns across the world.

has a keen sense of humour and never assumes that cloak of grandeur so often worn by eminent members of his profession. To him we are human beings first and patients second. He jokes with us in the ward and sometimes when we lie on the operating table; he will drink with us in the town; he enjoys life; he is one of us; and all this in spite of the fact that he is a very busy man, weighed down by great responsibility.

It was not long before Mr. McIndoe examined me. My hands had already been dressed and almost every part of my body had been photographed. I was waiting for lunch when he came into the ward. I saw that he was a man of medium height and solid build, with a bronzed complexion. His hair had begun to grey, was parted in the middle and brushed down and back from a broad brow. He wore horn-rimmed spectacles and behind them his eyes betrayed a keen sense of humour. His jaw was firm, and he radiated confidence. His hands were powerful, and the ends of his fingers squared.

In a few minutes of quiet observation, he had examined me, decided what he was going to do, and explained to me his plan in simple detail. He had none of the hesitation of many other doctors I had known. He told me that my first operation would take place the next day. Under an anaesthetic he would remove skin from my right arm and transfer it to my face to form new upper eyelids. This would be followed later on – when I had become stronger – by a similar operation that would replace my left lower eyelid. After these two operations had been carried out my eyesight would have been saved and the perpetual and irritating stream of tears from my left eye would at last cease.

I was then taken to one of the saline bathrooms and there my right arm was shaved, washed with ether, and bound up in a sterile towel by the Bathroom Boys.[9]

There is still a suspicion of strange irrational fear that shadows my mind at the thought of an operation. It is not the fear of pain, for I know that in the theatre I shall feel none, and that any pain that comes on after the operation can be conquered either by concentrating the mind on other things, or, if that fails, by the application of drugs. Pain at its worst is transitional, it comes and goes in rhythmic cycles; familiarity with it breeds for it a measure of contempt. No, it is not the fear of pain that clouds my mind at the thought of

---

[9]   This was a nickname given to the medical staff who managed the saline baths at the Queen Victoria Hospital. One of the techniques that McIndoe pioneered was to keep the burn injuries open, then wash the wounds with saline whilst regularly changing dressings. It is said that this process was the result of a 'serendipitous discovery', McIndoe having noted the improved healing rates of injured pilots who had landed in the sea.

the operating theatre; rather is it fear of the unknown, of something which is intangible, experience of which cannot be gained directly or vicariously during human existence.

This fear of the unknown which takes so many forms, particularly in childhood, is no doubt fundamentally the fear of death, for death to all but the fanatically religious means at worst oblivion, at best transference into a new form of existence. The imagination may strive to visualise it, but no one can find out what it really is and still live on. This fear of the unknown was alive in me on the morning of my first operation at the Plastic Unit. I had no desire to stop living in a world which interested and amused me vastly, yet curiosity as to what lay beyond this life moved me into a special mood of excitement. Death, to me, is not completely forbidding; there is bound up in the contemplation of it a desire to experience the unknown and search out the unexplored, which to some extent counteracts fear. To say that I believe in everlasting life would be untrue. To me *everlasting* is a most forbidding word. I prefer to believe that our purpose in this world is to develop human civilisation for the good of our own and future generations, and to think of life as being rounded off by death, the spirit absorbed afterwards by other human spirits, and the body disintegrated to dust, out of which new life eventually will grow.

It was early in the morning that the first preparations for my operation were made. I was given an injection of a soothing drug. This dried up my saliva, made me feel drowsy in body, and clear in mind. I have often noticed that, after these pre-anaesthetic injections, whereas my body has found peace through the calming of the whole nervous system, my mind, almost divorced from my body, has assumed a clarity and taken on an activity that I seldom experience under any other form of stimulation. Life seems ridiculously simple. I see no solutions to its problems, for the problems have disappeared.

Vaguely remembering that problems once existed I search for them in vain, and end by laughing at myself for being troubled by fantasies. Truth takes no form before my vision, but I feel conscious of its presence. I lose all fear. The whole process of thought becomes enchanting. There is no remorse, no striving, no shame. Every idea is bright and shining and I experience an almost physical glow of warmth – which brings my mind back to my body in sympathy with the warmth and peace that exists there.

This drug is administered about half an hour before the anaesthetic. In the first few minutes, accepting it gladly, I am able to increase its power, but it loses its potency when the trolley arrives at my bedside to carry me to the operating theatre.

That morning as I lay flat on my back on the trolley, dressed in a white operation gown and covered with gaily coloured blankets, I watched the roof of the ward pass and change to that of the passage outside, and felt the castors bumping over the concrete. Two theatre orderlies pushed me along. Their heads were capped with white berets, and they wore white theatre gowns. Their mouths and noses were masked. They chatted gaily with a forced callousness as we jolted along the concrete passageways.

Every theatre into which I had been carried in France had reeked strongly of ether. At the smell of it I still shudder, and my flesh turns cold and puckers. But I did not smell it in this theatre, in fact there was hardly any smell at all – only a faint odour of spirit. Ghostly white figures approached me and stretched out clean muscular arms that were strong and friendly. I found myself lying flat on the operating table looking up at my minute reflection in the great lamp that hung a few feet above my chest. A strange and fascinating scene filled my range of vision. I looked up into a hemispherical pool of air held in the white bowl of the ceiling. Centred in that pool floated the great lamp which later would light up my face after I had lost consciousness.

For the moment it was extinguished, and only the reflector gleamed. Around the edge of the pool floated the heads and shoulders of ghost-like figures. Only their eyes and cheekbones were completely uncovered. Those eyes were friendly, and because apart from them there was nothing else but the cold indifferent lamp to look at, I found my gaze returning often to those dark pools. Those eyes, soft, friendly and inspiring, I now know well, for they have changed seldom during the months I have spent in the hospital. They radiate sympathy and confidence. They have meant so much to me that when I see their owners unmasked I am filled with a vague disappointment, there is too much then to look at; the eyes no longer predominate; there are curls and pretty faces and symmetrical forms as well to distract my attention from the eyes I have learnt to love impersonally.

Jill,[10] who is McIndoe's theatre sister, and Russell,[11] the anaesthetist, comes in. Russell is dressed like the other ghosts, but Jill wears green silk and her

[10] Sister Jill Mullins. A key member of McIndoe's surgical team at the QVH, Mullins was one of the so-called 'Firm of Three' or the 'The Immortal Trio', the other two being McIndoe and anaesthetist Dr John Hunter. Having worked with McIndoe pre-war, Mullins accompanied him to East Grinstead in 1939.

[11] Dr Russell Davies. Having completed his medical training, Davies became a house physician, house surgeon and resident anaesthetist at the Westminster Hospital. He eventually joined

red gold locks are barely concealed. She smiles and places a warm hand on my shoulder. My right arm is then bared, stretched out, and held firmly. One of the ghosts binds a rubber tube around my puny bicep and the veins in the hollow of my elbow joint stand out like thin lines of faded blue ink. Russell takes up a huge hypodermic syringe; there is a tiny needle fitted into the end of it.

It looks clumsy. The glass body, full of straw-coloured liquid, is fat, and at the end the needle seems strangely small and thin. He holds my arm and chooses a vein. The ghosts all turn human eyes on mine, and I return their gaze, while the pentothal is driven by Russell firmly into my vein. A glow begins, slowly at first, to spread over my body. It accelerates suddenly and the last thing I am conscious of is a feeling between a taste and a smell going up the back of my mouth from my throat to the back of my nose. Oblivion descends upon me.

I am unconscious for only two hours, but blind for five days. I have been blind before, and I do not like it. I only know that I am conscious, and that the operation is over by the messages brought to my mind by my other senses. I can hear the familiar clattering sounds of ward life. From the tinkling of spoons on china, I guess it must be tea-time. Voices are slightly muffled, and I notice many soft gradations of sound which normally pass me by unheard.

Lead weights seem to be pressing down on my eyes. I feel hot and a little sick. There is a pricking sensation on the surface of my left eyeball, and a dull soreness in my right arm where it has been skinned. Someone is beside me. She has the accent of a Scot. I remember the voice as belonging to a rather pretty V.A.D. When last I had seen her just before I was wheeled away to the theatre she had seemed never to stop moving. Apparently she has stopped moving now. She is asking me how I feel. I say "all right"; and think how odd it is that I have no real pain. I had thought it was going to be worse than this. She tells me that when I came round I was talking French wildly, and furthermore was cursing her in very colloquial language. Worst of all, she understood every word, for, as she now tells me, she has lived in France for years. As her voice recedes another approaches. This time it is a soft Irish brogue belonging to Sister.[12]

---

the Emergency Medical Service and, following the outbreak of war, was posted to the QVH. He soon became a vital member of McIndoe's plastic surgery operating team, assisting the senior anaesthetist, Dr John Hunter. Davies was one of the founding members of the Guinea Pig Club in 1941, and was medical officer to the Club from its inception until 1991, providing medical and pastoral care.

[12] Sister Mary Rae.

I developed a cold, and they moved me to one of the regular wards of the Cottage Hospital. It was still used for local patients, and when I arrived in it, was filled with old men and small boys. At the far end there was a little room just large enough to hold two beds and called the balcony. In one of these beds, I was laid. I was still blacked out. In the other bed lay Noel. He was an R.A.F. officer who had held a short service commission which expired some time before the war. He then became a flying instructor and trained R.A.F. pupils in elementary flying at a training school in the Midlands. He was a bachelor and an individualist. He had a very dry sense of humour. He liked simple things; particularly the country, and pub life, flying, and his beer, and all simple people. He was very fond of children. He hated the *poseur*. His greatest personal admiration was perhaps, for McIndoe, who had just operated on him. He had had many operations carried out on his face – which had been badly burned as a result of a flying accident that had occurred about a year before.

We got on well together and he kept me perpetually amused by his wit. Of course, I knew his voice long before I knew him by sight. When eventually my bandages were removed I discovered that he was tall and of heavy build. He too had been given a new eyelid. It was covered with bandages and for a while he could only look at me with one blue and quizzical eye. Some of his thin brown hair had been burnt off in patches, but the bare portions of his scalp were covered by parting the hair that remained at one side where it grew long and brushing it across his head.

In this ward Sister and the staff nurse were both Irish. They were pleasant and efficient, and allowed us all the freedom we wanted so long as it did not interfere with our treatment.

As the days passed my cold cleared up. I got up and sat in a chair before the electric fire. I felt tired and weak and longed for light, sun and air – and the lifting of my blackout.

At last, on the fifth day after the operation the bandages were removed from my eyes. Layers of padding were exposed covering the marine sponges which were sewn with black silk to my face. Beneath the sponges, under the pressure of stent plastic mouldings, were my new upper eyelids. Each stitch was carefully cut by the staff nurse and removed neatly and painlessly from my face with fine forceps. At last, my lids were uncovered. Judging from the excitement they caused they were very beautiful. I tried to open them, but in vain, for my eyes were gummed up and remained firmly closed. The nurse bathed them in warm saline solution, and at last I could open them just enough to see out and down. In order to look up I was forced to lean backwards. Lastly she painted the lids with scarlet mercurochrome.

The next day, after they had been bathed, my lids opened sufficiently to allow me to read. The day after they opened still further, and I could see my reflection in a looking-glass when I held my head backwards. I looked like a giant baby bird, newly hatched, and taking its first look at the world, for I had great overhanging lids that almost completely shut out my eyes. These enormous lids – shading my eyes like the sun blinds of a shop front – were ponderous and brightly coloured. Basically, they were a translucent blue; but covered as they were with scarlet mercurochrome they had been transformed into a hideous purple. Round them were great ridges where they had been sewn to my forehead and nose. So, this was plastic surgery!

However, in a few weeks' time I had two grotesque but quite presentable eyelids, complete with lashes, which bore no resemblance to their early, horrible, blotchy purple appearance. I learnt from this experience that the first stages of plastic surgery do not always beautify; the final results have to be awaited with patience, sometimes for weeks and often for months. The most satisfactory aspect of this is, that from a first tendency to despair one is led on daily, through increasing hope, to a most satisfactory end. Plastic surgery is constructive, from the earliest moment after the rough image has been moulded, until the triumphal day when the finished moulding has achieved its permanent form, and one is ever conscious of the fact.

Now that I possessed my new upper eyelids, for the first time for eighteen weary months my eyes hardly watered at all. Imagine what a permanently running eye must mean to someone who cannot handle a handkerchief, and you will realise what this meant to me. Not only had the watering almost stopped, but at last I could close the upper lids at night, and sleep even when there was a strong light burning. How blessed and precious were these two reliefs. More precious still was to me the guarantee of the safety of my eyesight; for the prospect of losing limbs, health or hearing no longer could frighten me – but of blindness I was, and still am, afraid.

For several days after the bandages had been removed my lids had to be bathed. Then finally they were painted with their last coat of mercurochrome, and I was well enough to travel to Devon to the R.A.F. convalescent hospital for officers.[13]

---

[13] RAF Hospital Torquay was a medical facility run by the RAF in the Torquay suburb of Babbacombe, Devon, during the Second World War. It opened in 1939, having been

A short time before I left I met Kathleen Dewar.[14] One evening while staying at her beautiful house I told her something of my experiences and she became enthusiastic and encouraged me to write a book. A few days later she brought me a Dictaphone lent by the hospital welfare committee, and so forced my hand. It was then that I started work on my first book [Part I], which told of my hospital experiences in France.

---

established in the requisitioned Palace Hotel. In February 1940, it was stated that the hospital was equipped with 240 beds, and a complement of 200 staff; doctors nurses, dentists, administrative personnel. There was also at least eighty civilian staff who had worked at the hotel prior to it being commandeered for the war effort. The hospital was known for its convalescent status, and also for its work in psychotherapy..

[14] Kathleen Dewar and her husband, John Arthur 'Johnny' Dewar, of the famous whisky distilling family, were keen supporters of the Guinea Pig Club and the patients at the QVH. They lived in a property named Dutton Homestall, a short distance from the hospital in Ashurst Wood. Dutton Homestall became very popular with the Guinea Pigs who spent time there relaxing between operations in the large country house with its well-kept grounds to walk around.

Chapter 10

R.A.F. Convalescence

I left Paddington with the Bathroom Sergeant as escort, bound for the south-west coast, and the R.A.F. officers' convalescent hospital. I believed then that my convalescence would last until Christmas. However, I did not leave again until April 1942.

The train was crowded, and we were lucky to find two middle seats in a third-class compartment. Sitting opposite each other, securely jammed in to place by travellers on either side, the Bathroom Sergeant fed me, and then filled my pipe. He had kindly offered to take me down to Devon since it would have been difficult for me to travel alone. Eating once more in public was an embarrassing ordeal. In France I had become accustomed to being stared at and talked about; it was done in such an open, and often audible way that it was impossible to fail to notice it.

At first it had annoyed me, but later I grew accustomed to it. I felt that most people were interested and sympathetic, and perhaps filled with a painful knowledge that there was nothing they could do to help me. They did not turn shyly away when they found my gaze meeting theirs. I liked that; it killed my embarrassment immediately. Here in England most people reacted quite differently. Some of them studiously avoided looking in my direction. Others made a point of looking straight into my eyes, smiling with smiles that varied from kind understanding, through kind misunderstanding, to the inane grins of those who gazed at me with an expression on their faces which seemed to me to say: "I pity all poor cripples."

Some people gave me a glow of happiness by their obvious sympathy, but the inane – who thank God were always few, and probably incredibly stupid – made me squirm with suppressed irritation. Unlike the French, the English seem to be easily embarrassed, so that it was not uncommon for an Englishman to blush hotly when he found that I was watching him; often his inquisitive eyes, having roved over my hands and from there to my face, found that they were then looking into mine.

Often he looked so uncomfortable that I found myself, the *curiosity*, in the ironical position of feeling that it was necessary for me to put him at his ease. Sometimes I did this by asking for a light, or for help of some kind or another – always something fairly simple so that it would not draw too much attention to us and so defeat my end by increasing, instead of reducing, his blush of embarrassment. Occasionally when I was in an aggressive mood I amused myself by staring back fiercely at those who gazed too insistently at me. It was quite easy for me to win at this game, which took away most of the fun of it. This is a confession. I always ended by feeling ashamed, for I was sure that sometimes I inflicted a permanent hurt, which was quite unjustified.

Disfigurement has taught me to forget the diffidence which used to plague my childhood days – when any action of the simplest nature, likely in any way to draw attention to myself, was repugnant to me. Something of that feeling had stuck in my consciousness right up to the time when I first returned to the presence of normal people after my long illness. To say that I am now never embarrassed would not be true. Sometimes when I am tired or in any other way not quite my usual self I do still feel very shy on entering a crowded room, a restaurant, and so on, but at least now I have a wealth of experience to remind me that usually I am far less embarrassed than the other members of the crowd.

Whereas the more sensitive members of any such crowd are instantly filled with a feeling of helplessness – born of a desire to help me in some way and coupled with ignorance of the best thing to do – *I* have no such feeling. At worst I feel a little uncomfortable, but I can always see a sufficient number of ugly idiosyncrasies marking people around me, to cause me to appreciate ironically that nature can disfigure as cruelly as can man. In fact, the disfigurements of nature are the more cruel, for man can find more sympathy for those hurt and mutilated by his own kind than he can for those permanently scarred by nature.

When we arrived at the station of the South Devon town we were met by an R.A.F. driver who led us out to a Humber staff car, pushed my luggage into the front, and drove us through the town in the direction of the eastern outskirts to the hotel which had been converted into the R.A.F. officers' convalescent hospital.

Apart from the concrete strong points, anti-tank obstructions and masses of barbed wire which bordered the crescent shaped promenade and the walls of the little square harbour, the town had changed little. It looked very much the same to me now, as when in the days before the war it had been famous as a popular seaside resort. Considering it was winter the town was very full;

but the crowds consisted mainly of service men and women stationed nearby. Later I was to discover more about its fluid wartime population. For November the weather was unusually mild. The pale sun turned the sea in the bay to silver, and picked out a rich variety of colours on the fronts and roofs of the hotels and houses that rose up from the harbour and broke the skyline of hills that enclosed the town and the long-shaped inlet of the bay on all three sides. It was peaceful and pleasant; so much so, that I felt an involuntary twinge of guilt at the thought that here I was to spend many happy and quiet months away from the war.

The staff car climbed smoothly and steadily up the hill and we passed between the hotels and houses which stood solid and rather smug between the tall trees bordering the road. Then we dropped down a little and turned into a short drive leading up to a massive and ugly grey building. We had arrived at the hospital.

Before the war the hotel – now transformed into a hospital – had been one of the brightest and most popular centres of holiday life in this South Devon town. Here holiday makers who were sufficiently gregarious by nature could, at a price which was no doubt worth it to them, live and eat well. There were all kinds of facilities available for promoting good health and giving amusement. The air was a little heavy, but it was clean and good and came directly from the sea which was only a few hundred yards away. Although the entrance to the hotel was forbidding – the front entrance seemed to be logically the back – the interior was comfortable and the bedrooms, which overlooked the grounds and the sea beyond, were well appointed and well lighted.

Behind the hotel stretched terraces and gardens, and beyond lay a nine-hole golf course shaped like a boomerang, partly surrounded by woods and with a triangular view of the sea beyond. Hidden from view there was a small cove. It was still kept open but was reserved exclusively for the use of the hospital patients and staff. There were covered tennis and squash courts; an indoor swimming pool and a well-equipped full-size gymnasium; a billiard room and a cinema. The dining room and the various sitting rooms were reasonably comfortable, although some of the latter were badly lighted. It was, from the patients' point of view, an ideal convalescent hospital.

Inside it wore uncomfortably the signs of R.A.F. occupation. The hall was full of the grey-blue uniforms of airmen and airwomen clerks and orderlies. Behind the reception desk stood a corporal, and at the telephone switchboard sat a W.A.A.F.

Men and women officer patients, some with limbs in plaster, sat waiting and chatting in armchairs, or passed backwards and forwards from dining room to lounge. Others coming down the stairs from their rooms made their way towards the bar. The fact that there was a bar was to me symbolical of the general atmosphere of tolerance which existed in this hospital and marked it as outstanding in that respect from other service hospitals. Grey-blue uniforms dominated the scene, the monotony of which was happily broken by the white veils of the nursing sisters, and the white aprons emblazoned with great red crosses of the V.A.D.s. The walls were disfigured with notice boards covered with orders and sports announcements. The furnishings were sombre but comfortable – dull carpets, dark walls and dark leather chairs and sofas.

The corporal behind the reception desk made a note of my particulars and examined my documents. Then the Bathroom Sergeant and I went up in the lift to my room on the third floor, where I was greeted by the floor sister and given tea. After tea the sergeant left me to return to work in the saline bathrooms at the Plastic Unit, and I was left alone for a while with my thoughts.

They had given me a pleasant little room – just large enough to contain a single bed, a wardrobe, a dressing table and a built-in wash-hand-basin. The floor was covered with a Persian carpet of good quality, and the bed with a glossy pink cover. There was a straight-backed chair with a leather seat and a small, cushioned basket armchair. The only thing reminiscent of a hospital was a tall bedtable on castors, painted green, which straddled the bed. Otherwise, it was a typical hotel bedroom.

Leaning over the window sill I looked out and down. Far below small figures moved in a leisurely way over the golf course, which was beautifully green and obviously well looked after. Beyond, where the tall trees enclosed the grounds, there was a blaze of golden brown where the last slanting rays of sunlight caught and illuminated the leaves that still clung forlornly to the branches. Beyond I could see a triangular patch of silver-grey sea exposed by a gap in the hills and above it a pale blue sky mottled with great cumulus clouds that rolled rapidly along on the wind. It was difficult to believe that war existed while looking out on this scene of beauty and peace.

After a few days I began to settle down to my new life. There was a routine that was just sufficient to punctuate the day and mark off the passage of time without encroaching upon my freedom. In the morning, I was awakened either by Peggy, Mary Ruth, or Rosamund – three V.A.D.'s who shared the responsibility of feeding me with breakfast in bed. I had nothing to do but lie back and open my mouth and one eye. They were all three charming and cheerful, and although normally I detested being fed, they made it a real pleasure. There is a great art in the correct feeding of an invalid. It cannot be acquired unless a nurse is sensitive and imaginative and has a reasonable sense of humour. Food is sometimes mangled before it reaches the patient's mouth in such a way that he gets no pleasure from it and can even be disgusted by it. Any kind of mashing or plastering is revolting to me.

The great art of feeding lies first in cleanliness; next in a firm yet gentle proffering of the spoon to the patient in such a way that he is able to remove its contents without sticking out his neck; and finally in the preservation of the original appearance of the food on the plate just as it left the kitchen. English cooking is not suited for a mixing and mashing technique – for instance roast beef and vegetables become quite revolting if slashed into small pieces and then mixed up into one pile of mush.

Later Don, the R.A.F. orderly who looked after me, would come in and give me a bath and dress me, for I was still quite helpless until I was cleaned, dressed and up on my feet. After this I would go along to the sister's room and have my left hand dressed. This was done by Mary or Fluffy, the two nursing sisters who looked after patients' dressings on that particular floor.

Fluffy was *pétite*, pretty and Welsh. She had delicate rounded features, a neat figure and a graceful carriage. Her voice, with its soft sing-song Welsh intonation, was sheer music. She was sensitive and gentle – almost too much so for a nurse, for she suffered vicariously the pains of her patients to an extent far greater than most nurses. Her eyes were blue and her hair which waved naturally was light brown and shining. Her white uniform – although cut on regulation lines calculated to ruin the neatest figure – could not conceal her grace of movement and pleasing carriage. Her skin had a doll-like, almost waxen, quality.

Mary, on the other hand, was tall and heavily built. Her hands too were gentle – but they were also strong. They had a friendly, firm and confident touch which was invaluable for dressings and bandaging – in which art she was quick and skilful. Her face was full and her features regular; she wore no lipstick on lips that were full and sensual. The very paleness of her lips had an attraction of its own. Her eyes were large and possessed that quality of patience and compassion that is found in the eyes of a St. Bernard dog. She possessed depths of understanding which I have seldom found in anyone else. She adored her work and was impatient to have more of it; she felt she had no right to stay here but should be in the operating theatre of one of the more active hospitals, dealing with wounded men and women in their early and most critical days.

Actually, her value to the morale of convalescent men and women here was quite beyond measure.

There were in this hospital many excellent nurses – both R.A.F. and V.A.D. – but I always felt that of them all these two possessed the most outstanding qualities of skill and human understanding.

Later in the day I went for treatment to the physiotherapy department. There my right hand was treated with hot wax and my eyelids massaged with warm olive oil. The physiotherapy department was a converted conservatory and was presided over by Sister Mac, a very staunch and rabid Scot, a native of the Highlands. She had spent many years in the nursing profession, which included service in the Balkans during the last war. The purposes of massaging my eyelids with warm oil was to preserve their suppleness while they were shrinking into shape and so reduce the possibility of the formation of keloid scars, which latter, if allowed to grow, would later have to be treated by deep X-ray or surgically removed.

All my meals were served to me in my room. This was considered necessary since I could not feed myself. It was quite a pleasant arrangement but tended to shut me off in rather an unhealthy manner from the life of the rest of the community. This isolation was increased by the fact that I was soon busy at work on my Dictaphone writing *One of Our Pilots is Safe* [included as Book 1 here] but was countered to some extent by the efforts of some of my fellow patients and by Mary, who used to encourage me to go out into the town with them.

Most of the day I spent working with my Dictaphone. It was hard work and rather trying as I could not then manage to change the cylinders by myself. This meant that each time I had finished a cylinder and wanted to start on another I had to interrupt the flow of my thoughts while I looked for someone to help me. Often I wasted half an hour or so in this way, and then found it difficult to pick up the thread of continuity for some time longer. This mechanical difficulty was accentuated by the fact that I had never attempted to write a book before, nor had I any previous experience of the Dictaphone medium of expression.

Furthermore, I could not tell my story simply and directly, since exposure of all the facts would have endangered my friends in France and caused difficulties with the censors. I wanted badly to get the whole story off my chest, but even stronger was a desire to write as much of this story as possible in a way that would be acceptable to a publisher.

After completing recordings on the first two or three cylinders, however, I found myself sliding quite easily into the rhythm of the book. All the facts that I could use were so definitely ingrained in my memory that my only difficulty was to find words that would help my reader to grasp the essentials of the story I had to tell. It was hard work, but filled me with a great sense of satisfaction, which was only seldom broken down by a hopeless feeling that nobody would be interested in what I had to say. I suppose that feeling is common to anyone who embarks on the task of self-expression, whatever the medium may be – speech, letters, photography or art. I feel it now strongly as I write this book, and have to struggle against it, driven on by a force that is almost entirely nervous. For me writing is at once the most satisfactory and the most arduous of any work I have ever undertaken, and I am always filled with the frustrating knowledge that each one of us is really inarticulate, and that there is little that can be conveyed by an amateur like myself in a medium which has known only a few dozen masters in the whole history of civilisation.

The Dictaphone is a good medium of expression. After a cylinder has been recorded it can be listened to, and it is thus easy to tell whether or not the matter sounds right. If it sounds right it should read right. Also, it should be more likely to produce an aural reaction in the reader to amplify his visual reaction to the printed words he sees.

I used to hold the speaking tube between my wrists while recording. At first this was most tiring, due partly to my rather weak condition and partly to the fact that like most of us I was not accustomed to using my wrists or forearms for the purpose of gripping.

After a week or so I became quite accustomed to holding the speaking tube between my wrists for long periods on end. This inspired me to use the same technique for other things, so that now I brush my teeth and my hair in this way. Thus, I was forced into taking a small but important step in the recovery of my independence. I was then still quite unable to open round polished door handles, although handles of most other shapes were negotiable, but now, so accustomed have my wrists become to doing unusual things, that even the shiniest polished door knob responds to my grip.

Mary's sympathy and understanding were almost unique. There were few people who could, like she did, understand how one felt after an experience such as mine, unless they had experienced something similar themselves. Most people expected me to feel bitter, and to nurse a grievance against all mankind. Others thought it strange that I expressed no particular hate for the enemy. They expected me to hate the French too, because their hospitals were so bad. None of these feelings ever had any particular place in my heart – it was only very rarely that I had a feeling of great bitterness, and then it always passed quickly away. Rather I felt that I had been *lucky* to have experienced such a complete upheaval in my life; an upheaval which had forced me to readjust my scale of values. Even if the price was high it was still worth it all.

It is very rare for genuine combatants to feel a lasting and burning hate for the enemy – in fact fighting appears to induce some form of mutual respect between adversaries. Permanent hatred for the enemy seems to be enjoyed only by a few non-combatant persons, who are inwardly, and sometimes even outwardly, rather scornful of the tolerance of the combatants.

It was ridiculous to expect me to hate the French people. Their hospital treatment had been crude, and nearly fatal to me, but I had always received as much medical attention as any Frenchman. The French doctors and nurses did everything they could for me, but there was little they seemed to know about the modern methods of treating burns. Even when they did know what to do it was usually impossible to do it, for the right kind of treatment – since the Germans had removed most of their medical supplies – was unobtainable. I loved France and I loved the French people. I felt most grateful to them for treating me as one of themselves during those long months of 1940 and 1941 when it looked to Frenchmen as if England had no further feelings for France except those of hatred and contempt.

To explain these emotions convincingly, so that it could be appreciated that they were the normal and natural reactions of a badly wounded man starting out on the way of recovery, seemed impossible. I almost despaired of completing my first book, as often, while I write this book, I tend to despair. It seems so difficult to make people believe that a lack of bitterness is natural and not an affectation.

I am rapidly reaching the conclusion that it is impossible to appreciate the actual sensations which accompany any great physical-mental experience without having that experience oneself. That is why I see a great danger in psychiatrists, for no matter how powerful may be their imagination, and how astute their powers of deduction, they are still bound to fail to grasp more than the roughest suggestion of what is taking place in the patient's mind. Psychiatrists are usually men of great character and intelligence. They sacrifice their own lives and happiness in a most unselfish way, which is in itself, admirable; but I think they tend to work and study too much, so that they lose touch with their patients, who are usually more concerned with living than with thinking.

This is particularly so of R.A.F. aircrews. Then, since nervous disorders seem to arise as much from extremes of selfishness and self-centralisation as from any other cause, it must often be difficult for a psychiatrist not to feel irritated by his patient. This feeling of irritation must often partially, if not wholly, destroy the doctor's sympathy for the patient. And yet the preservation of sympathy is essential if the treatment is to succeed.

How often, I wonder, has a perfectly courageous but war-weary operational airman been convinced by the suggestions of a psychiatrist that he is too frightened to go on flying? Once a man is convinced by suggestion or by any other means that he is a coward, the rest of his life will be hell, unless someone later has the power to reassure him of his courage.

After a few weeks I managed to evolve a technique for feeding myself with a fork and spoon held between two of the three short stumps of finger that remained on my right hand. At first all my finger ends were so tender that it was painful and tiring to use them. I used often to drop the fork, until such time as the muscles had developed a new strength. As the weeks and months passed, however, the first two of these thin stumps developed a considerable extra power and also a new sense of touch. The strength became sufficient for me to lift half a pint of beer in a mug by gripping the top rim; and the sense of touch soon made it possible for me to distinguish between hot and cold, rough and smooth objects. Eating became much more pleasant – and quite an adventure, since I had continually to think out improvements and modifications of my technique.

And so, just as the first discovery of a method of gripping with my wrists had developed until I could turn door handles and unscrew jars, now the grip of my finger stumps has so developed that there spreads before me an unlimited field of development to be exploited. Soon I could write – using a miniature revolving pencil held between my finger ends – and could pick up and hold some light and thin objects. Imagine, if you can, what this meant to me who had been utterly helpless for so long.

Now that the problem of feeding was reduced to a question of who would cut up my food, I used to go and take most of my meals with George.

George was an Irishman who had sacrificed the last year of his university career to become an R.A.F. pilot. After completing his training, he was selected for instruction duties and posted as a flying instructor to a service flying training school. He was furious about this, as he wanted to be an operational pilot. He had been admitted to hospital with some kind of obscure trouble in his left hip. When first I saw him he was spending days and nights of severe pain and discomfort interspersed by occasional periods of complete calm – which unfortunately seldom lasted for long.

For the five or six months which we spent together in this convalescent home he was bedridden. Not only was he kept permanently lying on his back with his head and shoulders supported by pillows, but to add to this discomfort his left leg was secured in a Thomas' splint which drew it out from the hip socket. This was done by a complicated system of sticking plaster, cord, pulleys and weights, all supported by a heavy wooden framework so attached to the bed as to give it a four-poster appearance. The foot of the bed had been raised a foot or so off the ground and the castors rested on wooden blocks, so that the whole bed sloped downwards, from the elevated foot towards the head.

George had a keen wit and intelligence. His life so far had always been something of a struggle and his character had developed a certain toughness and scepticism during the hard years of his early youth. He was still in his early twenties, but apart from a certain roughness and an attitude of irresponsibility in keeping with his age, he had developed far beyond his years. I used to tell him stories of French men and women I had known and loved. Sometimes I showed him some of the completed typescript of my book and was greatly encouraged by his enthusiasm for it. Like myself he had undergone the rather bitter experience of never having been able to afford the way of life enjoyed by his school and college contemporaries. This had taught him to be self-reliant and had developed in him a wholesome hate of waste of all kinds. He had been encouraged by contact with that thin stratum of intelligent and well-educated people, who, having scorned personal advancement with all its financial benefits, have found a way of life that is selective, and is based on simple material things and rich intellectual experiences.

There were many links of mutual experience that bound us together. We had both known a certain amount of suffering of various kinds. We were both idealists at heart, but perplexed and frustrated by our inability to see any clear solution to the injustices of a national way of life that permitted such contrasts as slums and country mansions. Possibly we were aware of our own shortcomings, and were striving inwardly for a new, better and fuller life in which we would be able to play a part that was not selfish in its object. Condemning as we did the extremes of inequality in Society, we yet had no desire to lose any modicum of economic power we might gain for ourselves.

George had a gramophone and we listened for hours on end to recordings of classical music, which we both passionately loved. There is something at once mystical and sensual in the make-up of Celts which responds with peculiar warmth to good music.

Whereas our greatest source of mutual satisfaction was music, our greatest
hate was for the artificial and meretricious way of life that has done so much
to ruin the solidity and worth of English people – particularly in the cities
and large towns. We saw this exemplified in the popularity of flashy things
which we believed to be of little or no worth; the chromium-plated and neon-
lighted shops that thrived just before the war in large and small towns alike;
the incredible love of listening to jazz tunes, plugged relentlessly, with little
variety for months on end; the preference of music-hall to theatre; the parrot-
like repetition of American slang rather than the development of a lively and
colourful mode of speech of our own, such as existed in Elizabethan times.

We felt that the good life was both rich and simple; that it depended on
things that were good and solid, and yet not dull; on the companionship of
good friends and the enjoyment of conversation – which seems to be an art
which is rapidly disappearing in England: on the enjoyment of good food
which we felt should depend more on the cooking than on the purse: on good
music, which in common with all art has always been available to those who
seek it. It seemed to us that this country, although so rich in good things, was
being seduced by the cheap and flashy. However, we were somewhat reconciled
by the feeling that the war had in many ways driven us all back towards the
simple life and taught us to check carefully our scales of value.

George had much of that brand of wit and charm which is so common in
the Irish, and although I did not share all his opinions I liked to listen to the
expression of them and was greatly stimulated by his enthusiasm.

In the evenings just before sunset it was pleasant to wander from the
grounds of the hospital and to climb up through the woods and out on to the
downs beyond. These downs were grass-covered cliffs which fell abruptly at
their edge to the rocks and the sea below. There, on many an evening, between
autumn and Christmas, Mary and I used to stroll; Mary in ankle boots and a
coat buttoned over her sisters' uniform, struggling with her starched nurse's
veil which threatened to take flight at each little gust of wind; myself wrapped
up well with my hands enveloped in two or three thicknesses of wool under
which they were still blue and cold where the normal circulation was impeded
by scar tissue. Sometimes the breeze rose up at sunset, and the air, freshened
and cold, was stimulating and peculiarly satisfying. I felt my muscles flexing
and wanted to shout wildly and to sing.

The last slanting rays of the sun tinged with golden light the silver-grey
patches that covered the steel grey sea. When heavy grey clouds crossed
the path of the sunbeams they were frilled with gold lace and haloed in the

light trapped behind. Usually, the sea looked cold and forbidding when we approached the edge of the cliff and looked down at it breaking on the dark rocks three hundred feet below. While conscious of its grim aspect, I felt, as so many of us must have felt from time to time during this and other wars, that I ought to be eternally grateful for this very quality of grimness. All through history it has periodically saved us from invasion.

Mary was good and comforting company. Since leaving school she had spent eight hard years in hospitals and had never before known such comparatively easy conditions as she now enjoyed. She loved nursing. In particular she was devoted to work in the theatre, where she had assisted many leading surgeons. Here for the first time for years she had enough leisure to be able to think a little, and we did much of our thinking together and aloud. We soon developed a bond of sympathy which took me rather by surprise as I had for so long felt cut off from everyone and everything. She had been born in the Isle of Man and told me once she was sometimes called a Manx Minx.

Some nicknames are good caricatures, others are humorously and accurately descriptive. Manx Minx for Mary belonged to quite a different category. It was a good nickname because it was so obviously a complete contradiction of her character. It would have been difficult to find any woman with less feline characteristics than Mary. She was generous and sweet in all the things she said about other people. When she could find little to say that was good about anyone she was honest enough to admit it, but added that, she was sure that person had some attractive qualities which so far had not been apparent to her.

It was Mary who unobtrusively drew out from my inner self the feelings that troubled me. She alone at that time could encourage me to return to the normal life, for which I had begun to lose desire. England is so set in its habits, so contented with itself and so assured, that it seems almost indecent to introduce her to a new idea, or a new way of living. It was far more difficult for me to recover the semblance of normal life in England that it had been for me to feel at home and at ease in France. Perhaps in my Scottish blood I have inherited warmer feelings for France than are natural in most Anglo-Saxons. Anyway, I felt in those first few months back in England more of a foreigner than a Briton.

In England friends are made more slowly than in France, though they are made perhaps with greater discrimination. I believe that the English way is by far the best in the long run, for English friends are friends for life, whereas in France friendships easily made may often as easily be broken. However, the warmth of sudden friendship and the spontaneous acceptance of myself, a stranger, that I had encountered everywhere in France had delighted me; and for a long time, I felt that England was by contrast cold and rather dull.

Mary alone could break that feeling. She listened patiently to the long eulogies of France which I poured forth to her, and although she did not know France, and had no reason to love the French, she possessed a rich fount of sympathy and an inherent understanding of all nationalities that is rarely found in the English. Many a Pole or Czech would agree with me here. I had many good friends who would willingly have done what Mary did for me, yet not one of them succeeded as she did in penetrating the hard crust beneath which I jealously guarded my deepest emotions. She will be surprised if she reads this, for I am sure she does not know just how much she did for me in those first few months after I returned to England.

Sometimes we went together to the cinema or walked around the coast to tea in a neighbouring combe. Often we danced at the most luxurious of the hotels, and once we went to the ballet. Always she was the same – sympathetic and calm, smiling and gentle. Usually, we were two of a party of patients and nurses, for in this hospital nurses were encouraged to go out with the patients, partly as an essential part of the latters' recovery, and partly because it is the natural and obvious thing to do.

This South Devon town in those days knew nothing of war. There were still plenty of large hotels open to visitors and residents, for only a few had been commandeered by the services. The most luxurious of all was the most notorious as a haunt of escapists. I do not think this was in any way the fault of the management, who always welcomed patients from the hospital and other service visitors and gave us special attention and facilities. It just happened to be remarkably comfortable, and the escapists knew it. Attractively situated on a cliff overlooking the bay, it was still able to provide rich and appetising meals. There was always a number of service men and women staying there on leave, but even with special reductions the rates were prohibitive to any junior officer who depended solely on his, or her, service pay.

The only people who seemed able to afford to stay there for any length of time were the aforementioned escapists of all nationalities. There they sat in the lounge day after day, expensively dressed, overfed and bored. The women fed their lap dogs with scraps from the tea table, and their menfolk, who seemed little conscious of the selfishness of their existence in a country imperilled by war, drank their whiskies and smoked their cigars and talked of many things – no doubt among others of the profits they had amassed between and during wars. A few watched with interest the young, wounded airmen who came into dance with the nurses. Sometimes they tried to strike up a friendship with us, but not usually with much success, for few of us were in any mood to accept hospitality from people we could not help despising.

There were some among them, of course, who were charming, and had every right to enjoy an undisturbed life in their declining years. But they were few, and most of them were very old or invalids. The rest were just so many useless and unnecessary burdens to the national economy of which they had succeeded in cornering far more than their fair share. Some of them still ran cars and burnt up precious gallons of petrol which had been brought to this country at the cost of the lives of our gallant merchant seamen. The loss of life suffered to provide them with comfort did not appear to concern them. Their lives must remain undisturbed, others must make sacrifices for them. They would do nothing to help the country in which they lived safely. This was not their war.

At first when I danced there I felt very embarrassed. It seemed that all eyes were upon me and on my disfigurement. However, after the first two or three times it was no longer an ordeal, but a pleasure. All the same I never felt quite happy there, for when I saw all around me so many bloated and useless people, I could not forget the miseries I had left behind in France, and I felt ashamed to have any place in such luxury and indifference to the war at such a vital time.

You will remember how serious our national position was in the winter of 1941, and how many more great misfortunes were still in store for us.

A few of the families who lived in this South Devon town kept open house for the R.A.F. There were the MacLeod's, for instance, who gave a cocktail party for us every Sunday evening. They had practically adopted some of the patients and had provided a bus in which we could travel to and from the town every evening. This generosity was of the best kind – sincere and unobtrusive. Their only reward was the pleasure they gave to many of us. The Robinsons specialised in the entertainment of New Zealanders, but I went to this house once or twice with Mary. We had tea, and afterwards Mrs. Robinson, who was an exceptionally good pianist, entertained us for hours on end by playing Chopin to us. There were others who lavished money and attention on a selected few of the more attractive and interesting patients. On the whole, however, this South Devon town took little notice of the R.A.F. convalescent hospital, for few people there were wholeheartedly interested in us or in the war.

I enjoyed the musical afternoons particularly, for Mrs. Robinson played with great feeling and the music she made lived on in my memory, to recur at intervals for hours and even days afterwards. There are certain melodies which always haunt me. Each one has a number of associations, some sad, some gay. So it is that one particular ballad of Chopin will always bring back to my senses the memory of grim days in a dirty little town in France, brilliantly illuminated for an hour or two by a friend playing to me in a room full of junk.

Then there is a Tchaikowsky waltz, which for me has the most wonderful melody of all the music I have ever heard. I used to hear it in my head when I was confined, sick, hungry and lonely, in a bare room which was both ward and prison cell. I had been imprisoned by a country which I loved and for which I had been fighting, and I had almost despaired of ever being free and healthy again. The *Nachtmusik* of Mozart takes me back to a room in Lyons, a room that was almost as bare as my prison in Marseilles, yet its few furnishings were warm and its atmosphere *sympathique*. There are songs too, some of which I like and some that I hate, which recall different places, different people, different years. There are Gaelic laments and German *lieder*, songs from Italian opera, Hawaiian love songs and Cuban rhumbas, and a few – but very few, American blues!

On an earlier page I have said that I had no wish to pick up the scattered threads of my past life in England and elsewhere. But I was forced to do so from time to time. On one of these occasions fate was kind to me, for it put me once more in contact with Norman.

He arrived in the hospital with one leg in plaster, for he had suffered compound fractures of both the tibia and fibula after crash landing on his way home from a night bombing raid on Germany.

Norman joined the flight I then commanded about two years before the war. He was a Canadian, and one of that select number of Dominion airmen who had left their homeland to join the R.A.F. in the days of peace. He was a keen and sound pilot and had developed through many hours of peacetime and wartime flying into a first-rate bomber captain. He was inclined to be shy and over sensitive, which made his quality of great courage the more admirable; for his sensitiveness excited an imagination which was vivid enough for him to understand fully the risks he took.

In France, before the *phoney* war had finished, we celebrated his twenty-first birthday; and certainly, he looked no more than his age then. Immediately after I had been shot down during the Battle of France I was replaced by Don Garland – who won the V.C. for leading three Battles in a suicide attack which succeeded in destroying the bridges at Maastricht, over which the German panzer divisions poured on their way to France. Norman took over the flight and carried on the tradition inspired by Don Garland. He bombed by day and by night, sometimes with air force fighters as cover but usually leading two or three Battles unprotected except by their single rear guns. But somehow he survived – partly, perhaps, because he had my old observer to assist him. With the others he carried on, so that although there was little material result from the attacks, a tradition for courage under the most hopeless conditions was nourished in France and bore fruit later on in the Battle of Britain, as now in the Battle of Europe.

When the squadron was evacuated from one airfield after another as the Germans advanced, Norman was always one of the last to leave. He had developed a degree of conscientiousness more often found in a man of maturity. He grew up in those few weeks of continual fighting in France. Flying by night and by day and seldom sleeping for long, he was too worn out to think a great deal, until the return to England of the Battle squadrons sometime after the evacuation from Dunkirk.

Even after his return, when ragged, tired and dirty he at last found a little respite, it did not last for long, for there was still work to be done. The squadron had to be re-equipped – this time with Wellingtons. Norman was given a flight to command and had to train himself and a number of new pilots to fly the new twin-engine aircraft which were so different from the single-engine Battles. For over a year he was continually operating over enemy territory without a real break, until he ended up in hospital with his leg badly fractured. He bombed Brest and Lorient and nearly every one of the German towns that were attacked throughout that period. The example he had set to those who followed him in France was only eclipsed by his leadership in England. Twice he was mentioned in despatches and recommended for decoration, but for some reason decorations did not come his way. He did not particularly want them – but he must have felt that he had been left out. He was too self-effacing to make any enquiries.

When last I had seen him he was young and boyish in appearance. It was May 10th, 1940; the day that I was shot down. He was lively and had an excess of energy to spend. His manner was alternately bold and diffident, riotous and considerate. Inherent in him there was a graciousness and sympathy which one felt radiating from him in his more serious moments. He was tall and spare; and his carriage was straight. His light brown hair was brushed back – perhaps in an attempt to destroy its natural waviness. This exposed a good forehead and exaggerated the length of his face. His nose was thin and straight, and his cheekbones high and pronounced.

A certain eager yet shy humour was expressed in his grey eyes, which looked with a frank steady gaze into one's own. I had just come back from a short visit to London with an orderly. The train arrived at the station well after midnight, and it was after one o'clock when I reached the second-floor duty room, and reported to Fluffy, who was the sister on night duty. She told me that a great friend of mine had arrived. Margaret took me to his room, and I found Norman fast asleep. It was a strange sensation to see him lying there asleep; and then, as we shook him, to see him wakening to look up at me. No time seemed to have intervened, yet I was so different, and he was so much older.

I felt suddenly and overwhelmingly conscious of my disfigurement and my mutilated hands. When last he had seen me I had been reasonably good looking – at any rate I had had good hair and teeth and was fit and strong. As soon as Norman was fully awake he looked away from my hands quickly, and we began to talk. Instinctively he knew to fill my pipe which hung empty from the side of my mouth. Then he stuck it back between my teeth and lighted it. Sleep and the night were forgotten. On our watches were recorded the hours that passed while we talked, but we ourselves were outside and beyond time, or so it seemed. We were back in France; we lived through the Battle of France and the months that followed Dunkirk; we were over Bremen and Brest, Hamburg and Berlin; we were caught in searchlights and were flying through opaque blankets of cloud in the bitter cold of night at great heights, then we were landing together in East Anglia in the pale light that follows the dawn.

Norman told me about his crash; how, after flying for six hours and bombing Essen, he had a double engine failure when just back over the English coast, and had been forced to land, for he was too low to bale out. There was a full moon and its pale light picked out a road lined with trees. Norman decided to crash land on the road at a point where the trees fanned out on either side. At the last moment he saw that there was a bridge crossing the road just ahead of him; he pulled the nose of the Wellington up sufficiently high to prevent a head on crash, but as the belly of the aircraft hit the top of the bridge he was thrown from his seat through the cockpit cover and landed twenty or thirty yards in front of the crash.

When he regained consciousness he was aware of a nasty bump on the top of his head. A few seconds later he found that his left leg was immovable, and that any attempt to move it caused excruciating agony. Some of the crew had been killed; he felt very sick about that; but knew in his heart that it was not his fault. He had done the best he could to save them. When he told me of this a grey look spread over his face, and for a moment he seemed to become an old man. Clearly he had not yet recovered from that shock.

As he lay out in the moonlight waiting for an ambulance to arrive, a crowd collected, as crowds do at the most impossible hours and in the most inaccessible places on such occasions. In the crowd there was a policeman and a number of Home Guards. Norman's broken leg lay across a slight dip in the ground, so that when the policeman trod on it by mistake the fracture was changed from simple to compound. Before the ambulance arrived one of the Home Guards had repeated this mistake, and when eventually they laid him on the stretcher the jagged ends of the broken bones were protruding from the flesh of his leg.

It was several months later that Norman arrived at the convalescent hospital. He stayed for about two months, until his leg had healed sufficiently for him to return to flying – this time as an instructor. After meeting Norman again there stirred in me all kinds of old longings which for the time being at any rate I felt I ought not to possess. Nevertheless, it was very good to see him again.

The convalescent hospital had an atmosphere which I believe was unique. It had been created partly by the Matron, and it was due to her careful fostering that it continued. There were many other people who each in his or her own different way contributed a vital part to this atmosphere, but they would have been badly hampered without the humour and understanding of the Matron. The atmosphere was one of freedom from unnecessary and tiresome restrictions. Air crews wounded on operations or under training mixed freely with older men in need of a rest, and with W.A.A.F. officers suffering from many different complaints. In this way it was possible for the sick and despondent to be refreshed by contact with the more lively wounded – many of whom although in plaster were still able to get about and take part in organised games and exercises.

Over this *pot pourri* of all types of R.A.F. and W.A.A.F. officers of many different nationalities the Matron cast a motherly eye. She was a woman of enormous energy and great determination. She was short and slim and held herself square. Her chin and her tread were both firm. The searching look in her eyes was relieved by a humorous twinkle. She walked and talked briskly but had always enough time to spare to stop and chat to any patient who did not appear to be quite at ease. She always wore the R.A.F. matrons' uniform.

This consists of an air force blue dress of the same material as an officer's uniform buttoned up to the chin with small gilt buttons; over this and around the shoulders a small cape of the same material decorated with R.A.F. medical badges and any medal ribbons to which the owner is entitled; between the cuff and the elbow badges of rank – two thick red stripes centred by a thick white stripe; a veil of starched white linen coming to a point at the back just between the shoulder blades, with embroidered blue R.A.F. wings just above the point; black shoes and black silk stockings. Among her decorations she wore the R.R.C. and the O.B.E. and an active service ribbon – the latter earned in Palestine.

The C.O. was a reserved and unobtrusive man. He seldom contacted the patients except on the golf course or during his weekly round of inspection. He confined himself largely to the routine of his command, which no doubt was a full-time job in itself. This left the greater part of the welfare of the patients in the capable hands of the Matron. She in turn delegated her duties in all directions, but always kept in personal touch with the patients themselves.

Years of service in the nursing profession often leave a woman severe or sour, but those who escape severity and sourness usually emerge with outstandingly human qualities. Whereas many middle-aged, unmarried nurses do become sour, those who escape this often develop a delightfully rich and sympathetically broad understanding of other people's difficulties. Goodness knows that they see enough of the trouble of other people's lives, for hospital patients usually mercilessly expose their characters sooner or later during the worst hours of their pain. Our matron had survived the risks of sourness and had emerged from the danger period to a mature understanding. Her principles and standards were high, yet she was broadminded and tolerant of human weakness.

Any tendency to severity was relieved by a keen sense of humour. She loved to go out to tea-dances with her patients; dancing was one of her favourite relaxations and she danced with dignity and grace. She was equally fond of walking, particularly if the route lay along the path that skirted the cliff edge and led to one or other of the little combes that lay within walking distance of the hospital. She was good company for many reasons. Perhaps the main one was the fact that she could enter easily into the thoughts and feelings of people of all ages. She was a good listener; and on the other hand, her reminiscences were well worth listening to.

Sometimes in the afternoon when tired of working at my Dictaphone, I sat by the window and gazed over the golf course and out to sea. I used to think with nostalgia of the country which lay beyond the waters.

My life in the hospital, while it lasted, was good and pleasant. I was doing something I wanted to do, and I was recovering my health and putting on weight. I was among friends and had many reasons to feel satisfied. Yet I was unhappy. Not because I felt sorry for myself, nor because my married life had gone wrong, but because I had developed an obsession.

I was obsessed by thoughts of France. She had become like a mistress whom I loved dearly yet could not reach. I felt that I had deserted her, that I should never have returned to England and comfort until the war was over. These were serious feelings, and they still persist. It was, and still is, quite useless for me to try, by reason, to make myself accept, as a fact, the knowledge that I would have done no good by staying in France. Life seemed too good and undisturbed in England.

It seemed indecent to be well fed and putting on weight, to have plenty of tobacco to smoke, to have leisure and comfort, to feel an occasional glow of deep contentment. There, not so very far away, across the sea, lay France, prostrate under tyranny, and half starving. I loved France as a man loves a beautiful and intelligent mistress who has given him solace and understanding. My heart ached at the memory of the suffering I had seen there. I saw again the queues of small, shivering children, waiting for their paltry rations of blue skimmed milk. I felt again the cold unheated rooms in winter. I felt the hunger and the hopelessness which French men and women were feeling.

In spite of all my friends, here in England I felt lonely, I could not readily adapt myself to the calm air of confidence that prevailed all around me. I could think only of the misery that occupation by the Germans had brought to France. I was disturbed, too, by fear for the safety of the many friends of all nationalities whom I had left behind me in France. How, I wondered, were they managing to scrape together enough food? Were they still carrying on the multitudinous tasks of underground resistance, or had many of them been shot and imprisoned? How frustrated I felt in my desire to help them! I dared not, in the interests of their own safety, try to contact them, and there was, literally, nothing that I could do for them. Most of all, I feared for the safety of those who outwardly – even demonstratively – were pro-German, and pro-Vichy, while under cover of this mask, they were working hard for the downfall of the oppressors, and for the success of allied arms when the day of liberation arrived. Would they, I wondered, be the first victims of patriotic Frenchmen, unaware of their true role?

Each day that passed meant greater comfort for me and greater peril for my friends in France, and I was powerless to alter that state of affairs. One thing only I could do, and that was to write about France, so that as far as was in my power, I might present a case for her which would, perhaps, encourage sympathy for that great country among Englishmen and Americans. There was little I could say, it is true, for considerations of security would necessitate the omission of the material which could best prove my point – that the French were still a great people. Yet that little I was determined to write, in the hope that the discerning reader would use his imagination to read what lay between the lines. I felt that I had something to say and knew that I would know no peace of mind until I had said it.

There was another reason which spurred me on to write. Experiences such as mine fall seldom to anyone who is willing and anxious to discuss them openly. Most people who have been badly wounded, or have suffered a painful experience, are only too anxious to forget it as quickly as possible. I felt quite differently. I felt that my experiences should be made common property, so that others might learn from them something to their advantage. I could not define clearly in my mind just what exactly my message was to be but felt that by writing freely it would appear.

Chapter 11

Third Eyelid

At the beginning of spring, I returned to the Plastic Unit. I was sorry to leave the South Devon town, but glad to get on with the job of having my operations again. My book was finished except for a few alterations yet to be made. I had put on about three stone in weight and felt fit and comparatively happy. My left hand still gave me trouble and had not completely healed up; clearly it would be necessary to graft new skin over the open wound, which was still an ugly sight.

My right hand was still exceedingly tender, but I could already use it to quite a large extent. My new upper eyelids had shrunk considerably, and eyelashes which had once been stuck up on my forehead, were now flourishing on the ends of the new lids. My left eye still watered a little; but I could now bear to look at a strong light without dark glasses. There were still many more operations before me, before I could be declared finished, from the plastic surgeon's point of view. My legs were stronger, and I could flex my knees about thirty degrees. One knee was only thinly covered with skin and broke down repeatedly – perhaps here too a skin graft would be necessary.

This time when I arrived in Ward 3 at the Plastic Unit, I found many familiar faces. Peter was still there, lying in the corner bed, surrounded by books. He contrived to read, using the two thumbs which alone protruded from the bandages that covered his hands, for turning over the pages, and holding the book in position. He was still unable to walk, and when he was taken out, had to be pushed about in a wheelchair. He was in good form, although he still suffered considerable pain from time to time. Further operations had been carried out on Geoffrey's hands. Now some of the fingers that had been curled up into his palm were almost straight again. They were held in an outstretched position by splints made from a transparent plastic substance.

Sister was still there, as she has always been each time I have come back to Ward 3 in the course of over two years. It was comforting and pleasant to see all these familiar faces again, for a hospital ward is never very inviting to a stranger, until he has accustomed himself to his surroundings. Some of the nurses had left, others still remained. I had already grown to know most of them. One in particular, I admired.

She was a V.A.D. and wore service stripes for the last war as well as the present. She was a widow and had a grown-up daughter who was also a V.A.D. and worked in one of the other wards. The most impressive thing about her was her unobtrusiveness. She was completely self-effacing. There was an air of calm efficiency about her, and the times when I appreciated her most were when I was feeling at my worst, for then she would nurse me – as she nursed us all – gently and devotedly, knowing instinctively what was the most urgent need, and how to supply it. She was a very sweet person, and this was reflected in a certain softness in her eyes. When she laughed, it was quietly. What a wonderful thing it is to meet a woman who is content to serve humbly, the hard way, as she did, instead of aspiring to a far easier form of war service. I knew so many women who, younger than her, were doing absolutely nothing, so far, for the war. When this war is over, she will, no doubt, slip quietly away, possibly un-thanked, but those of us who were nursed by her will never forget her, and the fine standard she set for us all to aspire to.

Soon after I had arrived back in the ward, I was wheeled into the theatre again for my second plastic operation, this time to get my third eyelid. The space below my left eye was a half-moon of red, for the lower eyelid had disappeared, and the skin of my face had dragged it down, turning the lower end of the eye socket inside out. Below this, on the edge of the crescent, my eyelashes still grew. It was necessary, therefore, to make an incision just below the line of the eyelash and to graft a new eyelid from there, upwards, to meet the top lid when closed. The skin was shaved from my right upper arm, and the graft was sewn into position, pressed firmly against my eyeball by a moulding of stent of the exact shape required, covered first with a piece of marine sponge, then oily gauze soaked in orange-coloured acriflavine emulsion, and lastly securely bound up with a crepe bandage.

This may sound quite a simple process, but in fact it is extremely difficult, and is a most delicate operation. There are very few plastic surgeons in the world who are capable of carrying it out successfully.

The operation was a complete success. After the bandages had been removed, I saw that my eye would now close completely. In a few days time the giant lid had shrunk almost to shape. Further shrinking made it fit exactly, and at last I was completely free from watering eyes. This operation meant a complete relief from eye irritation, and the comfort this brought to me can hardly be imagined.

In the days that followed this operation, I began to find my way about the hospital, and visited the town. Petrol was still available in small quantities, for short excursions into the country. The major, veteran of the Boer War, used to take parties of patients out for drives in his Railton. It was very comfortable, and the trips were pleasant. It was good to see something of the surrounding country in this way. He drove us through wooded lanes and peaceful villages. Spring had begun and was everywhere in evidence.

The fields were a fresh new green. Buds were bursting in the hedgerows, and below last autumn's dead leaves primroses and violets were struggling to push their first shoots through the soft heavy mould. Somewhere along the route the major would pull up outside an inn, and we would go into the bar to drink beer, talk and eat sandwiches. The local publicans had got to know us well and were particularly well disposed towards us. We were a strange sight, some of us badly disfigured, with the added patchiness caused by plastic operations in their early stages. Few of us could handle with ease our tankards and glasses of beer, yet these parties were usually very cheerful.

Back in the Railton we used to argue politics and sociology with the major. The arguments were interesting, for we were advocating modern and somewhat revolutionary views, as against the more staid and settled ideas of the major. He stood up gamely under the weight of our arguments, and usually succeeded in getting in the last word. Most of us believed that radical changes in national and international ways of life were needed, and that now was the time to clamour for them. The major, while agreeing with the principle of most of our arguments, believed that our suggested reforms would have to be tempered with reason, born of long experience. To me he was representative of the old school; his views did not always seem to be quite logical, but one had to give him credit for a wealth of experience, which had begun years before any of us had been born.

This southern town boasted two cinemas; one stood by itself, but the other was part of a large establishment including a dance hall, an officers' club, a restaurant and a bar. This establishment was managed by Bill.[15] He took a special personal interest in our welfare. At the bar he would stand and drink with

---

[15] Bill Gardner. Bill was the manager of the Whitehall Theatre in London Road, East Grinstead. So welcoming was Bill, the Whitehall's owners, and its staff, to the Guinea Pigs that this large entertainment complex, which included a cinema and a ballroom, became known as 'Ward III's outpost in the town'. (See E.R. Mayhew, *The Reconstruction of Warriors* (Frontline Books, Barnsley, 2010), pp.158-9).

us, but he always had one eye on those of us who tended to drink too much. He contributed very largely to our happiness while we were in the neighbourhood. Whenever we felt particularly conscious of being ugly and deformed, we always knew that there was a welcome waiting for us at Bill's, and that he would soon laugh away any tendency we had towards gloom or depression.

Many houses were thrown open to us. In them we were never allowed to feel in any way peculiar. We were treated as members of the family, and from the contacts we made friendships grew which are unlikely ever to be broken. Here in this southern town, there was never any suggestion that disfigurement should be concealed, and that the disfigured should be confined to hospital until they had completed their beauty treatment; quite the contrary. Inspired largely by McIndoe himself, we were encouraged to circulate freely, no matter how bad our physical condition appeared, and the result was a complete success. I can only look back with horror at the examples that I had seen elsewhere in the past of attempts to conceal the disfigured. Here in this southern town, morale was kept high. I am sure that no one who saw us failed to be sobered by this evidence of the horror of war; and yet, seeing how cheerful we were, could not have felt despondent.

It is not easy for young men, who had possessed good and sound bodies, to accept disfigurement and the loss of physical independence. It was not easy for them to steel themselves to going out again in public. But the effort once made, under so much encouragement, was more than worthwhile. They soon realised that few people were rude enough to stare at them; and they always knew that their disfigurement was not considered dishonourable. They realised, too, that there was no cause for despair, and that by appearing in public, they were keeping the public aware of the realities of war. Yet in spite of all this, those first sorties into the world outside the hospital were painful, especially for the youngest amongst us.

Without hands, for instance, it was impossible to do anything without assistance. It was embarrassing to have someone pouring beer down your throat, wiping your mouth, blowing your nose, handling your money. It was even more embarrassing to have to make for the gentlemen's cloakroom in pairs. Naturally no young man experienced such a loss of his independence without resenting it strongly, for it made him as helpless as a small child and robbed him of all his dignity. But the resentment passed away – slowly at first, but steadily all the same – with the passage of time. There was always a funny side to it all; and I have met few R.A.F. crews who possessed no sense of humour.

The work of people like Bill, and all the others who accepted us so naturally, is quite immeasurable. They helped us unobtrusively. They made us feel normal again. They helped us to regain – if we had lost it – our self-respect. We shall always be grateful to them.

Somewhere between this southern town and the Ashdown Forest there lies a broad green valley. Shaped like a great green bowl, it is filled with paddocks of lush grass, interrupted here and there by fields of plough or growing corn according to season. It is fringed with woods of beech, oak and elm, which overflow from the skyline irregularly into the paddocks below. The woods that thus enclose the valley mark the boundaries of a single property; and wherever he may stand in the valley the owner looking about him can see only his own land. This makes the valley appear to be shut off from the outside world, and it is easy to forget that a public highway passes through its centre. It is easier still to forget that London lies only one hour's journey away.

The paddocks are separated from each other by hedges, out of which here and there grow great gnarled elms and sturdy oaks – standing out like sentinels on guard. Halfway up the eastern side spreads a long orchard, which merges with the woods beyond and above. Some of the paddocks are dotted with black, black-and-white, and dun-coloured shapes – for the owner's farm has herds of several different breeds of cattle. Other paddocks are grazed by sleek thoroughbreds from the racing stud, the stables of which can be seen on the west side of the valley. Cameronian, the famous Derby winner was born and bred here. Not far from the stables are the kennels where pedigree greyhounds are bred and trained for coursing. Near the kennels stand the main farm buildings. Behind and beyond these buildings stretches the poultry farm.

The owner's house stands on terraced ground near the summit of the south side of the valley. It is an imposing and beautiful home and provides a fitting memorial to some of the finest details of English domestic architecture of Tudor times. It is built of old grey stone and the gabled roofs are covered with Tudor tiles. The tall chimneys are also Tudor, as are the latticed windows set in stone frames. The central building encloses a courtyard. Two wings spread out to form with the central portion a three-sided hollow square. Inside the central portion there is a great hall which was once a part of Dutton Hall in Cheshire. Here it has been completely reconstructed, using the original oak beams. Unlike most houses built in the Tudor style, the interior of Dutton Homestall is warm and comfortable. It is essentially a home.

In the days of peace this house was the setting for big parties. Since the war it has been used variously – as a Red Cross convalescent hospital for officers; as a rest centre for operational fighter pilots of the R.A.F.; and now once more as a hospital. The owners have now retired to one wing. There they have entertained and housed from time to time many of my fellow-patients from the Plastic Unit. During my time in hospital, I spent many happy days there.

There were many other houses in which I was made to feel at home. One of them was a great grey Georgian mansion, situated within its own vast park, not far from the town. The exterior was to me rather forbidding, but the grounds were beautiful – great wooded parklands stretching out behind the house from the terrace and the enclosed flower and vegetable gardens to the lake and the woods beyond. Inside it was furnished lavishly – but with excellent taste. In particular the paintings were delightful. Here lived a Jewish family who kept open house for many of the patients.

There on many Sundays I have enjoyed their hospitality and sat in the deep couches set square around the log fire, drinking, chatting and sometimes listening spellbound to the symphonies of Tchaikowsky played on the great radiogram. Anti-semitism is perhaps the worst of medieval evils unearthed by Adolf Hitler and his team of illiterate barbarians. It was good to be here amongst Jews in England, who had become absorbed into our national life. It was good to find them justly proud of their race. I felt grateful to them for all their hospitality, and for the practical generosity they bestowed on us and on the hospital.

Another house that I visited frequently was an attractive red brick building partly covered by creepers and enclosed by beautiful gardens. A family who had lived for years in the East had retired here. The father was a keen amateur gardener, and his glasshouses and vegetable gardens were models of perfection. The mother was more concerned with the flowers. She it was who provided the blaze of colour in Ward 3, for every Sunday morning, and once or twice more during the week, she arrived with arms full of flowers cut from her garden, arranged them in vases, and set them out in the wards. She played an active part on the patients' welfare committee. Perhaps she was the most popular of our visitors, due as much to her whimsical sense of fun as to her inherent kindness and sympathy.

Chapter 12

Thigh to Hand

My next and third operation was carried out soon after the second. This time my hands were grafted with new skin. This covered up the ugly open wound on my left palm, and reinforced and revitalised the weak scar-skin on my right palm. It was also hoped to obtain at the same time more movement in my wrists, for I could not bend either hand backwards. Unfortunately, this was unsuccessful, for the tendons reaching to my palms from my forearms had been shortened by burns.

However, the main function of the operation was successful, and soon the grafts had taken. My left hand was covered with skin from the wrist to half ways down the palm, and my right hand, similarly grafted, was revitalised. The colour of both hands had been a blotchy red and purple, but this operation so improved the circulation of the blood supply that both hands returned to a fairly healthy pink – except under conditions of extreme cold.

The donor areas – from which the new skin was taken – were at the top of my left thigh; one on the outside, and one inside, near the groin. The healing of these donor areas and the grafts was completed in about ten days.

Operations on the hands are usually succeeded by acute pain. Nerves are often cut, and great pressure is maintained on the grafted area by tight crepe bandages. This causes a heavy burning pain which spreads right up the arm. So great is the satisfaction experienced, however, by realising that each operation is a step onwards in the direction of independence and normality, that the pain becomes of secondary importance. Moreover, it can be stopped by drugs. Whether or not it is wise to take drugs for minor spells of pain I do not know. Personally, I am inclined to believe that a certain amount of endurable pain provides such a stimulus to the powers of endurance that it should not be stopped. However, I am not sure that this is particularly good for the nervous system. Anyway, following my own inclinations, I seldom ask for drugs until the pain is preventing me from thinking of other things, or stopping my sleep for a whole night.

Although there seems to be no mechanism in the human brain for remembering past pain, every new experience instantly recalls a number of sensations that are familiar, so that it is possible to say afterwards exactly which form of pain was the most acute. So far my experience has been almost entirely confined to wound pains – and those have been on the surface. I know of none that are worse than a very severe stomach-ache. This is based on experience of a range of pain that has covered nearly every part of the surface of my body. To me pain that is internal is more alarming than pain that is superficial. Perhaps this is because to the layman internal pain is more mysterious in its origin. Certainly, it is possible to become accustomed to pain, for I now find that I can sleep through a degree of it which two or three years ago would have worked me up into a nervous and sleepless condition. When the exact reason is known why a certain pain exists one is instantly comforted – always excepting a case when one knows that it should not have occurred, and that the mistake is going to lead to disastrous results!

It is, therefore, I believe, a good idea to get to know as much as possible about one's wounds, and the nervous system that surrounds them. Then when one has acute pain in a certain place it is possible to say: "Oh well, that's such and such a series of nerve endings, and it will be all right in so many days." I have found this way of treating pain a great comfort to me. Usually, I deliberately exaggerate to myself the probable length of time it will last, and by this child's trick I am ridiculously gratified when it stops short of the time limit I have set.

There is a kind of brotherhood that exists in a hospital between patients when they are suffering. More often than not it is a silent one. One becomes accustomed to detecting suffering by the way different individuals adapt themselves to bear it. A few will groan and complain, others become nervous and bad tempered, some who are normally demonstrative become reserved, and so on. Most people give very little sign, and it is only by observing a certain unusual pallor in their faces, a firmer set of the mouth and a slightly strained look in eyes that have lost their lustre, that any indication of a period of suffering can be noticed. It is also true that few people can bear to talk very much when they are in pain.

For myself, I seem to get rather silent and often bad tempered. The bad temper is due, I believe, more to a liver reaction than to the pain itself. Certainly, I do not object to lying in bed, and am quite content to lie for hours day after day ruminating and reading; so much so, that the more practical side of my nature usually urges me to clamour to be allowed to get up as soon as possible before I sink into a torpor.

Getting up after an operation as soon as possible is, I am sure, the best way of getting better. To begin with, as we all of us normally spend the majority of our waking hours erect on our legs, or sitting up on our behinds, when we lie in bed the liver becomes sluggish. Few things have a worse effect both on morale and healing than a sluggish liver. After walking even only a few paces in the ward, or sitting up in a chair, it is much easier to sleep at night.

One of the most unpleasant of the before and after operation treatment is the administration of the drug, prontosil, as a means of preventing infection of the newly grafted area. It is administered in tablet form at regular intervals for a time varying somewhere between a day before and three days after an operation. The main tedious effects are a loss of appetite and an unpleasant sensation of nausea. In some cases, the patient turns a decided blue or green, and suffers from dreary depression. He often develops a foul temper. Fortunately, I seem to be largely immune from these unpleasant effects. No doubt my turn will come to experience them, but so far I have never turned a sickly shade of blue-green like Geoffrey and Peter and many of the others. In fact, I have reacted in no noticeable way at all. My appetite has so far remained normal, and I have felt completely at ease while taking prontosil.

After the operation the original dressings were changed by Sister or one of the staff nurses. They took particular care to prevent any chance infectious germs reaching the new graft. They covered their mouths and noses with operating masks, and their hands with rubber gloves. Before beginning to replace each dressing they carefully removed forceps and bowls from the boiling water of a sterilising tank. This tank was installed in the dressing room – a small compartment partitioned off from the end of the ward. Sterilised gauze was kept in drums which had been brought along from the main theatre sterilising ovens. In spite of all this care, streptococci infection did occasionally occur, but it was not the fault of the nurses. Its incidence was very slight in view of the vast number of dressings changed daily.

Sister, Pam and Johnny, were all experts in the art of dressing grafts and burns. They worked quickly, and neatly, and seldom caused any pain. They were proud of their work and took infinite pains to avoid the destruction of skin and tissue when it could be avoided. They removed stitches deftly; dressed and bandaged neatly. Thank God each one of them possessed a sense of humour. Like most of the other members of the Plastic Unit medical and nursing staffs, they tolerated and even encouraged suggestions from their patients as to the best way of treating each dressing problem. They were infinitely patient when we were irascible, and remarkably tolerant of our various individual whims.

Ideas still seemed to be fluid regarding the length of time it was necessary to leave in position the bandages that kept pressure on different types of graft. Usually, dressings on thin skin grafts were removed after two or three days, and seldom left on for more than five. When the bandages were removed, there was an instantaneous relief of pressure. This came as a great relief. Next the gauze was picked off with forceps and the stent moulding removed by cutting the stiches which secured it in position. Finally, the graft was exposed. It was then carefully examined. If satisfactory it was dressed with *tulle gras* and gauze soaked in saline solution. Sometimes it had healed sufficiently to be left exposed to the air, in which case it was painted scarlet with mercurochrome. A day or so later the stitches were removed, and the graft repainted with mercurochrome. When there no longer remained any danger of the graft becoming septic and breaking down, the mercurochrome would be washed off. The patient then was conscious of himself as the proud – or disgruntled – owner of a new patch, delicate in its shade of fresh pink but robust in its new role as eyelid, cheek, palm, knee, etc.

So much for Thiersch grafts – which are those made from thin skin. There are other much more complicated grafts, which involve bones and tissue as well as skin. (If you have the patience to read on, you will find some of them described in later chapters.)

When the graft has healed completely it is massaged gently with warm oil. This is done in the physiotherapy department by Miss Stevenson[16] and her team of trained *masseuses*. It prevents the graft from becoming too hard and dry and limits the formation of gathered – or keloid – scars. There are many people who possess skins that show no tendency to form scars, but others scar very easily. These scars form into hard lumpy lines which later have to be softened down and eliminated by X-ray treatment; or, if this fails, cut out during a future operation. Although oil massage cannot prevent the formation of keloid scars when a patient scars easily, it is invaluable for borderline cases.

The physiotherapy department of the hospital had only just been established in its new building a week or two before my third operation took place. Built of red brick to harmonise with the permanent building of the

---

[16] Miss W.M. Stevenson. By early 1941, it had been realised that the creation of a physiotherapy department at the QVH was 'one of the most pressing needs'. The Ministry of Health duly made two appointments, one of whom was Stevenson.

cottage hospital, it was surrounded by flower beds and vegetables. Inside it was clean, well lighted and airy.

In one room, along the polished parquet floor, couches were set out in rows each one of which could be isolated by dark curtains. On the walls were fitted mirrors, exercising bars, pulleys and weights. Heat ray lamps stood on their enamelled stands near the couches. In one corner there were small tanks filled with hot paraffin wax. This was used for softening up the burnt hands of patients before they were massaged with warm oil. In another corner stood the complicated electrical installations which provided shock treatment for moving tired muscles until they had regained their strength.

One door led to Miss Stevenson's office, another out into a passage at the end of which was a room filled with benches. At that time this room was used for weaving, model making and other gentle occupational therapy-treatment calculated to occupy the hands and minds of patients who, left to themselves, might become depressed and bored. It has now been converted into a tiny shadow factory, where patients can exercise their hands and minds in the assembly of parts for aircraft instruments. For this they are paid a standard rate per hour's work. This is a very popular idea, the work done is good, and the whole arrangement is a most satisfactory and practical way of occupying time, exercising wounded hands and making a patient realise that he has not by any means lost his place in the war effort and in industry after the war. In this way he soon realises – if he has not already come to that conclusion – that physical disabilities can be surmounted by concentration, and the exercise of patience and ingenuity.

The establishment of this little shadow factory of our own in the hospital in no way reflects unfavourably on the other more gentle forms of occupational therapy. Embroidery, the making of string belts with strings of different colours, model making and so on, still continue. They are undoubtedly excellent as far as they go, particularly for the bedridden. But the idea of the factory provides an advance in rehabilitation methods, for it offers a definite proof that normal civilian employment is possible to patients still undergoing operational treatment. It would be very satisfying to see this principle adopted in all other hospitals, for it carries the ideas of rehabilitation from the hobby to the work stage.

There are many other ways of occupying one's time in this hospital. Instruction is given in a large variety of subjects. There are libraries of books in English and several other languages. The electrician and the engineer, the wireless operator and the air navigator can resume their broken studies.

Languages, typewriting and shorthand are taught. The work is supervised by a welfare staff consisting of an R.A.F. education officer and a flight-sergeant physical-training instructor.

When the donor area from which skin has been shaved for a skin graft is beginning to heal, the dressing is usually removed and a fresh one applied. This can be a painful process but is made as easy as possible by the Bathroom Boys.

The Bathroom Boys have a character, language and method of working which is entirely their own. Working under the Bathroom Sergeant (now a flight sergeant), they rule over the saline baths and are a law unto themselves. Here they daily handle badly burned patients of both sexes and all ages. They remove all bandages and gently help the patient into the great bath of warm salt water kept at an even blood heat temperature. There the dressings soak and come away with a little assistance from the Boys who, masked and rubber gloved, lean over the edge of the bath with forceps in their hands.

When all the old dressings have been taken away they gently bathe the wounds, until they are clean and pink. Then they help the patient out of the bath and lay him down on a rubber covered trolley. Having dried the unaffected parts of the patient, they powder his wounds with sulphanilamide and cover them with soft, greasy *tulle gras*. Then they soak strips of gauze in saline solution and spread them over the *tulle gras*. Finally, the patient is bandaged and walks or is wheeled back to the ward, according to his condition. The worst cases are wheeled right into the bathroom in their beds.

This is the most up to date method of treating burns. It is ironical that it should have been used often in France – where *tulle gras* was invented – yet was never applied to me. This, of course, was due to the fact that while I was under treatment in France, medical stores were scarce, hospitals over-crowded and conditions extremely chaotic, due to the sudden debacle. As it was, in France my legs took over a year to heal, for each time they were dressed new tissue was destroyed and much blood was lost. It is unlikely that they would have taken longer than three months to heal had I received the Bathroom Boys' attention. My fingers might well have been partially saved, and all the suffering I had undergone limited to a small amount of pain and some discomfort.

In the saline bath, tissue is preserved. Dressings are never left on for more than twenty-four hours at the outside, and since they are kept soft, moist and greasy, they do not stick to the wounds and so prevent healing. The *tulle gras* consists of open mesh net impregnated with Vaseline, Peruvian balsam and halibut liver oil which nourishes the wounds and accelerates healing.

The saline gauze keeps the wound moist and protects it from infection. The sulphanilamide powder fights and destroys any germs it encounters and reduces or prevents the formation of pus. It is a wonderful treatment, especially when it is conscientiously and carefully applied. It is shameful that even now, more than four years since the first application of this revolutionary new treatment, the older methods are *still* employed in countless hospitals in Britain and elsewhere.

The Bathroom Sergeant has been in charge of the two saline bathrooms ever since they were installed. He is by trade a medical orderly of the R.A.F. Working under him he has a corporal and a number of orderlies. There is also one W.A.A.F. orderly, Betty. The work is hard but wholly worthwhile. It demands an even temper, and an absence of nerves. Some patients are very trying; some who are very extensively burnt take more than an hour to treat. This is a great ordeal for patient and orderlies alike. The Bathroom Boys and Betty have developed a particular blend of patience, firmness and tolerance. They never get ruffled, and when a patient can bear it – as nearly all can – he is ragged mercilessly from the moment he enters until the moment he leaves the bathroom. They have some strange customs and certain rites, such as the "walnut"; these are secret to all but the fully initiated.

Not all the patients of this hospital are in the services. The two large wards and a number of private rooms of the hospital building are still devoted to the treatment of local patients. One of the huts is full of women and children suffering from burns or facial injuries. One of the finest plastic dental centres in this country is housed on the premises, and wonderful work is done there by a staff of dental surgeons specialising in the remaking of broken jaws, teeth and facial bones.

There are furnished recreation rooms for both officers and men. Beer is provided and also games facilities. The officers' recreation room is particularly well furnished with sofas and easy chairs. It is provided with a radiogram, and a library. For these things we are indebted to many friends and organisations and to a large number of generous subscribers to our welfare fund. We are particularly fortunate to possess an energetic and enthusiastic welfare committee – to whom nothing seems impossible.

Chapter 13

Theatre

It is in keeping with the advanced ideas that characterise the Plastic Unit that patients should be encouraged to watch operations if they so desire. In this way, they can often see exactly what is going to happen to then at a future date. During my time in the hospital, I have seen a number of different operations. I believe strongly that to know what is going to happen to you on the operating table, is to lose almost all the fear which naturally attends operations. I have now no apprehension regarding certain plastic operations that have yet to be carried out on me, because I have seen for myself how easily Mr. McIndoe can perform them.

Two operations impressed me most of all. The first was a very complicated bone graft. A piece of bone was taken from the patient's hip and secured to his skull to cover up a large hole in the front of his cranium. The second was a skin graft. The patient's hands had been put into plaster after severe burning in the months before he had arrived at the unit. As a result of this treatment, his hands had become webbed. During the operation in question, McIndoe separated two fingers of one hand and grafted new skin between them.

Bob was a night fighter pilot.[17] He had commanded a flight of Boulton Paul Defiants. For outstanding operational flying in these single-engine two-seater

---

[17] Flight Lieutenant Robert Lionel Frank Day DFC. He was flying a Boulton Paul Defiant Mk.I of 'B' Flight, 410 (RCAF) Squadron, that with the serial number V1137, which crashed in Scotland on the evening of 8 December 1941. The following account is given in the squadron's Operations Record Book in its entry for the following day: 'It is known that [at] approximately 17.25 hours last night this aircraft was ordered to Scramble base [RAF Drem] on information being received that an enemy aircraft was in the vicinity … F/Lt Day was unable to locate enemy aircraft, and was eventually instructed to return to base. The weather and visibility was poor so the aircraft was taken over by "ZZ" for the homeward run. However, at approximately 19.00 hours on its approach towards runway in use, with undercarriage down, the aircraft struck trees some 6 miles East of base and crashed to the ground. It is assumed that the aircraft was flying at too low an altitude. F/Lt Day sustained severe head injuries and is reported to be seriously ill. His Air Gunner, F/Sgt Townsend,

aircraft he had been awarded a D.F.C. During a night flight he crashed and badly wounded his forehead. After the fragments of broken bone had been removed from the front of his skull he was left with a deep recess in the left side of his forehead. In order to secure him from danger to the brain, which was thus left unprotected, it was necessary to cover the area from which the fragments of skull bone had been removed with a piece of bone from his hip.

Before I was allowed to go into the theatre to watch this operation, one of the theatre nurses helped me into a spectator's gown, fitted a white cap on my head, and covered my nose and mouth with a linen mask. Inside the theatre Bob was stretched out on the operating table. Already he was unconscious, having been injected with pentothal in a vein of his arm. Lying there, with a rubber tube running from the corner of his mouth to the complicated arrangement of anaesthetic cylinders and controls, mounted on a chromium plated trolley near his head, he looked like a dead man, but I could see that he was breathing normally, for the white sheet that covered all of him except his head and face was rising and falling evenly where it passed over his chest. John Hunter, the anaesthetist, watched over him, and checked the dials of his apparatus from time to time.

Round the table nurses, enveloped in white, bustled about their various duties, making last minute preparations. Molly with sketch book and pencil in hand was waiting in one corner ready to sketch each stage of the surgeon's work for record and reference purposes.[18] Jill, McIndoe's theatre sister, dressed as usual in green, was sitting behind a table near Bob's head. On this table was spread a sterile towel covered with most of the operating instruments laid out in neat gleaming rows. There was an atmosphere of complete calm, for although this was a serious and complicated operation we all felt that it could not fail to be a success. These three individuals, McIndoe, Hunter and Jill are

---

was shaken but otherwise uninjured and showed great gallantry and presence of mind in extricating his Pilot from the aircraft (which had begun to blaze) and administering first aid treatment.' Initially taken to a military hospital in Edinburgh, Day was transferred to the QVH on 21 March 1942. He eventually returned to duty, but was killed flying over France on 18 June 1944. For his actions on 8 December 1941, Flight Sergeant S.J.J. Townsend was awarded the George Medal.

[18] Miss Mary Evelyn Lentaigne. Mollie, as she was known, was a Red Cross Voluntary Aid Detachment nurse at the Queen Victoria Hospital who had a great interest in art. McIndoe soon recognised the speed and accuracy of her drawings and took her under his wing to produce drawings to record his surgical procedures. East Grinstead Museum is now the custodian of some 300 of her unique drawings.

a perfect team, and to watch them together in the theatre is to see a marvellous example of teamwork.

When everything was ready, the two surgeons, McIndoe and Ross Tilley, came in together. They both wore white shoes. Their short-sleeved surgeons' gowns left their hands and muscular forearms bare. Ross wore a white linen cap, McIndoe one of light green. Masks were tied over their noses and mouths. They scrubbed their hands and pulled on sterile rubber gloves.

Behind McIndoe's horn-mimed spectacles there was a set look in his eyes. You could almost see him planning each successive move of the operation. He examined Bob's forehead carefully and made a last careful scrutiny of the X-rays which were fitted into an illuminated plate held in a tall stand at the foot of the operating table. He scrubbed Bob's forehead thoroughly with ether and spirit, then took a piece of pink plastic stent, and having softened it in the flame of a small, methylated spirit lamp, placed it on Bob's brow and moulded it gently into the shape of the dent.

This done, he dropped the moulding into a bowl of cold water. This moulding was now the pattern to the shape of which he would have to work the piece of bone that later he was going to remove from the hip. With a long needle on the end of a syringe he administered a local anaesthetic into half a dozen different points forming a semi-circle around the hair line of Bob's brow.

The first incision was a masterly, single stroke, quickly and firmly made with a scalpel. It left a pink line stretching from ear to ear around the top of Bob's forehead. Soon the whole of the skin and flesh of the forehead had been separated from the scalp and folded down, inside out, back over Bob's eyes and nose. The hole in his skull was revealed. Dozens of long artery forceps were secured in position and formed a metal circle fanning out from the edges of the open area. Bleeding was fairly profuse, and the electric blood extractor was brought into use, and gauze pads were pressed into place.

The next stage of the operation began. Bob's right hip, already raised and uncovered, was sterilised. McIndoe made a long straight incision along the line of skin stretched taut and pale over the bone. Next he cut deep down through skin and tissue on either side of the bone until it was exposed – a pink crescent arched up in the centre of a gaping red chasm. More artery forceps were secured here, and once more the blood extractor was brought into use, while McIndoe fitted the stent moulding against the bone. Satisfied that he had exposed sufficient bone for his purpose he set to work with chisel and hammer.

The dull thud of each hammer blow was disturbing at first, but I was soon completely lost in a fascination which excluded all other thoughts and sensations. When a piece of bone roughly the same shape as the stent moulding had been removed, Ross and Jill closed up the wound by drawing its edges together with a series of neat stitches. Meanwhile McIndoe was busy chipping pieces off the bone and comparing his work carefully with the stent mould. After a few minutes hard work, during part of which he began to whistle softly, he had transformed the piece of hip into an exact replica of the moulding.

This was a masterly achievement, because the mould was of a most uneven outline shape, and of a varying thickness all round from the centre to the edges; furthermore, because of the hardness of the material upon which he worked, McIndoe was forced to use instruments as powerful and heavy as wire-cutters.

Next, the bone was fitted into place on Bob's forehead and found to be satisfactory. With a neat hand drill, McIndoe made two tiny round holes straight through the new piece of bone and the skull beyond. Through these holes he threaded fine silver wire and twisted the ends until the bones were pressed tightly together; then he cut off the surplus ends. The artery forceps were removed, and the great flap of skin and flesh was replaced and sewn up with a long row of neat minute black stitches. I left the theatre with a thrill of satisfaction running up and down my spine. I had seen a wonderful example of the marvels of modern plastic surgery. I was encouraged beyond words by the realisation that the pair of firm, skilful hands which I had just seen operating would continue to operate on others and on me.

After Bob's bone graft the operation that most impressed me was on one of Peter's hands. In an earlier chapter I have explained that Peter was one of the unfortunate fighter pilots who crashed in flames before he had had a chance to get to grips with the enemy. This in itself was sad enough, but sadder still was the fact that during the weeks that passed before he was sent to the Plastic Unit, his burnt hands had been encased in plaster. The result was a complete webbing of his fingers. His fists were clenched and only his thumbs were free. This made his hands resemble a pair of boxing gloves of a purply pink colour.

As soon as Peter's hands were strong enough, McIndoe carried out a series of operations designed to separate each finger from its neighbour and to straighten it out as far as possible. It was one of the first of these operations that I witnessed. For me it was particularly interesting since I knew that later on a similar series of operations would probably be carried out on my right hand, where the stumps of fingers had partially webbed together in the same way and for the same reason.

After he had thoroughly scrubbed the whole of Peter's right hand, McIndoe took a special pen and marked a fine straight line down the centre of the web between two fingers. Since Peter's hand was permanently clenched, it was necessary to draw this line from joint to joint each time along a different plane.

Soon, after a number of quick incisions had been made, Peter's first and second fingers were separated by a deep cut running right through the centre of the web. After cutting away a certain amount of tissue and forcing the fingers to straighten as far as possible, McIndoe took a piece of stent, pushed it into the wound and moulded it until it forced the fingers open and kept them apart. Then he removed the stent, plugged gauze between the separated fingers, and turned to Peter's upper arm. It had already been shaved and thoroughly prepared for operation, but as a final precaution McIndoe gave it a last rub with spirit as soon as the sterile towel which covered it had been removed. Then he selected a long knife with a square blade, tested the edge and found that it was sharp enough for his purpose.

To remove the skin evenly McIndoe pressed down on Peter's arm with a special wooden plate which he moved along smoothly close in front of the blade of the knife, while he removed the skin with a delicate sawing movement. The skin was thin, pink and transparent, not unlike good quality sausage skin. He removed a piece about six inches long and four wide. He laid it carefully on a sterile plate. Nurses padded and bandaged the skinned arm, which was bleeding a little. McIndoe picked up the skin again, very carefully, and stretched it over the stent mould. Then, with the skin covering it, the mould was carefully wedged back, in between the raw sides of Peter's fingers and stitched neatly into place.

This was in turn wrapped in special soft gauze soaked in yellow acriflavine, and then covered by layers of gauze soaked in scarlet mercurochrome. Finally, the whole hand was locked tightly into position by a new crepe bandage which was wrapped round it and secured with a large safety pin.

This operation was a great success, and in a week or so Peter had regained some of the movement of both fingers.

It must have been about this time that John came back into Ward 3 for a final operation before going back to duty. John was an Australian air observer who had been burned when a Hampden in which he was flying during night flying practice at an operational training unit was involved in a collision and caught fire on the flare path. He was one of the more fortunate burn cases, for without delay he had been taken to one of the biggest R.A.F. hospitals and given there all the best and most up-to-date and detailed treatment for burns and shock. The result was that his hands, which had not been burned any less severely than mine, had been completely saved, so that now, since he has had them grafted with new skin, he can use them both fully, and has lost only the fingernails.

Whenever I saw his hands my mind went back to the days and months that followed my own accident and I could not help feeling sorry that I too had not been so well looked after. John's hands healed up within about three months, whereas mine were rotting by the end of the first fortnight and did not heal up completely for more than eighteen months – even then they were almost fingerless and stiffened at the wrists.

John had charm and a ready smile that won him instant popularity with everyone. He was just over thirty and had left a good job as a wool buyer in Australia to be trained in Canada as an air observer under the R.A.F. Empire Air-Training scheme. His home town was Sydney, and before the war he had worked hard in one of the most skilful and exacting jobs that the wool trade had to offer. I believe that there are only about two hundred skilled wool buyers in the whole of Australia. John had therefore achieved considerable success early in his career. The qualities that had carried him to the front in the wool trade had served him well during his training as an air observer. He was an exceptional pupil.

For months his burnt hands prevented him from returning to the job of air observer – a job which requires particularly delicate movement of fingers during the operation of sextants and bomb sights, and the plotting of courses and position-fixes on maps and charts. Apart from restriction of movement, the blood supply to his burned fingertips was poor at first, and with a low circulation in any of the extremities of the body it is impossible to work efficiently in the conditions of extreme cold experienced in bomber aircraft during operations. He hoped eventually to get into flying boats or land-based aircraft of coastal command, which did not normally fly high enough to experience the coldest conditions. McIndoe transferred skin from his legs to his hands, and greatly improved their condition. Now, I believe, he is back on flying duties again.

I met him for the first time at the R.A.F. officers' convalescent hospital when I went there after my first operation. We became good friends and often went out together, usually with one or two of the other patients and with Mary and some of the nurses.

Chapter 14

Devon Summer

My second long period of convalescence took place during the early summer months of 1942. I went back to the R.A.F. officers' convalescent hospital in the South Devon town in May and stayed there until the beginning of August. This period of convalescence was of great benefit to my body; it also improved the health of my mind, for all through those long summer months spent almost entirely out of doors, I had time to think of the past and make plans for the future.

Great opportunities for concentrated and prolonged spells of thought had already been granted to me while I lay on my back helpless in one French hospital after another. But the boundaries of my range of thought were confined to my immediate surroundings. Of the world beyond French frontiers I could learn nothing, for all unbiased news of the war was trapped in the fine mesh of the sieve of Vichy and German censorship.

I could not keep pace with the constant unfolding of events and the progress of the British and Russian preparations and operations. Now at last in the R.A.F. officers' convalescent hospital I could read up reports on the war in British and American publications – the latter having a special value as they were written by observers of a nation that was still neutral. Furthermore, I had a chance of discussion with my fellow patients.

Few of the patients stayed long at the convalescent hospital. A fortnight or a month were the usual periods for convalescence. Yet that time was sufficient for those who were engrossed in war operations to stop concentrating their thoughts within the rather narrow limits set by their work, and to give them free rein over a limitless plain. They represented many of the dominions and colonies that make up the commonwealth of nations of the British Empire. In addition, there were Americans who had joined the R.A.F.; many Poles; and a few Czechs, Norwegians, Dutchmen, Belgians and Frenchmen. Each member of this mixed community of peoples had something to offer his fellows from his own point of view. Here he had time and opportunity both to consider and express it.

Every Monday evening at eight o'clock it was customary for the hospital staff to ask four patients to give a short talk. There was no restriction on the subject chosen, with the result that nearly every talk was extremely interesting and provided a fund of general knowledge for all listeners, condensed into a short period – twenty minutes. Most of these talks consisted of accounts of the speakers' most interesting experiences in or before the war. One of the older patients told us how he had bought a fishing trawler some ten years ago and described his struggle to maintain it at a profit, in the days when fish was plentiful and market prices low. Another recounted some of his adventures as a policeman.

One of the Poles spoke with hardly suppressed emotion of the bloody fate of his country under the Nazi boot, and of his experiences in a Russian concentration camp. The head psychiatrist gave us a long description of his experiences during a visit paid to America, during which he flew many thousands of miles backwards and forwards across the States trying to convey to the American people an impression of the reaction of Britons to blitz bombings and other forms of acute war strain. Occasionally visiting speakers addressed us. They included Commander Campbell of the Brains Trust, who held our attention for over an hour with a host of anecdotes, delightfully told, covering the lands and oceans of the world.

These talks inspired discussion, and with time to think and talk, the trend was usually to discuss the future and the kind of world each one of us hoped to help to create after the war was over. Ideas were so many regarding this immense subject that it is impossible for me to attempt to record here in detail the views that I heard expressed; but I can give some indication of them in a very general way.

We were the fighting class. We came from all grades of society and from many different parts of the world. Comradeship of arms – or call it what you will – had drawn us closely together. We had all experienced something in the war that was both stirring and disturbing, and we were all striving, each to a different degree, to set up for ourselves a new and better scale of values. Under these conditions, and in view of the directness of attack to any problem that is bred in airmen and those connected with flying, it was natural that we should have made some considerable progress towards discovering what were the fundamental principles governing a full and practical way of life. Lack of experience in deep thought, however, made it difficult for most of us to decide exactly what these were.

Most of us were sick of the old pre-war way of life that had condoned the worship of money as the only god and had often mocked at patriotism. We sought for a purpose that went deeper than the struggle for wealth and mechanical progress. We wanted to see social security as a concrete thing, so that each living human being could be provided by the community of which he was an integral part with a certain basic rate of living, when in need, from funds to which he and his fellows would subscribe. We believed that from this basic form of existence – sufficient to guarantee a certain peace of mind and ensure a feeling of security – all men would feel free to devote themselves to a struggle for better and more beautiful things. We believed that every member of the community should have equity of opportunity in life and that even before birth his parents should feel confident that the child would have a fair start followed by an equal chance – irrespective of parents' position and economic status – to reach as high a level as he was fitted for, according to his character and ability.

We hoped for a better understanding between all nations, particularly those sharing the English tongue, and for a vigorous suppression of all forms of exploitation of the common people in the interests of a privileged few. We were of course whole-heartedly against power-politics and all forms of political and social tyranny, calculated to impose the will of either a dictator or a dictatorial state on the community. We did not believe that absolute equality was either possible or desirable, but we were very conscious of the sacred duty of the stronger members of the community at all times to aid their weaker brothers. We believed that the present war was caused as much by the apathy of living generations nurtured in a broad measure of freedom as it was due to the ambitions of dictators, the greed of powerful nations and the weakness of British and French leadership.

We had been told in the past so much about Russia – particularly during the Finnish campaign – that seemed now to have been amply disproved by the magnificence of the Russians' resistance to German invasion, that we were anxious to know far more about the truth of this great country, which many of us believed had as great a contribution to make to the plans for a new world as any other nation. We wanted to know the truth – and the whole truth – about the Soviet way of life, for we could not help feeling, many of us that the Russians had found some of the solutions to problems that we would have to meet while revolutionising our way of life in the British Commonwealth of Nations. We had been taught for long that Russian methods were totalitarian like those of the Nazis and the Fascists and that they would not suit us here in

Britain. We wanted to find out for ourselves. In the fact that, irrespective of the wide geographical and political differences of our various backgrounds, we had all come to think along more unselfish and more responsible lines, we were aware of a state of revolution of heart common to us all, both in its range and influence. Above all, we hoped that at the coming of peace we would neither weaken, sit back, nor submit to suppression from older generations which after past wars had failed to reap a rich harvest in peace, because they had sown no seeds in the broken soil of war.

Of course, not all the patients were prepared to devote much time to thought. Many of them preferred to make full use of the various facilities for entertainment and refreshment that were available, to an extent that robbed them of the benefits to be gained from consistent thought. Some of them seemed to wish to submerge in rivers of alcohol the bitter memories that troubled their minds. When they talked, it was lightly. They pooled reminiscences of their various adventures, experienced in the air and elsewhere. Men of action do not usually take kindly to contemplation while they are still young, and it is not surprising that in the R.A.F. there should be many who hate to think deeply at all – especially since they have little reason to expect a long life.

What surprised and interested me most about the officers' convalescent hospital was that here there were far more men and women who were ready to discuss any subject, than I had ever come across before in the R.A.F. either in peace or in war. To some extent this can be explained by the fact that the hospital provided a cross-section of all the men and women from countless different walks of life, swept into the R.A.F. for "the duration." But it was a fact too great not to be significant. I believe that it was symbolic of a new awareness that was affecting each one on us, an awareness of our rights as common men and women to influence ourselves and each other, an awareness too of our responsibilities to community, country and world – responsibilities which in the past most of us had vigorously evaded.

In the services an ambitious man is beset by few temptations to exploit his fellow men and women. There are few ways in which he can do so without the fact becoming obvious, and when this occurs his powers are quickly removed. Improved positions and higher pay are won on merit more than is usually the case in civilian life. While serving, it is impossible to *make* money inside the service organisation. One receives one's pay and allowances, and that is that.

Development inside the service is limited by the orders and dictates of the powers above. In this way a service man is restricted to an extent that would not be tolerated by many civilians in peace or war. Ambition, although not entirely destroyed, is confined within very strict limits. When a serving man faces the larger issues, therefore, his mind is not contaminated by the tempting thought of: "If I do so-and-so, how much money will I get out of it?" He is trained to a communal form of life, and he does not usually find it unpleasant – even if it is sometimes boring.

Flying enforces directness of thought and complete harmonisation of mind with physical reaction. Without this, the airman cannot survive, for if he is unable to think quickly while in the air, and turn his thoughts into quick action, certain mistakes will occur and will eventually become fatal. When he turns his mind on to problems other than those connected with flying and air force administration, he usually tackles them with the directness and frankness he has developed in the air. There is a good chance therefore that he will arrive at sound conclusions fairly quickly, after one or two false starts, and not easily be led away from the point. And so, I believe that it is the duty of the flying men and women of my generation to force their way after the war into positions from which they can influence greatly the planning of our post-war national and imperial way of life.

With the soldiers and sailors, we have fought, and will continue to fight, to destroy our enemies, so that we, and all other peoples of the world, may be free to start the struggle for a better post-war world. We have earned the right to raise our voices when the time is ripe. We would be incredibly foolish if we failed to avail ourselves of this privilege, and if when peace comes we allow ourselves the luxury of sitting back and letting things slide – worn out by the many trials and strains of war – we shall not only be refusing a privilege, we shall also be neglecting our duty to generations as yet unborn.

Most service men and women in Britain believe that they are fighting to destroy Hitler and the Japanese. By this they mean those malicious forms of oppression that eventually, if allowed free rein, destroy all vestiges of the freedom to choose his own way of life inherent in every living human being. It is imperative that they should fight to destroy. It is more important still that after destruction they should fight to build. The destruction of Hitler and the military caste of the Japanese is the beginning. The beginning of the end, however, is the creation of a full and free way of life for all men, born both of body and spirit and planned for purpose, colour and beauty. To all this must be added the principle of a basic level of social security, from which the individual gains sufficient peace of mind to free him from many nagging worries and permits him – even if he does have a wife and three children – to aspire from this level to better and more beautiful things.

There are few things more irritating to a nature as obstinate and pernickety as mine than to have to submit to being washed and dressed by someone else. I am a creature of habit, and I like to do everything my own way. I don't believe that I am particularly intolerant on large issues, but I am fussy about small details. It was therefore a considerable trial to me to have to submit myself to the hands of another for each small detail of my toilet, but it would have been impossible for me to have been in better hands than those of Owen.

Medical orderlies are not well paid, nor do they command much respect from their fellow airmen and airwomen, but to those of us who have been attended by them, no praise is high enough for the consideration they habitually give to the needs and comfort of their patients. It is a trying and arduous business looking after someone who is quite helpless; especially if he is often in a bad humour. Owen was perhaps the best of all the orderlies who looked after me. Always quiet and calm, he was also sensitive to my feelings of ridiculous helplessness, which were often but barely conquered by my sense of humour. He realised that I had to struggle to repress an acute exasperation born of a complete loss both of dignity and independence of action.

He came into my room every morning shortly after I had been given breakfast in bed. Then began the complicated business of getting me up. He washed and dressed me with care and patience; never leaving me until I felt completely comfortable and contented. All this took about three quarters of an hour – each minute of which was crowded with a series of small operations and adjustments, each one, though small in itself, of cumulative importance.

At some time or another there must be few people who – since reaching adult age – have not been partially or wholly dressed by someone else. Such people will remember no doubt the ridiculous importance they attached to the way their ties were knotted, their socks put on, their hair brushed, and so on. They will understand me then when I say that such small matters as a shirt rucked up under my braces or a shoe lace a little too slack have been sufficient to disjoint my good humour for hours on end. But with Owen I felt that I could ask him to pay attention to the most ridiculous of these small things, and I knew that he would understand.

Owen was slim and had a neat figure, preserved no doubt by an abstemious way of life and his activities with the Boy Scout movement. He ran a troop of scouts in this South Devon town and persuaded me once to go and talk to them – a terrifying experience since the subject involved aircraft on which the boys were far better informed than I was. His other main relaxation was music, and he was always happy whenever his off-duty time allowed him to hear a good classical concert. His had no doubt been a hard youth, for he was born and brought up in one of the most unattractive of London's Thameside slums.

It is a criminal indictment of our educational and social system that anyone possessing his qualities of sensitiveness, will power, and unselfish devotion to others had not had the chance of a good education to develop his qualities to the full. As it was, he was rather too self-effacing to rise to prominence without encouragement. Fortunately, I do not believe that that worried him, for he seemed perfectly content to devote himself to others without thought for material reward.

He was the second orderly who had looked after me for any length of time at the officers' convalescent hospital. The first time I went there I was cared for by Don. He too was sensitive and considerate. It was a wonderful stroke of luck that over two such long periods of complete helplessness the rough edges of my life there had been smoothed down so efficiently by two such orderlies. Don I saw frequently at the Plastic Unit, for he was now one of the Bathroom Boys.

In spite of all the care which I received from Owen I still longed to be able to fend for myself. Perhaps the most marked Scottish characteristic in my nature is a form of "rugged independence". I do not regard this as a quality – although it has its moments of advantage – for it causes me to hate to feel indebted to others. I am kept consciously aware of the fact that there are always people who will gladly help me in anything I ask of them, and still, I always want to help myself. I realise that this is a fault, yet in some ways it is fortunate that I do feel like this, for it spurs me on to greater effort and discourages me from sitting back and accepting every assistance without making an attempt to progress step by step towards the goal of complete independence.

The first day that I contrived to visit the lavatory by myself assumed what may seem to the reader ridiculous importance. But it meant that in future I was no longer a complete slave to nature for every movement beyond my room. After this it was not long before, with the help of clips, zip fasteners and press studs fitted to my clothing in place of buttons, I was able partially to dress and undress myself, sufficiently anyhow to be able to go about with no fear of becoming stranded at an awkward moment. The modifications to my dress were made by a lady who very kindly used to come in to the hospital to repair patients' clothing and darn socks.

So skilfully did she work that I am still wearing the clothes modified by her. It is no exaggeration to say that provision for a prompt answering of the calls of nature was far and away the most important step in the recovery of my independence. The solution of this problem released nervous energy that had been stored up for many months. I was freed from one of the worst embarrassments that can plague a member of so-called civilised society.

There was one other character whom I met for the first time at the officers' convalescent hospital in South Devon, and whom I have come to know better still at the plastic surgery unit. This was Chris, a Fighting French army officer, a little over thirty, who had been trained as a leader of paratroops. His face and hands had been badly burned when the bomber in which he was flying crashed and caught fire during a night exercise.[19]

He was deeply troubled by the sad sequence of events which had subjected his beloved country to so much long-protracted misery, and lived only for the day when he could return to France and help to rid her soil of the hated invader. He was an idealist and an intellectual, and throughout the long periods of hospital life suffered acutely from the abnormal activities of a mind tortured not only by the misery of the present, but by the manifold problems of reconstruction that would arise before France could work out for herself a new way of life from the ruins created by German arms and lying propaganda.

Often over a game of chess – which he invariably won – he would tell me of the problems, as he visualised them, arising in the future. He would flatter me, as a lover of France, by asking for my views regarding their solution, although he knew that the subject was far above my head. I could give him nothing but my sympathy and my assurances of an abiding faith in the powers of re-birth of a country which had known and bred greatness in the past.

Whenever the weather was hot, and the sun seemed to promise us a few consecutive hours of warmth, we scrambled down on to the beach, there to bathe and then tan our bodies in the heat of the sun. The distance separating the beach from the hospital was small, but the way was rough. First you had to walk up a winding path through the trees that bordered the grounds, then cut across the rough grass of the downs to the edge of the cliff. The vertical distance from here to the pebbles of the beach below was about three hundred feet. There were stone steps and a rough path leading all the way down.

It was pleasant before going down, to linger for a while at the cliff edge and gaze out to sea. On a clear sunlit day, the view was magnificent, and looking

---

[19] Captain Christian Boissonas. A member of the Free French Air Force, Boissonas was a member of the crew of a Armstrong Whitworth Whitley Mk.V, Z6727 of 1419 Flight, which suffered engine failure and crashed-landed near Newmarket, hitting a telegraph pole in the process, on 25 July 1941. The aircraft had been involved in 'testing secret equipment' at the time. All eight persons on board were injured to one degree or another.

across the many bays and inlets of the South Devon coastline it was sometimes possible to see Portland Bill away to the south-east – its chalk cliffs pale grey in the distance where they jutted out into the Channel. All around there was a lovely variety of colour; the blue of sea and sky, the white of the clouds above, and the foam below where the waves broke over the rocks; the green of the downs backed by the reddish brown and green patchwork of the countryside behind; the red cliffs of Devon in the middle distance replaced beyond by the grey ones of Dorset, paling as distance lengthened the view. Far below, the tiny cove which had looked forbidding when the sea had been cold and grey in winter, was now warm, inviting and full of colour.

The water, deep blue and patched with violet, looked deceptively warm; and when it was calm there were thousands of jellyfish – discernible as a translucent scum undulating lazily on the surface of transparent water through which the bottom of the sea could be seen. Once down in the bay and settled on the pebbles with my back against a large rock, I was compelled to look up and back. Here was seclusion and complete separation from an alien and busy world. A strong feeling of detachment was heightened by the fact that the beach was reserved for the air-force patients and staff of the hospital. The airman, standing on guard on the cliff edge at the point where the path down to the cove began, was a minute dark silhouette outlined in black against blue sky or white cloud.

Often a few miles out at sea three mine sweepers ploughed along in arrowhead formation. All around and overhead the wheeling gulls cried plaintively as they soared on the up currents, and then curved down to land beside their nests on the cliff side.

There with the others I lay in the sun for hours on end all through the summer months, until my hair was bleached, and my body tanned a deep patchy brown over the healed burns. Sometimes I went for a swim but found that my blood had not found sufficient new routes of circulation through my burned body to withstand the cold of the sea. My legs and hands turned purple, and I was obliged to scramble quickly from the water after only a few strokes, rub myself dry and soak up new heat from the sun. Sometimes I stayed down there all day, only returning to the hospital for meals.

One of the most frequent visitors to the beach was George Weston. He was a New Zealander and a Squadron Leader. His command was a flight of giant four-engine Lancaster bombers in a squadron that had bombed at tree top level such targets as Le Creusot and Augsburg – raids that meant protracted periods of grave risk while flying in broad daylight to and from targets situated hundreds of miles inside territory controlled by the enemy. For his outstanding leadership throughout these thrilling flights on many occasions he had recently been decorated with the D.F.C.

He was stocky, and very solid in build, with fair hair, a freckled skin and blue eyes. His features were clear cut. He was not particularly good looking, but his face bore unmistakable witness to the sterling qualities that composed his character. He was a grim and earnest realist. Just under thirty years of age, he was experienced enough in life to know exactly what he was fighting for, and to have no doubt that the struggle, with its attendant sacrifices, was worthwhile. He was aware too of the fact that ideals can only be realised by the concentrated efforts of enlightened and earnest men and women. He set an example which others quickly learned to follow.

George Weston taught me something about New Zealand; he also taught me something of the art of living. He made it all seem so simple. Starting from basic Christian principles he tackled each problem with that same directness, courage and determination which he applied with such good results to the stern task of leading a flight of giant bombers both on the ground and in the air. He was neither saint nor prig. The good qualities in his character were no doubt counterbalanced by others; but I learnt little about his faults, whereas I was impressed and inspired by his virtues. Now only his spirit remains amongst those who knew him, for a few weeks after I last saw him at the convalescent hospital he was killed. As a mature man he accepted with complete understanding the dangers of his operational flying duties. He had retained the fire of youth, but long outstripped its blindness. He knew exactly what he was doing and why he was doing it, and he believed that any sacrifice was worthwhile to shorten the period in which tyranny could reign unhampered over large areas of the world.

George's point of view was very like that of Angus. One of Lord Beaverbrook's journalists before the war, Angus, as I knew him in his early thirties, was a talented and brilliant young Scot. I had first met him at the headquarters of the Advanced Air Striking Force in Rheims during the first few months of the war. There he was still a journalist but wore the uniform of an R.A.F. press-correspondent. Our first contact was a fleeting one and I retained only the memory of a tall clear-eyed Scot with a broad brow and fair hair. I did not know then that he was a brilliant athlete as well as a first-class journalist; nor did I know that he was married and had two small children. These things I was to learn nearly three years later when I met him again during my summer convalescence in South Devon.

Perhaps it was in France that he first decided that journalism, even in war garb, did not bring him into close enough contact with the enemy that he wanted to fight. At any rate, when he returned to England from France he volunteered for aircrew duties in the R.A.F. and was accepted for training as a pilot. At the end of his flying training, he was sent to an operational training unit where he had a flying accident, as a result of which he arrived at the R.A.F. officers' convalescent hospital with a compound fracture of the leg.

At the convalescent hospital he was a prominent figure. His enthusiasm was apparently without limit, and it was with difficulty that he channelled it within a limited number of activities. Some of these were the exercises and games in force for all orthopaedic cases. They included strenuous P.T., swimming, and games of volleyball and basketball. To these activities he gave abounding energy but had still plenty in reserve for acting and for editing the hospital magazine. He was one of those fortunate versatile personalities who always seem to reach success in everything they attempt. It was natural therefore that he should be an outstanding pilot and a devoted husband and father.

Angus belonged to that select band of men who had given up everything in this war – success, fame, and future prospects – for the single purpose of fighting the enemy. Like George Weston he had already matured and knew exactly what he was doing and why he was doing it. He had the added responsibilities of a wife and a young family. For them alone it is a tragedy beyond words that he should have been killed on active service, for he would have devoted great talents to the task of parenthood. His loss is also our loss – the loss of all fighting men who are determined to play a prominent part in the future peace-time struggle for the realisation of the ideals for which we are now fighting. Had he lived he could have led and inspired us as it is we have only the memory of his example and the endurance of his unseen spirit amongst us to spur us on.

There was at that time at the convalescent hospital one other patient, who has since been killed, who interested and inspired me. His influence upon me was again different. Unlike George Weston and Angus Williamson, he was very young – only just twenty-four – and whereas they were both expansive and little concerned with themselves, Richard Hillary was introspective and a professed egotist. While George and Angus and I lay on the beach for hours talking together, Richard preferred to isolate himself on the top of a rock where he sat reading a book.

Richard Hillary has been so much publicised through the press and through his own brilliant writing in his book, *The Last Enemy*, that his name is now better known to the public than most of the other outstanding flying personalities of this war. I believe that it is right that this should be the case, for he was an exceptional person. Shot down and badly burned during the Battle of Britain, he had already undergone a long series of plastic operations when first I met him at the Plastic Unit just before the summer. He had evidently been extremely good looking. Burns and plastic surgery had played strange tricks with his face and left it with a certain, almost terrible, attraction. Good looks had been replaced by a distinction which was individual and arresting. The slight disfigurement that remained about his new upper lip and his new eyelids and eyebrows, added to, rather than detracted from, his physical appeal. His hands were whole, but the fingers of each were curled in towards the palm.

Although he professed a completely egotistical outlook towards life, I do not believe that in so doing he was expressing his real self. He was experimenting in egotism, and, I imagine, finding the result unbearable. He was unusually sensitive for a fighter pilot and could not bear to be disliked. Yet he never made any attempt to make himself popular with his fellow patients; on the contrary, he tended to follow quite an opposite course from that which would have made him popular, as if constantly defying a sentiment that had no place in the egotistical viewpoint to which he attempted to subscribe.

I would have liked to have known him better, but he was always rather reserved in his relationship with me. This was my great loss, for I felt that we had many things in common. To begin with we had shared a terrible ordeal by fire. We both wanted to write, and we had both produced a manuscript. His had already been published in America and was soon due to appear in England. Mine had yet to be accepted by a publisher. We were both conscious of a great feeling of dissatisfaction with the way of life which had preceded the war, and which still continued in a lesser degree during the war. We were both in quest of an ideal to follow, although our means of pursuit were vastly different; for whereas I hoped to find it through the contact and influence of other people, as much as from within my own spirit, Richard Hillary – as far as I could gather – was searching his own spirit, and that alone, in his introspective and feverish search for truth.

While we were still both in South Devon I gave him the manuscript of *One of Our Pilots Is Safe*, and as a result of this he undertook to present it to the publishers who eventually accepted it. Soon after that he left the convalescent hospital, and I did not see him again for several months. In the meantime, I had read his book.

I bought *The Last Enemy* in London on my way back to South Devon after a visit to the Plastic Unit about the middle of my period of convalescence. It held me spellbound from Paddington to my destination. That night, back in my bed in the hospital, I finished it. When I laid it down I felt profoundly moved. Richard Hillary had written a very great book which had expressed many of the emotions which I myself was unable to put into words. He had done a great service to all of us who, like him, had been burned. He was ruthless in his description of people, and although this caused a certain amount of pain to others, I felt that he was fully justified by the fact that he had not spared himself. The courage with which he had recorded his emotions and reactions at times when he felt at his worst was beyond all praise. Fine courageous writing such as his serves a very great purpose, for it alone gives a true picture of life, painted both in its most attractive and its most clashing colours.

I only saw Richard Hillary once after he had left the convalescent hospital. It was at a cocktail party in London to celebrate the acceptance of my manuscript. He was working on a script which he was writing for a film about the R.A.F. Air-Sea Rescue Service. So great had been the impression that his book had made upon me that this seemed neither the time nor the place to attempt to put into words to him my feelings for it. I have since deeply regretted this, for some months later he was killed.

Richard need never have returned to flying; in fact, he was discouraged from doing so by good advice from many different sources. But for some reason he felt that he had to get back into the air. He succeeded in doing so; and soon after joined the very select ranks of those who, badly wounded and severely handicapped, have returned to the air and to their death.

There is a great dearth of courageous young authors who are prepared to risk everything in their desire to express faithfully their emotions, and their reactions to those of others. Richard Hillary had the courage to paint an absolutely faithful portrait of himself, and of others as he saw them: if he had lived to use his gift again as he used it in *The Last Enemy* we should all have been greatly enriched by his writings. He has left behind him a great gap which may never be filled by one of his own generation.

Often while going to and from the beach I wore nothing more than a pair of shorts and sandals. One day while I was crossing the downs in this state of undress I saw a man approaching me. As he drew nearer it became obvious to me that his interest had been aroused by something peculiar about my hands. This interest increased to a wide-eyed astonishment when we had approached each other near enough for him to absorb each detail of disfigurement which marred my body, so generously exposed.

By the time we met his mouth had fallen open. In a voice that was a strange mixture of horror and pity he exclaimed: "Gawd. They ain't 'aif made a bloody mess of you." So sudden was this remark and so incongruous, particularly as the accent was cockney and we were in Devon, that I burst out laughing. He drew quickly away with his face further distorted by shocked surprise. Apparently it was bad enough to meet such a spectacle as I presented, but devastatingly horrible to find me capable of laughing at a condition which he considered catastrophic.

That is the remarkable reaction of some people to disfigurement and disability. They treat one as an object of pity, and it is at once infuriating and amusing. Often people have said to me: "I do pity you"; or "I am so sorry for you; it must be terrible to be like that." It is quite useless to try to laugh off these remarks, for the speakers are then strangely offended, and shocked that you yourself should treat so flippantly the disabilities to which you have become accustomed.

When, I wonder, will the majority of people realise that we, the disfigured and maimed, do not want their pity, and that the last thing we want to be asked to do is to indulge in self-pity? When will they realise that we want only to be accepted as normal human beings, and our disfigurement and disabilities to be accepted quite dispassionately. We do not object to discussing the subject in a matter-of-fact way, but to be pitied is embarrassing in the extreme, and makes us feel that we are not being admitted to society as normal human beings – which, apart from differences that to us appear insignificant, and which, given a chance, we can often forget, we feel ourselves to be. The cheaply sentimental expression of pity, as distinct from practical and useful sympathy, is unbearably condescending.

It makes us wonder whether some people who have not shared our misfortunes consider themselves to be superior to us. We cannot, and should not, tolerate this. We have retained our pride and our self-respect and can see no reason why we should be classified as pitiful human ruins, inferior in character and intelligence to the physically unharmed, and forced to throw ourselves on the mercy of society.

We do not want pity, and we intend to make our own way, goaded on to greater effort by very reason of the fact that we are handicapped physically. We need your help and your encouragement, but, if you value our friendship and companionship, seek it on equal terms and for goodness sake spare us the humiliation of your pity.

After a few weeks, spent lazily lying in the sun, I had regained sufficient strength to take part in the morning P.T. parade. Of course, there were many exercises which were beyond my limited powers, but on the whole I managed to get full benefit of it all with the other patients. While the others were doing press-ups and other exercises which involved the use of hands, John and I broke off to do special exercises of our own together. I discovered that I could still run and that my wind was reasonably good. As for my heart, it seemed to have suffered absolutely no ill effects from a long and trying period of infirmity. Thank God that in the past I had concentrated on the pursuit of athletics, even if it had retarded my mental development! How exhilarating it was to feel once more hot blood coursing swiftly through my veins, while the exercises flexed one set of muscles after another! How good it was to feel muscles swelling and subsiding, and to stand square and steady on my legs with arms outstretched breathing in lungful's of fresh cool air.

Whenever the weather was fine these parades were held on the lawns outside the hospital between the terrace and the golf course. When it was wet we retired to the gymnasium. It was an excellent gymnasium; spacious, airy, well lighted and spring-floored with smooth narrow pine boards. Into it was packed a mass of complicated exercising equipment. There were stationary bicycles and rowing machines; climbing ropes and wall bars; a vaulting horse and mats; rings and parallel bars; exercise tables and long mirrors; mechanical horses and a camel; punch balls and weights; Indian clubs – and a long bowling alley.

There were few patients who could not use some of this wide range of equipment. Here, when P.T. parades were over, they could continue their exercises under the supervision of the P.T. staff. Whereas all this equipment was common to a well-appointed gymnasium, it was still not sufficient to provide for all the needs of rehabilitary treatment, and so a complicated arrangement of ropes, blocks, pulleys and weights of different values to provide resistance for the exercise of special groups of muscles had been added. Attached to these ropes at all times during the day were groups of convalescents patiently working to regain the use of muscles that had deteriorated while their damaged limbs had been encased in plaster. Many of them were still in plaster when this treatment began. In this way it was possible to prevent any risk of withering muscles. Often when the plaster was finally removed the muscles concerned were found to be already in good condition.

One side of the gymnasium had been partitioned off and divided into three compartments. In one room three skilled *masseuses* worked hard at their job of softening stiff muscles and restoring power to wasted limbs by means of massage, special exercises, heat and electrical treatment. In this room and throughout the gymnasium there was an eternal babble of sound, for spirits were always high, and there was never any suggestion of despondency among the injured men.

Another was a small office where the R.A.F. Surgeons and physicians examined patients when they arrived. There they noted their records, prescribed the necessary remedial treatment, supervised the work of the P.T. instructors and masseuses and generally watched carefully over the progress of the diverse and numerous cases who passed through their hands. I was under the orders of a tall, thin Squadron Leader Surgeon. He was a first-class surgeon and took an unusually keen interest in the fate of his patients after they had returned to some form of duty. He was full of ideas and practical schemes for finding employment for patients during any further period of advanced convalescence that might be necessary after they had completed their special treatment at the convalescent hospital.

The Squadron Leader had a hurried manner and seldom finished a sentence. He hardly ever closed an interview in the conventional manner – usually disappearing in a rush in the middle of it, leaving behind him a patient who was completely confused regarding the future course of his treatment. It was therefore all the more surprising when, on the next visit to the squadron leader's office, one discovered that he had completely grasped the situation and had already produced a solution to problems that other doctors had failed to solve in twice the time. His personality was the strangest mixture of scatterbrain and precision of any that I can remember having contacted.

My first impression was that he was completely disorganised mentally; but I soon found out what a mistake I had made. The many schemes instituted by him for the temporary employment of his patients, were quite outside the scope of his normal duties. One of the best of these was an arrangement by which we could go to work on a farm before we were quite fit for the strain of flying duties.

The third room, situated between the two others, had been converted into a snack bar. This was opened every morning at eleven o'clock, and to the accompaniment of lively badinage, Connie and Sheila served us with milk shakes. Connie was the talented and charming wife of Dan Maskell, the squadron leader in charge of our games and physical activities. They were a delightful couple. Dan was well known as the tennis professional who, in peace time, had trained several Davis Cup teams. He was slight and wiry, a brilliant and versatile athlete, and a perfect selection for a difficult and arduous job.

He had an extraordinary fund of physical and mental energy and took part in all the games. I don't think he ever lost a set of tennis or a game of squash, and on the golf course he was a formidable opponent.

Dan and Connie played an enormous part in promoting the health and welfare of all of us. Connie, like her husband, was full of energy and ideas. She too was very athletic – although extremely feminine and the mother of a baby boy. As an amateur actress she was enchanting.

Working under Dan and the doctors there was a team of air-force physical-training N.C.O.s. Their leader was Sergeant Mann. A distinguished marathon runner before the war, he had developed on a slim frame the perfect physique of a Grecian athlete. Nature had blessed him with wavy fair hair, clear blue eyes, clean features and a flashing smile; add to this a remarkable zest for life, and dry humour matured in Covent Garden – where he had worked in the family fruit business – a breadth of vision and a tolerance of differing points of view – developed no doubt through travel over many parts of Europe and North Africa – and you have the salient points, as I saw them, of his character. He was well suited to the monumental task of persuading hilarious-minded young pilots accustomed to having much of their own way to take an interest in physical exercises essential to their return to flying fitness. He succeeded in making them enjoy exercises that could have been painfully dull. He had a way with him that made the simplest of exercises and the most childish of games become really good entertainment. Most important of all, in the difficult position of an N.C.O. in charge of squads of officers – some of senior rank – he preserved complete control without ever causing offence.

Like Dan's, his was a long and healthy day, and he appeared to enjoy fully every moment of it. When P.T. parades were over he used to swim with as many of us as were sufficiently fit to jump into the swimming bath. Many a man with a fractured leg still in plaster must have been surprised the first time he was expected to leap into the swimming bath, plaster and all, for plaster is no deterrent to exercise, although of course special care had to be taken to ensure that the exercises did not interfere with the knitting together of broken bones. A broken back – or even a broken neck – was not admitted as an excuse from taking part in all forms of P.T. It was remarkable how proficient some patients became at swimming with one leg in plaster.

At other times he would join the patients in games of basket-and-volley-ball – and here again plaster was much in evidence, so that by the time the plaster was finally removed patients were already nearly a hundred per cent fit and had preserved and even developed muscle elsewhere on their bodies.

Perhaps Sergeant Mann's most pleasant duty was to lead us on rambles that varied in length between three and fifteen miles and were exceedingly strenuous. We set out from the hospital in our own bus and went far into the interior of the surrounding countryside. Sometimes the bus would stop in the middle of a moor, and at others near the banks of the Dart, or the Teign. Then we would get out and follow the sergeant at a pace and over country rough enough to satisfy the keenest commando. Nettles and brambles, barbed wire and almost sheer declivities were sought out and conquered as we made our circuitous way to the hotel predestined to provide us with lunch or tea. Parties were always mixed. They included W.A.A.F.s and nurses.

By these walks we were brought into the closest contact with the rich variety of the Devon countryside. The routes, though hard, were always beautiful, the air and the exercise exhilarating, and I found each expedition increasingly pleasant, and beneficial alike both to mind and body. The long months of infirmity – at least as far as my legs were concerned – receded into the already half-forgotten and grim past. Every day I felt fitter, stronger, and younger; the dormant zest for a full physical life flared up almost to its former heights.

Inspired by these organised rambles, some of us used to go in small parties on excursions of our own. We rowed up the Dart, fished in Tor Bay, or walked a few miles around the coast to Maidencombe for tea. Arriving back in the evening, we would perhaps be in time to see the cinema show which took place on three nights a week. If there was no cinema there would be short talks, bridge, a dance, or a concert to amuse us, there was always something on in the evenings.

It was at one of these concerts that I heard the Poles singing for the first time. There were many Polish officers at the convalescent hospital that summer, and to me and to many others they provided a constant reminder of the terrible state into which Hitler and the Germans had plunged most of the people of Europe. Many of the Poles had fought at home and in France before winning their prominent place in the forefront of the R.A.F. Some of them had been prisoners both in Germany and in Russia. They could tell horrible stories of their ordeals, but they told them seldom, for many of them felt a great sense of helplessness when trying to describe to us the life of concentration and prison camp.

There was one, however, who spoke of his experiences in Poland after the Germans had taken over control. It was one of the shortest talks we heard, and one of the most inspiring. With a voice that was calm and steady he told us with simple clarity the fate of members of his own family, his *fiancée* and his friends. It was a terrible story that inspired awe. Although outwardly he was calm and his voice perfectly controlled, all the time he spoke one felt that he was fighting a deep emotion. There must have been few of his listeners who were not deeply moved by the story he had to tell.

Our Poles were not trained singers and they had no real choir, but when they gathered in a group around the piano at the end of one of our concerts the quality of their singing prolonged the entertainment for another half hour. They sang their national anthem and ours; the songs of the Polish Army and Air Force; the yodel airs of the mountains. In perfect harmony they revealed to us the beauty of the songs of many different regions of Poland. The applause was thunderous – especially for an English audience that could not understand one word of the songs.

They poured into their singing all the emotions of love and longing for their country – a country nurtured in sorrow, never free from wars and strife. Like most Slav melodies, theirs were sufficiently rich in flavour to cause acute pleasure, and the spine shivered in an ecstasy that harmonised with the emotion of their voices. From the first night that I heard them I contrived always to be near at hand when a group of Poles gathered round a piano.

Once while I was lying on the beach, a little girl – the daughter of one of the doctors – engaged me in conversation with the remark: "You've got no hands." Foreseeing a rather difficult discussion, I tried to avoid it by saying: "No, but I don't really need any." This was obviously so unacceptable to the directness of a child's mind, that immediately she burst out, with devastating logic: "Oh, yes you do!" There she had me.

One of the saddest things about disfigurement and disability is the fact that small children are often terrified by it. This has been particularly painful to me, for I love children, and I am afraid that I have become diffident in my approach towards them. I am afraid to touch them or offer them my maimed hands, for fear of killing at birth what I often hope will be a long friendship. Nature hates and despises disfigurement; civilisation on the other hand tolerates it and even ignores it. Children, being nearer to the animal state than adults are, react more naturally than their elders. They are often cruel, often insensitive, in the things they say and do. As I am very much concerned with the friendship of children I have usually been at a loss to know how to treat them; how to gain their affection without striking horror in their hearts.

What the solution is I am not quite sure, but I do know of one child – admittedly very small – who has no horror of my hands or face. Perhaps that is because he is of the same blood as mine, for he is my sister's son. He is a sturdy, healthy little boy just under three. Although so young he is quite old enough to realise that I am not normal. With him I always try to treat disfigurement and disability as a subject of acute interest rather than something that is to be feared and avoided, so that when he asks me as he often does: "Have you got a hand, uncle Bill?" I make some such answer as: "Yes, but it's very small." Then he takes it and examines it with interest. When I walk about with him, still tightly holding my hand, I am full of an incredible happiness, for through John I am given faith that my own children of the future will feel as he does.

All through the summer I had been wondering how and when I could get back to work again. I was physically fit for work in every way except one, and that was the most important of all – I still could not use my hands sufficiently even for office work. It seemed to me, however, that since I could now write with a small pencil – small enough to be held between the stumps of two fingers – I was rapidly approaching the goal. I asked myself just what would be demanded of me in an office and was surprised to realise that fingers played only a very small part in office routine. There were, I discovered, only four things that I would have to master before I could work at an office desk. The first, to be able to write in pencil and sign my name in ink; the second to be able to handle a telephone with my left hand while making notes with the right; the third to be able to carry papers, turn them, and separate them; the fourth, to be able to open and shut doors while carrying papers.

Although it would still be some months before I would have been beautified sufficiently to be able to present myself in public without risking a chance of being turned down on the count of disfigurement, it was as well to make plans in advance. Although already I could write in pencil, before being able to write in ink I would have to design a special pen and persuade someone to make it for me. Opening doors, I had already mastered by using my wrists, while carrying papers locked between one arm and my side. Handling papers no longer presented an insoluble problem, since I could pick them up clamped between my two hands and turn them over with my finger stumps after moving them to the edge of a desk or table. But how to operate a telephone with a fingerless hand while writing with the other – that was a real problem I had yet to solve.

Just before I left the convalescent hospital I got to know a fellow patient who solved this problem for me. He was a group captain who had specialised for years in pilotless aircraft and other special aircraft instruments. He had played a leading part in the development of the Queen Bee radio-controlled-target-aircraft. To him my problem was child's play, and he solved it in this way.

First of all, he took an old leather glove and remodelled it to fit exactly over the stump of my left hand. Along the palm he sewed a zip fastener which I could operate quite easily either by means of my teeth or with the stumps of my right hand. Then with a piece of copper wire, bent carefully to shape and held in place by loops of leather, he made a hook which fitted on to my palm at right angles to the line of my hand. He wound leather neatly round the end of the hook. He took particular care to make everything fit perfectly and comfortably on to my tender stump and spent hours bending the wire carefully into shape. With the glove and hook attachment – so simple in design, yet so effective – I could pick up a telephone and hold it to my ear without effort.

And so, before I left Devon, thanks to the group captain's kindness and patience, I had regained complete confidence in my ability to work in an office again.

Chapter 15

Forehead to Nose

W hen in August I at last left the R.A.F. officers' convalescent hospital and went back to the Plastic Unit to be operated on once more, I had no sensations of apprehension about returning to a hospital bed. In fact, I found it difficult now to think of the plastic surgery unit as a hospital, for already I had made so many friends there both inside and outside Ward 3 that returning was like going back to a well-loved squadron where I could find those of my own kind. Also, I had no idea how serious and complicated was the first operation that was about to be performed on me.

I knew, of course, that the hole exposed by the disappearance of the wing that should have covered my left nostril would be covered by means of a graft. I thought that a piece of skin and flesh – known as a Wolfe graft – would be removed from my stomach, which by now was bronzed and well provided with flesh, and that this piece when sewn into position would be sufficient to form a new nostril.

However, as soon as McIndoe had examined me after my return to Ward 3, he decided that the most efficient way of repairing my nose would be to remodel it almost completely by means of a Rhinoplastic operation. I agreed to this with some apprehension, for I knew it was a complicated operation and sometimes resulted in acute pain that lasted for days.

My hair, which had only just returned to its natural length and shape, aided by the sun and fresh air of Devon, was shaved off in front, back to a line running from ear to ear straight across the peak of my scalp. Feeling that I already looked ugly enough I resented this addition to my grotesque disfigurement. Then in the operating theatre McIndoe set to work.

Of course, I was under an anaesthetic at the time, but I was given a full description of the operation afterwards. Briefly it was as follows. After very careful measurement, the Boss made a long curved incision around my forehead. The first part of the incision ran from my left ear along the border of my hair and across the top of my scalp to the other side. It was exactly the same as the first incision I had watched being made on Bob's head, during the bone graft operation described in an earlier chapter.

Once arrived at the other side of my head he went straight on down to my right eyebrow, then along above the eyebrow to the line of my nose, and back to halfway up the centre of my forehead. Thus, the whole incision was outlined in the form of a "G" lying back to front on its stomach. Next he raised the skin and flesh completely from my scalp and forehead inside the line of this first incision. After that he cut a small flap of skin and flesh above the hole of my enlarged nostril on the left side of my nose and folded it down inside-out to form a lining for my new ala. (A wing-like gristle-filled piece of skin that arches over the nostril).

Then with a deft movement he twisted the raised portion of my head and forehead until the last bend in the "G" – the bottom and left side of my forehead – was over the left side of my nose and secured it into position as a new and integral part of my nose. He also sewed it securely to the rest of my nose along a line passing from the top across the right side around the bridge, and up to my right eyebrow. In this way I was left with the rest of the flap twisted like a sausage back to my left temple. Through the sausage ran an artery which supplied blood to my nose. To assist the future task of shaping my ala, he pierced it through and inserted a wad of gauze as a plug, so that when later it was removed, a recess would be left which in turn could be moulded to the exact shape of the recess above the nostril.

Over my right temple and back from the right side of my scalp Ross Tinsey grafted a piece of skin which he had shaved from my stomach with a special dermatome cutting machine that he had imported from Canada. Of this machine he was justly proud, for it could be adjusted to remove skin and flesh of the exact thickness required so smoothly, that after a few months the only sign of its work on my stomach was a light, slightly indented oblong shape – about eight inches by four – similar to a vaccination mark. This graft covered the area of forehead and scalp which had become part of my nose. The rest of the flap would be returned to its original position on my head during a future operation in three weeks' time – as soon, in fact, as the disturbed tissue had recovered. In the meantime that part of my head was carefully padded with gauze, secured in position under strong pressure by a crepe bandage surrounding my head.

When I came round from the anaesthetic I was relieved to find that after this long operation, lasting between two and three hours, I suffered no pain at all – just a dull and uncomfortable feeling that spread over my head and face. Even my tightly bandaged raw stomach was painless so long as I remained absolutely still. My nose was bleeding a little, but I felt quite well, for although I had lost a great deal of blood it had been replaced in plasma form while I was still under the effect of the anaesthetic.

John Hunter had done his usual thorough job of carefully balancing the mixture of the anaesthetic so that I did not vomit at all and had no worse sensation when I regained consciousness than a very faint one of nausea, which passed away within a few hours. My left eye was half covered by the flap and closed for a day or two until the swelling had died down; but I was not blind, for my right eye was quite free. I never felt at all ill in the days that followed, and it was a great tribute to my long convalescence and the skill of surgeons, anaesthetist and nurses, that I was well enough to get out of bed for a short while the first day after the operation without feeling either weak or giddy.

As the days passed by hair began to sprout on the sausage shaped flap stretched between my head and my nose. This of course was the hair of my shaved scalp, and eventually would be growing once more in its proper place after the flap had been cut off my nose and restored to my scalp and forehead. As it was it looked most grotesque, growing short and bristly, fanned out around the rolled flap like prickles on a porcupine.

Geoffrey and a flight lieutenant called Bill were both in the ward at the time. Geoffrey had been given a new eyebrow – a crescent shaped deep graft of skin and hair having been removed from the side of his head and sewn neatly into place to form an eyebrow, that already realistic, would eventually settle down until it was indistinguishable from normal. Geoffrey had already gone back to flying duties and was hoping soon to get into an operational Spitfire squadron. Bill had been given a new forehead which added to the temporary patchiness of his face on which had already been grafted two eyelids, eyebrows and a patch across his nose. In the course of time, he would lose the patchiness completely. When all the grafts had finally settled into his face he would probably retain only a number of very faint lines – or possibly nothing at all. The present patchiness caused one amusing incident.

Bill was in a bus, and when the conductor took his fare and noticed his face he asked: "Been in the wars, chum?" "Yes, a bit," answered Bill, amused, and the conductor went back to his step. He kept looking at Bill, and from his expression it was obvious that he was still thinking of the disfigured face and searching in his mind for something comforting to say. When Bill was about to get off the bus at his destination, the conductor, plucking up his courage at the last moment, caught Bill's arm and asked: "Ever heard of plastic surgeons?" "Yes". "Well, you get in touch with one of them, chum. They'll work wonders with all those scars on your face." As the scars had been caused by plastic surgeons this remark had a certain irony. It was repeated to McIndoe, who roared with laughter. Plastic surgery is a slow process, and results have to be attended with patience for months and sometimes even years.

No doubt encouraged by the success of my rhinoplasty; McIndoe produced two others in quick succession. Paul got one and it was enormous.[20] After the flap had been replaced he was left with a protuberance. The whole of the rest of Paul's face had already been replaced – chin, cheeks, eyelids – so that this new burden was hard to bear; but the final result was no doubt worth the original embarrassment. It was adjusted to roman, and from roman changed to *retroussé* – more in keeping with the shape of a face that was on the small side.

Stan, on the other hand, was given an excellent nose from the outset, and it did not need more than a final touching up to be quite normal. Many more noses were remodelled during the next two or three months – all on burned airmen. Most of them were enormous to begin with and were later reduced to normal size. This fitted in with the theory that it was better to err on the large side, since excess can easily be removed later, whereas little can be done to remedy a grafted nose if it becomes too small, after shrinking, due to insufficient material.

Not all the noses were made from forehead flaps. Many of them came from a flap transferred from stomach to arm and then to nose, or direct from chest to nose. These methods were usually employed when the patient had scar tissue covering the whole of his forehead. The flaps were rolled up like long pale sausages. They always contained a main artery. They were attached at one end to chest or arm, where the skin was sound and the blood supply good, and at the other end to the burned nose.

As soon as the displaced tissue on nose and flap had become adjusted to this new function, and after all swelling had subsided, the flap was cut free from the chest, cut to shape and sewn into position on the nose. Tim, Jock, Taffy and Chiefie had all been through this experience – either for noses,

---

[20] This is almost certainly Leading Aircraftman Paul Rounds Hart. He suffered burns to his face, hands and thigh, when the aircraft he was flying, Miles Master N7442 of 5 Flying Training School, crashed into a hillside in fog near Wrexham during a training exercise on 30 October 1940. He would endure a total of twenty-five operations at the QVH.

cheeks or chins. Taffy had to lie for about three weeks with his head bent down and to one side. In this cramped position he could not read, but we all contrived to keep him amused by talking to him.

One of the latest arrivals in the ward was Henry Malin. American by birth, he had joined the R.C.A.F. before Pearl Harbor had brought America into the war. In the R.C.A.F. he served on operations in Hampden bombers, and during a mine laying operation was forced to land in the sea through engine failure.

It was summer and the North Sea was, he said, fairly warm. He floated on it for over a fortnight, cramped up in his rubber dinghy. He had no food and no water. One member of the crew shared the dinghy for a day or two before dying. The others had been killed outright or drowned. The dinghy was very small, and Henry's feet trailed in the water. One day he trapped a seagull on his chest and drank its blood – for the rest of the time he neither ate nor drank. His endurance was terrific. It was wonderful that he should have lived through that fortnight of exposure before he was rescued off the Dutch coast by a British naval patrol. His feet, deteriorated through exposure, had to be amputated at the Plastic Unit after the failure of a long-drawn-out attempt to save them. He was very quiet at first and never showed any signs of glorying in his own qualities of courage and endurance which had preserved him for so long under such appalling conditions. He was very attractive. His hair was grey and his eyes deep brown.

In bed, propped up with pillows, it was impossible to tell how tall he was. Betty used to wheel him down to Bill's bar and the cinema in a wheelchair. She also took him swimming. He swam beautifully, in spite of the fact that both legs had been amputated just below the knee. Now he has been fitted with two artificial limbs. Only a few days after they arrived he was walking – a little awkwardly at first – without a stick. I noticed now that he was about six feet tall. Already he is driving his car again, and his one predominating ambition is to get back to piloting as soon as possible. To him the idea of allowing his artificial legs to prevent him from flying is quite unacceptable. He has become so much an accepted part of Ward 3 that we shall all miss him very much when he leaves us.

Three weeks or so after the first operation on my forehead and nose, my elephant's trunk – now generously covered with short bristly hair – was separated from my nose and neatly sewn back into place on my head. The nose that remained was large and swollen and extremely ugly; particularly after it had been painted scarlet with mercurochrome! Paul, whom I had named Ikey, My head looked no better. It would take six months for the short bristly hair in front to grow back to its full length to match the longer hair behind. From the front it looked rather like a coconut. An awful mess had been made of me temporarily, but it was well worthwhile for the results that would follow in time.

I was still in this horrible state when one day into the ward walked one of my old friends – the doctor of the bomber squadron in which I served in France. Once before, since my return to England, I had met him in London. Since France he had been to Murmansk with the R.A.F. Hurricane fighter wing, which was stationed in Russia for some months while the Russian air force was being equipped with Hurricanes.

Now back in England he was the senior medical officer of a nearby fighter station. He took me over there to see his wife and baby. Afterwards we paid a visit to the aerodrome. This was the first time I had been back on an R.A.F. aerodrome since I had been wounded, and I did not like the experience. I was conscious of a strong nostalgia for flying at the sight of the trim little Spitfires dispersed round the landing ground and flying overhead. The desire was reborn in me to be in the air again, a desire which I had almost forgotten. This was the station from which Paddy Finucane – whom I had met in hospital in South Devon – led his famous wing on sweeps over France, until he was shot down and crashed in the channel.[21]

The attack on Dieppe took place sometime before I left the hospital. Many jaw and burns casualties were admitted to the hospital, and Ward 3 had its share. King Cole, a very senior R.A.A.F. officer, was there. He had been shot through the jaw when a low flying German fighter raked with fire the bridge of the naval vessel from which the naval, land and air forces were controlled. Jimmy, R.N.V.R. master of a tank landing craft, had also been shot through the jaw in the same way, right at the end of the action, while only a few miles from port on the last return journey. Scottie, flight commander of a squadron of Blenheims engaged in laying a smoke screen, had been hit by the fire of the pom-poms of our own naval craft, and was burned when his damaged aircraft caught fire after he had carried out a brilliant, forced landing just across the south coast.

---

[21] Wing Commander Brendan Eamonn Fergus Finucane, DSO, DFC & Two Bars, known as Paddy to his colleagues, was an Irish Second World War RAF fighter pilot and flying ace. His Spitfire Mk.Vb, BM308, was hit by anti-aircraft fire during a sweep over the Channel on 15 July 1942. The fighter was seen to ditch, but Finucane did not survive and remains posted as 'missing' to this day.

King Cole was the most senior patient who had ever been admitted to Ward 3. Like all the other senior officers who had preceded him, he settled down immediately to our free and easy ways. Furthermore, he added a new jargon all his own to our mode of speech, and we missed him very much when he left us. The cannon shell which had pierced his jaw and broken many bones had left a nasty hole in his face. With his jaw locked up while the bones were resetting he could hardly talk and was on an all-liquid diet. Jimmy was in the same condition, and at meal-times there was a continual sucking sound as the two of them contrived to soak up nourishment through rubber tubes and spouted mugs.

Scottie arrived in the ward with his face and hands painted with gentian violet. He had sandy hair and a freckled skin which showed in places through the gauze mask – pierced by holes for eyes, nose and mouth – which covered most of his face. His burns were not serious and after a fortnight of saline bath treatment hardly any evidence of this ordeal remained visible.

In spite of everything they had been through all three of them were soon in most hilarious spirits that harmonised well with the customary cheerful atmosphere of the ward.

One more operation was performed on me before I left Ward 3 to go back to work. McIndoe decided to improve the condition and shape of my left hand-stump. Completely covered in a sac of thin skin and not too robust scar tissue, there still remained the knuckles of each finger and some short, pointed stumps of finger bone. The knuckles were apparently decalcifying rapidly, and the pointed bones sometimes injured the surrounding tissue, with the result that the skin was broken, and did not heal again for some time. While I was under an anaesthetic McIndoe opened up the stump, removed the offending pieces of bone and the knuckles, and trimmed off the metacarpals in an even line. This left me with a stump which, after it had healed, became eventually firm and neatly rounded off.

This was the most painful operation that I had experienced. Many nerves had to be severed and the condition of the skin and tissue cut during the operation was so bad that for a long time my hand was a nasty swollen mess only just held together by the stitches, which strained against the swelling. However, in a few weeks' time the stump had healed and shrunk almost to its present neat, rounded shape. It was no longer tender, and I could submit it to fairly rough handling. Best of all it was now in a fit state to carry an artificial appliance.

And now at last I was fit to go back to work. By the end of November, I was working a full and normal day in an office in the Air Ministry.

Chapter 16

Work Without Fingers

Before I left the Plastic Unit I was presented with a neat little pen, specially made for me by one of my fellow patients, with which I could sign my name and write in ink. With this pen, a special small revolving pencil, and the telephone-hand made for me by the group captain at the convalescent hospital, I was now completely fit for the physical side of my duties in the Air Ministry. Two further problems remained to be solved. The first was to assure the authorities concerned that I was physically fit and able to do all the things necessary for efficient office work. This was accomplished, and only one last problem remained.

Long before, when first I landed in England, I had decided that not until I had been patched up would it be fair to see my mother. Shortly before I left France to return home she had undergone a serious operation, and I was afraid – perhaps unreasonably – of causing her acute distress by my appearance.

For months I forced myself to the painful duty of putting off my reunion with her until my face and hands had reached a certain state of restoration, and I did not feel that by the time I returned to work that stage had been reached. My nose was still grotesque and swollen and my hair short in front. My hands were much better – but they were still tender and a very ugly colour.

And so, separated from my wife and not wishing to disturb my mother, I was faced with the problem of finding somewhere to stay in London, where I could be looked after. My search did not last long, for before the date due for my entry into the Air Ministry, I was adopted into a family to whom I owe the deepest of all the debts of gratitude which I have incurred since the day when I was wounded. There I was looked after with a kindness, tolerance, and care which alone made it possible for me to get back to work.

On Monday, November 23rd, 1942, I returned to work. On the same day my book, *One of Our Pilots Is Safe*, was published. To be back at work was the one thing for which, above all others, I had hoped and longed for during my two and a half years in hospitals. The publication of my book released pent-up emotions which for long I had nursed and concealed. With its appearance in print, I felt that the last chapter of pain was for ever ended.

After such a long time spent largely in idleness and contemplation, I found the routine of work arduous and difficult. Physical disabilities did not handicap me at all, but my mental machinery was rusty, and my memory for details of the kind that I encountered had almost vanished. With the passing of days and weeks, my mind regained its former powers – such as they were – and I was exhilarated by the feeling of at last being once more able to earn my own living.

When one has known a full and complete life, unhampered by physical or mental defects, the acceptance of a state of crippledom is extremely trying. But after the first few months of shock, pain and embarrassment, it is possible to sink quite easily into a state of existence dependent almost entirely upon help given by more fortunate people. This is a necessary state of mind to attain, for obviously when certain things have become inaccessible, the sooner the fact is accepted with resignation, the sooner one recovers composure, and something of lost peace and happiness. In this state of resignation and acceptance mind and body are relatively at peace, and healing is accelerated.

Yet all through this period of resignation one must keep one thing alive inside oneself – the spark of adventure, the desire to go forward. One must never allow oneself to become so resigned to what appears at times to be a blow predestined by Fate or God, that one is no longer able to call up enough courage and enthusiasm to embark as soon as possible on the great adventure of overcoming disability and regaining independence.

It is indeed pleasant to be nursed by cheerful and pretty nurses, and to be waited upon hand and foot, both inside and outside hospital. There is a certain sense of well-being that warms a man when he knows that there are other people who are willing to sacrifice their leisure and their own amusement in order to look after him. It is easy to lose the desire to fend for oneself.

It is easy, too, to forget to cultivate and express gratitude – particularly when it becomes impossible and undesirable to keep repeating words of thanks for every single act of help given all through the day, day after day. Also, there is a danger of hurting the feelings of others by refusing help sweetly and kindly offered, because one knows that it is within one's power to do a certain thing, if only one can have a little practice. How often, I can remember, I have brusquely refused help and hurt tender feelings – yet I knew that I must regain my independence by my own efforts, and so remove the drag I was imposing on the lives of others.

The resigned acceptance of a disability, while necessary at times up to a certain point, must never be allowed to reach ascendancy over the desire to regain independence. The struggle for independence of a man who has virtually lost both hands is not bitter when the spirit is sound. I know that my struggle, which still goes on, has seldom been unbearable. It is true that there have often been moments when, alone, I have almost screamed with mortification and rage, because I have been unable to do something which I wanted badly to do – often something trivial in itself, yet necessary to the completion of a scheme involving other more important movements. For the rest of the time, however, I have been so keenly concerned with the recovery of control of my body, until it reaches harmony with the independence of my mind, that it has been a great and thrilling adventure.

The most important things that have been denied to me in disability have been by far the easiest to bear. My greatest tormentors have always been petty things. It does not now upset me to know that I cannot handle with physical satisfaction a host of things pleasing to the touch. It no longer worries me to know that I shall perhaps never be able to do a number of important things necessitating two strong hands; but I am furious when I cannot adjust my tie, or wind my watch, or some such other thing of no real importance. Why this should be so is beyond me; but perhaps the psychologists can find an answer.

When I first went back to work I had very little confidence in my ability to travel by myself. I could not handle small change, remove my coat, use a torch in the blackout. I hated asking conductors to delve into my pockets, and was a little frightened in the dark, realising that if I fell down I could not get up again without help. Yet there was no way back. I had to go on, and necessity forced me to improvise, until within a short time I had evolved ways and means of looking after myself. I discovered that by carrying everything that I needed – money, pocket-book, pens, pencils, tickets, etc. – in my right hand trouser pocket, or in the right hand pocket of a great coat, it was possible for me with practice to extract and replace everything at the right time.

I had only one pincer grip – between the stump of my first and index fingers – and this grip had to do everything. Looking back now, I can remember hosts of petty problems that once seemed insurmountable, but which I can now solve unconsciously and without effort. The strength in that one grip of mine became formidable. With it I could withdraw coin after coin, and drop them one after the other into my lap – or hold them in the crook of my arm – until I had found the right fare for bus, taxi or tube; with it, I could carry papers, bank notes and a wallet; write in pencil and in ink; extract matches from a box and light my pipe; handle a fork and a spoon in turn; drink from a glass, tankard or cup; operate press and zip fasteners on my clothing; hold a comb – and many other small, but essential things that needed to be done by day and night.

I knew always that this was only the beginning – and that in time with the help of special apparatus and my own will-power, I could conquer all the things that were necessary to the full and complete civilised form of life to which one is accustomed. The struggle for the recovery of complete independence was advancing well, but there was one other personal struggle which concerned me, and which must have concerned all others who have known infirmity and disfigurement. It was the struggle to force my way back into human society, to regain for myself acceptance by all persons in every walk of life and to impose on them recognition of the fact that I was a human being who was not subnormal.

This struggle, parallel with that for independence, still goes on. It will continue for ever in a degree that will diminish as my powers increase and my appearance is improved, for it is my aim to be restricted by nothing, and to be accepted everywhere. By forcing myself upon society in my present unfinished state of repair, I believe that I can help not only myself, but all with whom I come in contact, to get away from the idea that disfigurement and infirmity should be concealed.

Had I lived and been wounded in savage times I should no doubt have been killed or ignored until I starved to death. In medieval times I should have been shunned, and had I shown any attempt to conquer my disabilities, I would probably have been drowned like a witch. After the last war, I should probably have been shut away until the doctors had restored me, as far as was in their power, to normality. Thank God those days have passed; but there still remains the necessity of educating men and women to the natural and unemotional acceptance of ugliness and mutilation.

At this southern town and in other towns, where wounded men are allowed liberty to circulate irrespective of the horrible nature of their wounds, people have gradually become accustomed to us. They have come to realise that inside ourselves we are the same as they are, and that a maimed body does not necessarily harbour a maimed mind and a warped character. Each one of us must have come into contact with someone who, in spite of physical disability, has risen to a position from which he may guide men stronger in body than himself, but weaker in mind.

Consider for instance the character of Nelson – or to be more topical, that of Franklin D. Roosevelt. No matter how odd my appearance may be, while I am in this southern town nobody stares at me; nobody is surprised or particularly interested, because they have seen far worse sights than me too frequently before to be affected with horror. Yet I only need to go to London, or elsewhere in England where disfigurement is rare, to be stared at and discussed in whispers charged with fear, horror and distaste. I have even heard of cases where people have expressed to each other the conviction that we who have been wounded or maimed in peace and war should be shut away out of sight. What a revolting suggestion! In the streets of London, the centre of British culture, I have heard passers-by – usually well-dressed women – draw in through their teeth a hissing breath. I have heard them click their tongues, then say: "Isn't it terrible to be like that." Even after Bill had lost nearly all signs of his disfigurement he overheard a woman, who passed him with a friend, say: "Coo. Ain't 'e awful!" And this, mark you, is the attitude towards men in uniform; it is much worse when one is a civilian.

All this can be quite amusing – if one can take it like that – but tragically stupid and unworthy of such progress as we have made towards a state of civilisation. Someday I am sure we shall all be educated up to the state of accepting naturally the fact of disfigurement. If it is possible in this southern town, certainly it is possible elsewhere. Wherever I go, I make an attempt not to conceal my disfigured hands. Sometimes I weaken and hide them in my pockets. When I do this I am furious with myself, for I believe that it is my duty to accustom to disfigurement as many people as I know and pass by. In this way, perhaps I may be able to carry on a struggle that for long has been maintained by many other wounded and disfigured men and women. Thus, I hope to prepare a small part of the road for those who follow me along it.

And so, when my first book had circulated sufficiently for me to make new friends, I was glad of this opportunity of widening the range of my human contacts. I tried to mix with different nationalities, creeds, interests, occupations and classes, for I wanted to infect them all with the idea that was so strong in me, that disfigurement must never again be a brand on any man or woman, forbidding them a full life and freedom to move about as they desired.

To the reader all this may appear a little far-fetched; yet it is true, that in spite of eight years of world war within the last thirty, the men and women of this and other countries are peculiarly unprepared to witness and accept the marks that bear witness to the real horrors of war that are worn by their fellow beings. Our leaders have told us that in their opinion this war cannot be brought to a close without a considerable sacrifice of blood, and so the sooner we can accustom ourselves to the reality of war scars, the better it will be both for the unharmed and for the wounded.

As my confidence increased and my appearance improved, I began once more to long to see my mother and my family. The reunion was planned for Christmas 1942. I spent it with my mother, sister and my nephew John. You may remember, if you were within the London area at that time, that Christmas Day was cold and shrouded in gloom. We were in a suburb of North London, staying in the house of a friend. It was there that I first met my only nephew.

For many years I had been away from home at Christmas, so that I had almost forgotten what it meant to small children. John restored my realisation in full. He was then between two and three years old; a sturdy little boy rather than a baby, with blue eyes and curly fair hair. He accepted me immediately – perhaps because his mother had schooled him well in advance for the first shock, but I like to believe that it was because of the natural hidden link of common blood. Soon he was climbing all over me, and for the first time since I had been burned I discovered that I was not necessarily repugnant to a child too young to have learned the good but insincere manners of sophisticated adults.

It surprised me to realise how proud I was to have a baby nephew – how much I was moved by his spontaneous affection, and by the sober evidence in him of a new-born generation which looked up to mine for guidance. John restored in me nearly all the gaps left in my self-confidence. He did much more than that, for he made me long, as never before, to have a family of my own. I knew through him that my life had become selfish and self-centred, and that only with a family of my own could I obliterate my too great interest in myself.

What is a man to do when he first feels the desire to bestow all the inner floods of affection and love cooped up in his nature on a wife and children? What is he to do if he is disfigured and maimed and in part helpless? Can he really ask any girl to accept a life with him which will involve embarrassment and much self-sacrifice for her? Will he ever find the girl who can love him physically and mentally to the extent he desires and needs, irrespective of his ugliness?

These questions rose repeatedly to the surface of my mind for long after my first meeting with John. You will probably agree with me that such a man should not let his handicaps stand in his way; that if he has much to give he will find someone to whom he can devote himself – who will be proud of him, and glad to help him. For myself I know that with the aid of plastic surgery and my own spark of adventure, I shall strive for and win complete independence; then turn part of it to the completion of love and devotion of a family of my own.

The war has deprived so many of us of our home life, and for that reason alone war is horrible. It has split up marriages, and removed many of us from the influences of those to whom we are tied by the marriage contract or by blood. In the coming peace, surely one of the greatest of all our aims must be the restoration of the home, the firm welding of marriage, and the creation of future generations of children, born in and into parental love. How easy it is in wartime to forget the fundamental principles of the good life; and there is little opportunity to give to a family the devotion and time that it needs. Yet only out of the family background is it possible for a new generation to grow up healthy in mind and in body.

Office life has no charms to enthral me. Eight years ago, after two years imprisoned by office walls, I had broken loose at last, and searched for new horizons and greater variety, when I joined the air force to train as a pilot. It was therefore galling to find myself back in London after all these years and once more a slave to the office desk. However, I had no real cause for complaint. My work was interesting, and although my part of the war effort was obscure and infinitesimally small, it was better to play it than to remain idle. When last I worked in London I was still in my late teens. I arrived there fresh from a school life that had been full and exhilarating.

I worked in a small advertising agency. My day was full, like that of older men and women, yet for two years I was paid a salary fluctuating between a pound and thirty-five shillings a week. They told me that my salary was kept so low because I was only learning the job. Although I lived at home, it was forty minutes by electric train and shanks' pony from the office; and it was impossible for me to return for lunch. On my meagre pittance I found for myself railway fares, clothes, and lunch. Practically nothing was left over for even the cheapest forms of entertainment. As the work was interesting, I stayed on in the belief that therein lay my future.

In my spare time I wandered about London. I spent hours in the east end and on Thameside. I grew to love the Thames. Grey, dirty and depressing though I found it, it had yet a character that was impelling and peculiar to itself. There was always bustle in the docks, and on the broad dull waters moved the trim little tugs, fussily impressed, it seemed, by their own importance, officious in their attitude to the docile lighters that trailed behind them. The east end appalled and fascinated me. I shall never be able to shake off completely the feeling of disgust that I developed then at the sight of so much poverty, filth and misery lying around the heart of London, like scum thrown out from the centre of a stagnant pool to cling to its edges.

But now, back in London, as an air force officer, I saw something of the work and play of the other half – of the west end. I became familiar with Mayfair and Belgravia, Chelsea, Knightsbridge and Kensington. I was well paid and lived a comfortable undisturbed life in the midst of cheerful influences and surroundings. The great parks called me. Often when I had a free day, I would walk for hours on end all over them. In spring they were lovely. I fell particularly in love with St. James – when the new green grass and the spring flowers were in bloom; when the lake was alive with ducks, and when by standing on the bridge that spanned the lake, it was possible to see the buildings of Whitehall standing out like white fairy castles skirted by the trees clustered at the side of the water, the whole lit up with a new sun that promised summer.

Perhaps I was equally in love with Regent's Park, particularly in the early summer when the roses were in bloom. What a contrast all this was to the heavily blitzed east end. How sad it was that the great parks of the west end should be so far from the people in the slums. In autumn Hyde Park was beautiful, for the trees were growing old, and as their leaves turned from green to gold, and from gold to brown, the parklands wore gracefully the mantle of maturity, and the sad appeal of old age.

It was in autumn that I returned to work – but for me it was spring, for a new life was awakening within me. The old one of pain and distortion is almost forgotten now, for the mind has no strong memory for pain – it cannot dwell on the dismal retrospect of unhappy thoughts. I was reasonably happy, that autumn and winter, for many of the things that I wanted to do were now within my powers of achievement. Reasonably happy only, for my life was not complete. Yet it was good, and I had regained a strong zest to live it to the full. It was in this spirit that I returned to the southern town in January 1943, for the Annual Dinner of the Guinea Pig Club, an R.A.F. club which I will describe in the next chapter.

Chapter 17

Guinea-Pig Club

There are several clubs and institutions that are peculiar to the flying men of the air force. Some of them are very exclusive. One is the Caterpillar Club, membership of which is confined to officers and men who have been saved from death by a parachute jump from an aircraft. Another is the Goldfish Club, which accepts as members only those who have been forced down into the sea, and subsequently rescued from the water. Fate, alone, can choose the members of these two clubs. She also appoints the members of the Guinea-Pig Club.

Of all the many clubs formed all over the world, surely the Guinea-Pig Club must be both one of the strangest and most exclusive. To qualify for membership would be the desire of no one; yet, to become a member is at once a privilege and a pleasure. Membership is open only to flying men of the air force who have been burned and disfigured, and then treated by McIndoe and his staff at the Plastic Unit.

The idea of the club was conceived by a group of four or five officer-patients who were still in McIndoe's hands about Christmas time, 1940. One of them, then a squadron leader, is now a group captain. Another, Geoffrey, has since returned to operational flying and has won a D.F.C. Two others have returned to ground duties and have also been promoted. Yet another, who like Geoffrey returned to fly once more against the enemy, has since been killed.

They called it the Guinea-Pig Club because they regarded themselves, light heartedly, as the guinea-pigs upon whom McIndoe practised and improved his skill. They made Peter the treasurer, since he was at that time still unable to walk, and it would therefore have been very difficult for him to run away with the funds. They called in Bill to advise them on club rules. Then, seated around a table in one of the recreation huts of the hospital, they declared and recorded their object in forming the club, and laid down plans for its development and expansion in the future. Their object was to create an organisation by means of which they, and their fellow patients, might maintain contact with each other long after they had finally left the hospital. They laid plans for a dinner, to take place in the coming January and thereafter annually.

The next thing they did was to invite McIndoe and the other doctors on the hospital staff to become members. This invitation was unanimously accepted. Then they declared the existence of a society, to be known as the Society for Prevention of Cruelty to Guinea-Pigs. To membership of this society, they elected a number of individuals – one of the first of whom was Bill – who had, by means of that practical friendship to the patients, made as pleasant as possible their long periods of hospital treatment. Later it was the members of this society who provided most of the funds necessary for the purchase of food and drink for the dinners. In this way the Guinea-Pig Club was created and controlled by patients, supported by their doctors, and largely financed by their friends.

The first dinner provided, as had been hoped, a means of renewing that fellowship which had developed during long months in hospital; a fellowship that knew no differentiation of rank between those of us who had become brothers, first in misfortune and finally in hope, as each one of us recovered under the care of McIndoe. At the second dinner it became obvious that something big had been started, for the sight of past patients, partially or completely restored to normality, provided a powerful source of hope and encouragement for all newcomers. By the time the third dinner took place many of the original patients – some of whom had been injured at the time of Dunkirk or later in the Battle of Britain – had recovered their good looks and regained their former efficiency and mobility. It was then quite clear that the Guinea-Pig Club had to offer to all wounded men present, and those there with them, a message of hope. It had by that time absorbed into honorary membership Air Marshals and other leading officers of the home and dominion air forces, and a body of members of the society for the Prevention of Cruelty to Guinea-Pigs who could be relied upon to extend permanent friendship towards all the patients present.

Naturally it was difficult in the middle of the war to collect together the members of the club. However, each year it was essential for the Boss to call together his guinea-pigs – at least, as many of them as remained scattered over the United Kingdom, for some had already gone overseas. Records of progress had to be brought up to date and appointments arranged for any operations that might be necessary in the future.

Plastic surgical treatment may often be spread over two or more years. During the long periods in between operations, most patients returned to full or light duty with the R.A.F. In order to condense the work involved in checking a number of cases that ran into hundreds, McIndoe arranged a month or so in advance for a convocation of all his guinea-pigs to take place on a particular day each January. The evening of that day was set aside for the annual dinner of the club.

So far I have been able to attend the last two dinners, and I hope to be present at the next and at many more. The last one took place on a Friday in January 1943. All day, patients were arriving back at the Plastic Unit. They came from many different R.A.F. stations scattered all over the United Kingdom. The dentists' lecture room, in which they congregated and awaited their turn to see McIndoe, was filled with an excited hubbub of sound. Everyone present had been operated upon at least once. Some had lain as many as twenty and thirty times upon the operating "slab". Each one bore some signs on his person to bear witness to his right to membership of the club. Many of the signs were slight, others much more pronounced.

It was almost possible to date a patient's stay in hospital by the type of scars he still possessed. One saw new eyebrows and ears; jaws and chins; lips and cheeks; legs that had been restored by graft and hands that had recovered their lost usefulness. Those whom many of us had last seen with faces that were distorted and ribbed with scars or lying in beds with their hands and heads obscured by dressings, were now fit and robust, their grafted hands and faces bronzed and healthy. They were nearly all still in uniform, for few indeed of the patients of McIndoe left the hospital still unfit for ground or flying duties. It was difficult to believe that they were the same men who had lain – not so very long ago – mutilated, sick and weak in the beds of the service wards. There were no long faces. Everyone there must have felt within him – as I did – a glow of pride, confidence and satisfaction. Each one, a miracle himself, was surrounded by similar miracles of surgical skill. For McIndoe and his assistants this was indeed a great day.

It reached its climax that evening when we all sat down together at the dinner tables. There were more than a hundred past and present patients seated at the long tables set out in the officers' club room above Bill's bar. The tables were arranged in the form of a three-sided rectangle, with an extra table running up the centre. Our guests included Australian and Canadian Air Marshals, the Director General of R.A.F. Medical Services, the Air Officer Commander-in-Chief of Fighter Command and the members of the Society for Prevention of Cruelty to Guinea-Pigs. Of all the happy faces there, perhaps one of the happiest was that of Bill. After dinner there were toasts and speeches.

Warm tributes were paid by grateful patients to McIndoe and his staff of experts. In his reply, McIndoe, looking round at the satisfactory evidence of the work of his hands and brain, urged us never to lose the feelings of brotherhood which had united us, irrespective of nationality, and rank, age, and creed, in his hospital wards. There were amongst us Australians, South Africans, and New Zealanders; Canadians and Americans; Frenchmen, Dutchmen and Belgians; Norwegians, Poles, and Czechs; Englishmen and Welshmen; Irishmen and Scots. In rank we ranged from air marshals to air craftsmen. Each one of us had seen something of the stark reality of war. We had a message to carry away with us wherever we went. It was a message born of a mutual ordeal, later transformed into recovery. It was a message of courage and brotherhood for the present, and hope for the future.

After dinner we were entertained by Arthur Riscoe, Frances Day and Harry Jacobson, who had been with us in the hospital many times before. When eventually we broke up and returned to hospital, or to the houses where we were guests for the weekend, there must have been few of us who did not feel, as I did, that this inspiring assembly was one man's great triumph. Without the inspiration, skill and devotion of McIndoe, such a meeting could never have been possible.

Chapter 18

Limb Workshop

I n the outskirts of London[22] there is a hospital, that since the last war must
  have become well known to disabled service and ex-service men and their
  relations. Its main entrance is approached from a lane, leading up from one
of the many commons that separate the monotonous blocks of suburbia that
encircle London at its outer fringe.

It is an attractive lane. It winds up gently past semi-detached villas, a block
of modern flats and enclosed sports grounds. At the summit of its rise stands
the hospital. The main building was once, I imagine, a country mansion.
It is an attractive red-brick building covered here and there by clinging
creeper. Around it are clustered groups of huts – less attractive, but of infinite
importance for the work that takes place within. These huts spread out from
the main building in most directions. Some of them contain wards, operating
theatres, offices, and the other varied apartments essential to a hospital. In
others there are workshops. There disabled men and women are encouraged
during their time in hospital to rehabilitate themselves to work. There, if they
so desire, they may learn a trade, which will be of use to them upon their
return to the outside world and the struggle for existence.

There are other buildings and hutments, satellite to the main pile, wherein
Ministry of Pensions surgeons and doctors receive the maimed who arrive
there in quest of an artificial limb. Behind these buildings stand two that are
larger than the rest. They are the factories in which civilian firms, contracted
by the Ministry, design, construct, and fit the new arms and legs. One factory
specialises in legs; another in arms and hands.

One day in March 1943 I found myself outside the wrought iron gates
that separate the hospital grounds from the lane. The Air Ministry had sent
me there to ask for an artificial hand to fit over my left-hand stump. I passed

---

[22] Queen Mary's, Roehampton. The history of Queen Mary's began with the rehabilitation of
service personnel who had lost limbs during the First World War. Amputee rehabilitation
has continued to be a service at the hospital ever since.

through the gates and along the road that led me past the circular lawn in front of the mansion, past the rehabilitation workshops, past the signpost marked "To Limb Fitting Centre".

Finally, I arrived at the waiting room, and I went in. Sitting on armchairs pulled up to two long tables set in the middle of a bare, but warm, room, was a number of soldiers in hospital blue and a few ex-service men. Silently they perused bound editions of *Punch* – editions that had first appeared at the beginning of the century – and more recent tattered copies of *Picture Post*. I presented myself at a small hatch window, handed in my chit, watched a clerk enter my particulars in a file, then sat down at the table with the others, there to await my turn to go before the surgeons.

When my turn arrived, I was shown into a consulting room. A number of Ministry of Pensions doctors were there. They examined my hands with sympathetic interest. They asked me questions regarding the nature of the accident that had brought me to them. They were surprised to hear that I was already back at work, and examined the leather glove, complete with its wire hook, with which I handled a telephone.

Although impressed by the neatness of my stump they expressed surprise at the fact that my hand had not been completely removed. Gently they handled it, next checked its range of movement. This was very small – between fifteen- and twenty-degrees forwards. It would not move backwards at all because of the shortening of tendons surrounded by scar tissue on my burned forearm. This short stump of hand, stretching from my wrist to a point where the metacarpal bones had been trimmed and shortened after the removal of my knuckles, was to me a very precious possession. Equally precious was the movement in my wrist. I wished to preserve and use both of them, small though they were. However, the doctors did not altogether agree that they were of much real value. After consultation among themselves, and with an expert from the arm factory, they told me that it was their opinion that I ought to submit to a further amputation – this time removing my hand, wrist and forearm back to within five inches of the elbow joint.

Now this suggestion came as something of a shock, for I had been treated both in France and in England with a view to keeping as much of my arms and hands as it was possible to preserve in a healthy state. Furthermore, I believed that there must be some way of utilising the wrist movement that through exercise I had worked so hard to preserve and had succeeded in developing from zero to between fifteen and twenty degrees. It seemed to me that on to an artificial hand fitted over my stump and attached to my arm – fully articulated over the wrist – it should be possible to fit some kind of mechanism, which would increase the movement, and be so designed as to open and close an artificial thumb – or alternatively four fingers in unison – by the movements of my wrist. With such an appliance I believed that it would be possible to pick up light articles and to hold and release them at will. This view was not shared by the surgeons.

Unanimously they repeated to me their advice to submit to an amputation that would leave me with only a stump of forearm five inches long from tip to elbow joint. They argued that on this stump they could fit one of their standard arms with hand attached; that this arrangement would give me a strong hand on one side of my body with which I should be able to carry heavy articles and hold light ones between the permanently curved fingers and a thumb operated by a strap fitted round my right shoulder. They did not consider that any real use could be developed out of my small wrist movement, and pointed out that any hand they fitted on to the end of my half-hand stump would be grotesquely long.

As I did not feel disposed to accept the offer of an amputation without giving the matter careful thought, I asked them if they would be prepared to make something in the way of an appliance suitable for me to fit on to my existing stump. They agreed to that readily, and I left them somewhat relieved.

A few days later I returned and was admitted to the casting room of the artificial hand factory. It was one of several rooms contained in the new brick building of the factory. All round the walls there were shelves loaded with plaster of paris stumps. Each one was marked in indelible pencil with the owner's name. Most of them were forearm stumps, but there were also shoulders, and a few partially mutilated hands – those from which some of the fingers had been lost. They were grey and ugly, and reminded me of a repair workshop for wax models. In the centre of the room there was a wooden table; they asked me to sit beside it.

One of the limb-fitting experts emptied a pile of white powder into a basin, added water, and began to mix it with a pestle. In the meantime, one of the others covered my stump and part of my arm with Vaseline, and then prepared the plaster box. This was made of wood, had detachable sides, and was open at the top. From one end had been cut out a hemispherical opening, against which my forearm rested when my hand and wrist were in the box. When the plaster was ready it was poured gently into the box, until it was smoothly settled around my hand, wrist and arm. It was the best quality white Italian plaster and looked like icing sugar. My hand was firmly embedded in it but only half covered.

When it had set completely, they told me to remove my hand, which I did somewhat gingerly, until I found that the Vaseline had prevented any adhesion of plaster to the hairs on my skin. When they had scraped the top level, covered it with Vaseline, and fitted higher sides on to the box, I replaced my hand. They poured on more plaster to complete the second half of the cast. In this way the negative cast was made in two sections. Later they placed the two halves of the cast together and poured plaster into the hole made by my hand. When it was set, they drew out an exact replica of my hand and wrist, and they then marked it with my name in indelible pencil.

Afterwards the foreman showed me round the factory. There must have been about forty men, most of them over middle age and some of them wearing artificial limbs themselves, at work at long deal benches, set in long rows up and down the length of the main room. They were closely packed but had sufficient room to work comfortably. Overhead ran the belts that conveyed power from plant to machine. Above the room – the ceiling, arched, as in the old style aircraft hangar – was high for the size of the factory. The arrangement of lights and ventilation was good; there was warmth and light without stuffiness and glare. The first impression I had was one of extreme ugliness. Closer inspection of the work going on at the benches made me forget the drabness of the surroundings.

Everywhere men were working on the various details that combine to make artificial arms and hands. Some were moulding wet leather onto plaster casts; others were assembling the intricate steel mechanism that controls the working and free swinging of the arm. The workmanship was beautiful – no matter whether it was the stitching on leather, the moulding of plastic fingers, the assembly of mechanical parts, or any of the other processes and assemblies. The finished arms, complete with hand attached, were beautiful and strong. They were made of polished leather, plastics, and chromium plate. Every arm and hand was "tailor made". Each one was vastly different, for no two stumps were alike, and few men's arms would fit another.

Naturally my interest was centred on the hands. They were beautifully worked and very realistic, were painted flesh colour, and shaped almost perfectly – even to grooves around the cuticle at the base of the nails. Casts were drawn from tallow wax mouldings, which formed the base for the next process. From this the fingers were removed and replaced with others cut out of cork. These were glued to the wax, then filed and polished until they had a smooth finish. Next, in an adjoining room, they were taken by girls, who began to cover them with strips of linen. On to the cover of linen was painted a special glue. Further coats of linen and glue were added, one after the other, and the resulting sticky plastic substance was smoothed carefully and left to dry.

Later the wax mould was removed, leaving the cork fingers inside the linen and the rest of the hand hollow. The result was a white hand of extraordinary strength. It was now painted pink and sized with varnish. It was then returned to the main factory, where it was fitted with a detachable block at the wrist of the artificial arm to which it was destined to belong. These were the "dress" hands – particularly in demand for women. Usually, they were made with the fingers bent inwards, so that the forefinger touched the thumb.

Sometimes the thumb was made separately out of wood. It was articulated at the base by means of a ball joint and socket, and fitted with mechanism by means of which it could be opened and closed. In this way, small light articles could be carried between the thumb and forefinger and loops held within the bend of the four fingers. They were light, yet so toughly made that it was possible to beat them against a bench without causing them damage. As they were sized with special varnish, they were also waterproof.

Since some people preferred to have a hand which had fully articulated fingers and thumb, these too could be provided. There was one craftsman of outstanding skill, rare master of an unusual trade, who modelled articulated fingers out of hard wood. At each knuckle there was a neat, perfectly fitted, fully articulating joint. By using the other hand, it was possible to bend these articulated fingers into most shapes required. However, although they would stay in position, they could not be locked and were therefore useless for carrying anything heavy. This did not matter as much as one might reasonably expect, for if necessary, it could easily be removed and replaced by one or other type of mechanical device designed to fulfil a special *rôle*.

For the gardener and manual labourer there was a detachable spade grip; for eating, there were special knives, forks and spoons; there were also nail and hairbrush holders. For carrying heavy articles with loop handles, the best appliance was a Williamson hook – made in the form of a circle, broken in one place. So efficient were some of the hooks and other special appliances however, that many men preferred them to the hand itself, though it was the most unobtrusive thing of all, and the one that had the most natural appearance. Of all the many appliances, I was personally impressed most by the split hook.

The split hook could be locked into the same fitting at the wrist block that held the hand which it replaced. As its name suggests, it is a rounded hook split in two from the tip right up the middle to the base. Made of steel and coated with chromium plate, it is quite neat in appearance, and has a rounded narrow spike. I have often wondered why some men preferred a black patch to a glass eye. I think it must be because there is a mysterious romantic glamour that goes with the patch. It is rather the same with a hook. Its normal position is tightly closed, so that the split is not noticeable. This is the best position when it is desired to use the crook of the hook for carrying anything heavy and is an excellent substitute for four curled fingers. It even has certain advantages over nature since it is insensible. For more refined movements usually made by fingers – either individually or combined in pairs – the split comes into operation. On the side of the hook there is a lever arm, at the end of which is attached a strap which passes through loops in the artificial arm, and then across the back to the opposite shoulder, over which it is passed in the form of a loop. By moving the muscles of the back or shoulder, the hook is opened.

When the strain is released the hook closes, under the influence of a simple arrangement of rubber bands wound tightly round the base of the hook at the lever arm. This may sound rather involved and complicated, but actually it is not. Control is quite easy to obtain and becomes automatic in a few hours. The width of the split can easily be limited to most dimensions required, and such small articles as pins can be selected from a pile. In some ways it is even more efficient than human fingers – for instance, with the split hook it is easy to pick up a length of cigarette ash without breaking it, whereas this is well-nigh impossible by using forefinger and thumb. (If you don't believe me, try it and see.) To prevent slipping, the inside surfaces of the split in the hook are serrated; alternatively, they may be lined with thin rubber.

Hands have often been made that have been fitted with mechanism to open and close fully articulated fingers and thumbs. I saw one at the limb factory. It was made of steel, was hollow at the palm and wrist, and was articulated at the base of each finger individually and the ball of the thumb. The metal had been cut away from the inside of each finger and the thumb and replaced by shaped cork.

Inside the hollow – between palm, back and wrist – were fitted springs to hold the fingers and thumb united so that the tip of the thumb was pressed firmly against the tips of the fingers. Also, inside this hollow there was a simple mechanism controlled by a steel rod that worked in opposition to the springs and pushed fingers and thumb apart. On to the end of the rod was fitted a wire cable that was threaded out through a hole near the wrist and led back to the shoulder of the opposite arm, where it was secured by a loop. It was operated by moving shoulder or back, exactly in the same manner as the split hook.

It was very neat and seemed to me to be an excellent appliance. However, they told me that it was not very popular – possibly because it was rather heavy.

My first artificial appliance was a split hook, set in a special mounting on the back of a leather glove that was fitted to my hand stump. It was neatly made, and I find it most useful. Now they are making me an artificial hand with fixed curled fingers and a movable thumb. This will not be quite as useful as the split hook, but when covered with a glove, will be practically indistinguishable from the real thing. I am most grateful for all that has been done for me in this limb factory.

Great advances have been made since the beginning of the first world war in the design and construction of artificial hands. Yet there still remains an unlimited field of scope for improvement. Nothing has yet been invented and constructed that reproduces more than a vague suggestion of one or two of the natural movements of the human hand.

This is not surprising, for there have been few more glorious achievements of Nature than that of the human hand. It is a mass of intricately interleaved joints – each one perfectly fluid and free from friction – held together by muscles so cunningly interconnected that they are capable of moving the fingers separately and in unison in a most varied manner. The whole system is linked to the brain by a system of nerves that carry instantaneous messages to and from the distant brain which controls each movement. This extraordinary system is even waterproof and guaranteed to withstand the harshest treatment with no appreciable signs of wear for a whole lifetime.

When attempting to replace this intricate miracle of Nature by a man-made substitute, one comes up against problems that seem insurmountable. For instance, there is the problem of how to reproduce mechanically a system that can be controlled remotely by the brain; how to reproduce the sense of touch; how, in an area as small as a hand, to create a mechanism as light, yet as powerful as that of Nature. There are, however, other problems that should soon be within the powers of man to solve, and here is a chance for anyone who can afford to spend time and money on research and experiment. He is unlikely to have strong competition, for the limb factories are overworked on routine demands, and there is no evidence that the government has given the matter weighty consideration.

There are certain methods by which surgeons can prepare the extensor and flexor muscles of an amputee's arm in such a way that they can be harnessed to an artificial hand and operate it satisfactorily. These methods do not seem to have been tried frequently in this country but have found some favour with surgeons of other nations – in particular in Germany, Italy and the United States of America. The interesting and well-illustrated *Cine-plastic Operations on Stumps of the Upper Extremity*,[23] by Rudolf Nissen, M.D. (New York) and Ernst Bergman, M.D. (New York) covers this subject.

One method applied is the creation of tunnels in the muscles into which are placed ivory pegs which are connected to a mechanical hand appliance.

---

[23] William Heinemann Medical Books, Ltd., London.

Chapter 19

Tonsillitis

It was in the summer of the year 1943 that I returned to Ward 3. For long McIndoe had been itching to start work again on my face. After working for six months at the Air Ministry I was at last ready to return to the hospital bed. Here a surprise was in store for me, for when the house surgeon examined me the day before my first operation was due to take place, he reported that my tonsils were swollen. I had come back to Ward 3 for plastic surgery only to find that I was suffering from tonsillitis! This was a great anticlimax, and extremely irritating as it was bound to delay my plastic treatment for some time.

They sent me away on sick leave until such time as the swelling in and around my tonsils had subsided sufficiently for it to be safe to remove the offending glands without danger of complications. This was a complete deadlock as far as I was concerned, and an infuriating waste of time. I returned to London and spent most of my sick leave there.

While I was still in London I was approached by the B.B.C. and asked to take part in a broadcast. It was to be one of a series destined for the United States and designed to give Americans some idea of the hopes held by ordinary people here for the reconstruction of our way of life after the war. For this broadcast, the first of the series, a discussion was arranged and recorded. Four of us took part in the discussion, each one expressing his own views and hopes. There was a Trades Union official, a lorry driver, the wife of a lighterman and myself. It was both interesting and entertaining for us – I hope it was equally so for the Americans who listened to it.

This was my first experience of the microphone. As a result of it I was soon afterwards asked to give two further broadcasts. One was for transmission to France. It was in French, and was part of the programme "*Les Français parlent aux Français*" transmitted regularly by the French section of the B.B.C. It had as its purpose the forewarning of the French people of large-scale air bombardments of France by the R.A.F. and the American 8th Army Air Force.

The subject of this broadcast was naturally painful to me. I wondered whether any of my friends still in France heard it and recognised my voice. It was like talking to oneself in the darkness, unaware whether or not one was being overheard. Broadcasting in my own peculiar French was a most moving experience for me, for when I left France I had pledged myself to friendship for her, and here at last was an occasion to express it publicly.

More moving still for me was a broadcast which I made on July 14th on the Home Service. It was part of a programme entitled *France Fights On* [see Appendix II]. It gave me a wonderful chance of expressing my faith in the ultimate liberation and rebirth of France – a rebirth which would, I was convinced, restore her as a great and powerful nation. I felt, as I spoke, that at last I was making a real effort to fulfil a promise I had made many months before to my courageous French friends. Under the pressure of the evil forces of occupation a new purpose, a new patriotism had been born in French hearts.

A great deal of preparation takes place before most broadcasts are delivered to the public. First of all, I visited the producer and gave him an outline of my ideas on the subject of my short talk. He then told me the lines on which I should prepare my script. After I had finished writing the script, he checked it, and then transformed it from a piece of writing into a broadcast. About two thousand words were needed to fill in five minutes of talking time.

I was told that sentences should be short, that words full of sibilants should be avoided, that long pauses should be made for effect at certain points. "You should try", he said, "to concentrate on the effect of silence. In fact, your broadcast should appear to you as a long period of silence interrupted at intervals by moments of sound." Then he made me rehearse the delivery of the script several times, while he briefed me and checked the timing, until I had reached as near the stage of perfection as was within my power. I was impressed by the practical psychology of this producer; with his human understanding of the great importance I attached to this particular broadcast, he transformed a rather nerve-racking experience into a great pleasure.

On the evening of the broadcast the producer took me to a studio. On the way we stopped at the B.B.C. club bar where I took some Dutch courage in the form of whisky. We were now below ground. The air conditioned and electric-lighted studio was shaped like a box and resembled a padded cell. In fact, the walls were actually padded with thick, perforated white panels of sound absorbing material, which prevented echo and kept the studio soundproof. In the centre of the studio stood a solid square table, the top of which was covered with a thick mesh of twine.

On the table stood the microphone – the most alarming thing in the room; even more frightening than the electric clock on one of the walls, ticking out sharply and relentlessly the passing seconds marked on its face by the long arm that jerked around the dial. Plain armchairs were drawn up to the table. One of the walls was broken by a glass window, through which I could see the engineer. He was sitting beside the controls, ready to put the broadcast on the air, and then regulate its transmission. On the table in front of him was a copy of the script approved by the B.B.C. and the Air Ministry. At the slightest deviation from this script, it was his duty to throw a master switch and cut out the broadcast.

I was told to relax, and to smile. The effect of a smile on the voice is to alter its tone – in fact a smile might almost be said to be audible. My imagination ran rife, and I was momentarily scared almost speechless at the thought of the enormous power of the microphone that was about to carry my voice all over the world. It was uncanny to be sitting there with only the producer beside me, particularly as my speech had to synchronise with a number of other speakers in a different studio. However, when I began talking all nervousness disappeared and the broadcast went without a hitch. When I stopped speaking I was conscious of a strange sensation – although I had been speaking to a vast audience no one was there to hiss or clap – there was no other sound but the staccato ticking of the perpetually moving clock.

Broadcasting is something which can be done without hands, and even without a presentable appearance. It is sometimes well within the scope of a crippled man, provided that he has something to say, and has a suitable microphone voice with which to say it.

The day after this broadcast I returned to Ward 3. At half past eight the next morning my tonsils were removed.

When on sick leave recovering from my tonsillectomy operation I paid a visit to Oxford. There I stayed in St. John's College as the guest of the senior tutor. Oxford had always attracted me. I was now toying with the idea of trying to enter St. John's College, with the object of getting a real educational background, which I had missed after leaving school. I was very kindly received and well entertained. In the atmosphere of antiquity that surrounded the wonderful old sixteenth century buildings of the college I found a welcome peace. It would have been pleasant to rest there for a year or two studying and writing. However, I was advised against entering the college. I was told that in my case and with my disabilities it would be wiser for me to start once more on the worldly business of settling my future employment. After all, I was twenty-nine, and although that was not a very great age, it was better for me to work than to study.

I hope that other wounded men, younger than I, will be given a full and fair chance of pursuing a course of study at the great universities after their war service is over. It seems to me that the universities and the country as a whole should make a great effort to induce young men who have been wounded in the war to enrich their lives and improve their future prospects by means of a university course. Many of them would probably have entered a university instead of one of the services had there been no war. Others must have broken off their studies; they should certainly return to them.

I had expected to have finished this book before returning to Ward 3 for further operations. However, I was once more back in bed before I had time to write this and the following chapter. I am glad of that, for it gives me a chance to give you one last glimpse of the life of the ward before I close the subject for ever.

For a long time, the Plastic Unit had become like a second home to me. I had come to know the doctors and the nurses, and many scores of patients. Ward 3 had changed little. Sister was still her same self – slight, fair, Irish, temperamental, conscientious to a degree, and as skilful as ever. The nurses were still maintaining their reputation for charm and good looks – their facility for hard work providing a strong contradiction to the popular assumption that work and beauty do not go hand in hand. The Bathroom Boys were still there, cheerful and busy.

I lay in bed recovering from an operation by means of which McIndoe had transferred a large area of the skin from my stomach to my left cheek and my forehead, to replace the last remaining pieces of burned and red scarred tissue left on my face. I watched the nurses moving about the ward, and listened, still unwillingly, to the radio. It was good to be back. My operations were more than three quarters over. My face had been transformed, and only trimming would now be necessary before it was completely finished. There still remained two or three major operations to be carried out on my right hand. I was along the way to recovery.

As I lay there thinking, I wondered what would become of this hospital after the war. I hoped that the huts would be demolished, and that a great new modern building would arise from the present foundation. I hoped that McIndoe would continue his miraculous work long after the war, and that the disfigured and maimed would be treated as we had been treated and would be given new hope – with their new skin – to regain a normal way of life.

The majority of the beds were occupied by Canadian airmen. Assisting McIndoe, and responsible for the Canadians was a group of surgeons and nurses of the R.C.A.F. Their leader was Wing Commander Ross Tilley, who would soon have a twin plastic surgery unit of his own; for in a field adjoining the hospital grounds Canadian troops were erecting a Canadian Wing. It was to be dedicated as a memorial to Canadian officers and men killed on air operations during this war. As soon as it was ready it would be filled, at first by Canadians in this country already wounded and disfigured, later by repatriated prisoners of war in need of plastic treatment. It was to be constructed in stone and brick and especially designed for plastic surgery.

When I was fit to get up I went and sat in my dressing gown in the officers' recreation room. Chris, Fighting French paratroop officer, was there. He had returned for an operation on one of his hands. His right leg was encased in plaster. Not content with having been severely burned, he had returned to parachuting and broken his leg during his fifteenth jump. McIndoe once described him as "indestructible." There was another Fighting Frenchman there. He had commanded a French Spitfire squadron and had been shot up over France. His Spitfire caught fire. His eyelids were burnt before he could get out. He landed by parachute in France. A few weeks later he was back in England. His eyelids were remodelled with grafts. At present he was completely blacked out. When his new eyelids had settled down he was determined to return to flying again – once more over France in his Spitfire, this time perhaps covering the landing of Anglo-American troops. To me they were fine examples of the courage that inspired young Frenchmen all over the world.

Let no one dare to try and tell me that the French lack guts.

There was also an Army doctor, a Scot, who had been burned in Tunisia. He boasted that his grafts were the best that had ever been given to anyone. Certainly, they were beautiful. His early treatment of saline was instantaneous, for he had been thrown, a burning torch, straight into the sea. There were others; Ken, who had been blinded – but retained humour and hope to the full; a New Zealand airman with wounds in his back; a Canadian flying officer, journalist in peace time, itching to be back in the air in spite of a nasty leg wound; a radio officer of British Overseas Airways, whose broken jaw was being restored to shape by the dental plastic surgeons.

We sat around the stove and listened to records of a Chopin piano concerto. We were a strange and varied community. We might be classified as victims of war, but we were all confident in our surgeons – and happy. The spirit inspired by McIndoe and kept alive by everyone in the hospital will serve always as an inspiration to all of us. I know that the months I have spent in this hospital have been predominantly happy.

Chapter 20

Wounded Youth

Whereas we may all hope that this war will end soon, we have been warned repeatedly by our leaders against the dangers of complacence. We have been told that almost certainly great and bloody battles have yet to be fought against both Germans and Japanese before we can bring this war to a victorious conclusion. If these battles take place, badly wounded men in large numbers will eventually return to this country. What kind of a reception will they find waiting for them?

There are other countries that believe in attempting to conceal from their people the sight of mutilated and disfigured men. There are some people in this country who favour such a policy; fortunately, they are, I believe, in a very small minority. If this policy were pursued in these islands it would mean the sacrifice of the happiness of men who sacrificed many other things for us.

Anyone who has come into close contact for a reasonable period of time with disfigured and maimed men and women, will, I am sure, agree with me that when the first shock has worn off they have found that it is easy to forget surface disfigurement after contact has been made with the personality that lies beneath it. We, the disfigured, are not abnormal. It is of vital importance that everyone should realise this fact and treat us as normal human beings. We have our burden to bear, but you can lighten it until we become unconscious of its weight. How can you do this?

In my opinion it is mainly the responsibility of state departments to restore us, rehabilitate us and ensure us of either employment or pension. Thereafter it is our individual responsibility to strike out for ourselves. To compete with the physically fit we will have to struggle. You can help us to achieve our ends. We need your help. You can give it to us in many different ways; first of all by trying to understand what we feel and what we think; secondly, by your friendship and encouragement.

We do not want sympathy contaminated by sentimentality. We do not want cheap hero worship. We do not want pity. Two things we all aspire to attain; the first is to be accepted by human society as completely normal human beings; the second is to regain our independence. Fortified by your help and our own spirit, nothing is impossible to us.

Epilogue

After some two years of treatment, William Simpson was able to return to RAF service, in his case a 'desk job' at the Air Ministry. There he came to the attention of Lord Beaverbrook, who, as *The Times* pointed out in its edition of 7 December 2005, 'sent him as an air and war correspondent for the *Sunday Express* to Belgium as its territory was liberated, and later to Germany before the end of hostilities.'

Simpson retired from the RAF in 1948, by which time he had attained the rank of squadron leader. He joined British European Airways as a press officer.

On the evening of Monday, 9 January 1961, Simpson became the 146th subject of the BBC television programme *This Is Your Life*. Having been surprised by Eammon Andrews at the BBC's Lime Grove Studios, he was presented with the famous red book in front of an audience that included Sergeant, later Warrant Officer, Edward Odell.

In 1973, as BEA merged with British Overseas Airways Corporation to form British Airways, William retired from his role as public relations director – though he continued to undertake consultancy roles in the aviation industry.

As well as advising the Housing Corporation and the Leonard Cheshire Foundation, Simpson gave unremitting service to the disabled. For more than thirty years he was a member of the National Advisory Council on the Employment of Disabled People, for which work he was appointed OBE.

Squadron Leader William Simpson, OBE, DFC, passed away on 15 November 2005, aged 91.

APPENDICES

No.12 Squadron Operations Record Book
10 May 1940

Battle I
L4949, "V"

       F/Lt. Simpson, W.

       513884, Sgt. Odell

       550950, LAC. Tomlinson

Bombing Operations Order No.1

Time Up   1705

Time Down   F/L

Battle I
L5190, "P"

       P/O. Matthews, A.W.

       517089, Sgt. Maderson

       580311, LAC. Senior

Bombing Operations Order No.1

Time Up   1705

Time Down   -

Battle I
P2243, "U"

       F/Lt. Hunt, P.H.M.S.

       516479, Sgt. Wilks

       537207, LAC. Cooke

Time Up   1650

Time Down   F/L

Battle I
L5249, "D"

> P/O. Hulse, C.L.
> 563811, Sgt. Young
> 611633, LAC. Aitken

Bombing Operations Order No.1

Time Up   1650
Time Down   1830

Details of Sortie or Flight:

Two half sections had to attack column on road between the town of LUXEMBURG, JUNGLISTER and ECHTERNACH. Aircraft were routed S. of the town of LUXEMBURG and to avoid main roads over enemy occupied territory up to target area.

F/Lt. Simpson of "B" Flight dropped four bombs low level on the road while under intense A.A. and machine gun fire on that part of the road between LUXEMBURG and JUNGLISTER at 1752 hrs, photographs of the bomb bursts were taken by LAC. Tomlinson. Immediately afterwards Sgt. Odell reported a leak in the petrol tank and course was set for the frontier.

Just after passing north of VIRTON in Belgium the pilot informed crew that as engine was missing badly he was going to force land; this took place with wheels up in a rough field at 1815 hours. Immediately the aircraft struck the ground it caught fire.

The observer – Sgt. Odell and the W.T. Operator – LAC. Tomlinson jumped out of the machine and pulled F/Lt. Simpson clear, his hands being badly burnt. LAC. Tomlinson suffered from burns on the hands while doing this. On the crew reaching a point about 150 yds from the machine it blew up. For this exploit F/Lt. Simpson was subsequently awarded the D.F.C., Sgt. Odell the D.F.M. and Cpl. Tomlinson the D.F.M.

P/O Matthews of "B" Flight and crew failed to return but were last seen by F/Lt. Simpson immediately after attacking the target, they turned in a N. Easterly direction, aircraft appeared under control and to have landed at about 1800 hours.

F/Lt. Hunt of "A" Flight had to force land at PIENNES before he got to target owing to the bomb control being shot away.

P/O. Hulse of "A" Flight attached the target low level under heavy cross machine gun fire, just before reaching it his observer Sgt. Young was wounded in the shoulder. One bomb landed close to the road on which A.F.V's were moving south.

The National Archives, AIR 27/164

Appendix II

Citations for Gallantry Awards

Distinguished Flying Cross

Flight Lieutenant William SIMPSON (37235)

In May, 1940, this officer led a half section of aircraft carrying out a low level bombing attack on troops and convoys on a road between Luxemburg and Junglister, with the object of checking the German advance after the violation of Holland and Belgium. Despite intense anti-aircraft fire after crossing the frontier, he pressed home the attack and scored four direct hits on the convoy. After the attack, owing to a leak in the petrol tank, it was necessary to make a forced landing. As the aircraft touched ground flames arose from the bomb aimer's trap. The pilot was only saved by the prompt action of the crew before the aircraft exploded. Flight Lieutenant Simpson has consistently done good work.

Distinguished Flying Medal

513884 Sergeant Edward Nelson ODELL
550950 Corporal Robert Tod TOMLINSON

These airmen acted as air observer and wireless operator-air gunner respectively in an aircraft piloted by Flight Lieutenant Simpson engaged on a low level bombing attack on enemy troops and convoys. After the attack a petrol leak compelled a forced landing, and the aircraft caught fire. These airmen, without thought for their own safety, immediately went to the aid of the pilot (who was enveloped in flames) and pulled him clear of the aircraft which afterwards exploded. Valuable photographs of the bombing and convoy were obtained by Corporal Tomlinson.

The London Gazette
No.34860, 31 May 1940

Appendix III

'The French Fight On'

The following is a transcript of a recording that William Simpson wrote, and which was broadcast on the BBC on 14 July 1943.

I am going to say something for a few minutes about France and the French. I feel I have to say it, because since I got back here I have found so much misunderstanding of the French people.

As a country, I think we are always prone to underate other countries and some people, I find, in view of what happened to the French are busy now writing off France. Well, that doesn't square with my own experience. It happened to come to me unusually intense in concentrated form, in fact I spent the worst eighteen months of my life in France. So, the little things I have to say about the French are nice things; well you will agree, I had good opportunity to judge for myself.

When the war began I was a bomber pilot commanding a flight of Battle bombers based in northern France. I was shot down behind the Allied lines on May 10th, 1940 – that was the day the Germans invaded the Low Countries. I was trapped in the cockpit in the middle of thirty-foot high flames and would have been burnt to death if my Observer and Air Gunner had not pulled me out.

As it was, I was burnt so badly that after three years of hospital life I was still in the hands of plastic surgeons. I have lost all the fingers of my left hand and have only a few stumps left on my right. My face is disfigured and my legs and body are scarred. I think the French doctors quite thought I was going to die, but that didn't deter them from passing me from one hospital to another to keep me out of reach of the rapidly advancing German Army.

For eighteen months I had lived the life of a cripple. I was so helpless during the first ten, I couldn't even sit up in bed. I had to learn French to make myself understood to the nurses.

Slowly at first, but steadily all the same, I began to understand the French people and to like them very much. I wasn't seeing them, you understand, at a favourable time. In less than two months after the German offensive,

France had suffered the worst series of calamities and indignities she had ever known. First the Germans broke through the French lines, then the Belgian Army surrendered, then the BEF was evacuated from Dunkirk and then, when France was fighting alone against the Germans, Mussolini joined in and stabbed her in the back.

When the French people came to after the Armistice, they found that two million of their young men had been taken prisoner and marched to Germany. Other casualties were very high too; there were millions of refugees clogging the roads and railways. The food stocks that had not been commandeered by the Germans began to run out. The misery of the people was terrible.

They felt bitter of course, and when they searched their minds for the causes of their defeat among other things they reckoned was the evacuation of Dunkirk by the British. They felt that we had ratted on them, and on top of all this came our attacks on them at Oran and Dakar and later on in Syria.

No doubt these things were necessary, but exploited as they were, of course, by the Germans they made for very bitter feeling. Not the best conditions for an Englishman, who was now entirely dependent upon them, to see the French for the first time. Nevertheless, as I watched them in their worst hour I was filled with admiration for the courage they showed. In past wars I knew they had been famous for their courage and as I watched them now I became convinced that individually they had deserved it, for in this war they had been given bad leadership and old fashioned equipment and ideas.

But the mass of the people I saw was still tough and strong. If they had been given a respite, such as we were given, I believe the French Army would have developed into a formidable fighting force ... I knew myself something of what they had done in the air with their old Morane fighters – these were no match at all for the Messerschmitt, but many of the squadrons had averaged a bag of about seventy German planes. I knew one that had shot down over a hundred.

During the Battle of Britain, the French learnt to admire us and the way we stood up to the Germans. They began to realise that we were fighting in their cause as well as our own. They were grateful too and became almost universally pro-British. They developed a particular affection for the RAF – every time we bombed their towns they were delighted. The courage and logic of that struck me as remarkable.

When they heard that an Air Force officer was in hospital, people came to see me from as far away as Calais. They said they would like bigger and better bombs, so long as plenty of Germans were killed and plenty of German ships sunk. They seemed quite indifferent to their own safety. One thing struck me especially through all of this – they never lost their sense of humour. They always found something about the Germans to laugh at, even though they hated them so bitterly.

Over here I know you have heard a lot about the quarrels and differences of opinion that divide Frenchmen and France from elsewhere. You must remember not only are their problems enormous, but for three years the Germans have been working to divide the French. Can we suppose that if the Germans had managed to invade England they wouldn't have found differences to exploit here too?

As to French collaboration with the Germans, my own opinion is that there are no more collaborators in France than there are black marketers here. I can tell you that many a prominent collaborator was really working hard underground in the opposite direction. I went to France as a typical Britisher, [and] although I saw them under the worst possible circumstances, the French people have come to attract me strongly.

I admire their courage, their intelligence, their logic and, most of all perhaps, their individualism. But France is done with being a great people I simply can't believe. When the Germans are cleaned out, the French will have big readjustments to make. I am convinced they will make them. I shouldn't be surprised if it were a French formula, the French spirit of association, that leads Europe into the new world she did it once with her *Liberté, égalité, fraternité*. Well, she may do it again.